The Fall of the Philippines

ALSO BY DONALD J. YOUNG

*Final Hours in the Pacific:
The Allied Surrenders of Wake Island,
Bataan, Corregidor, Hong Kong and Singapore* (2011)

*The Battle of Bataan:
A Complete History,* 2d ed. (2009)

# The Fall of the Philippines

*The Desperate Struggle
Against the Japanese
Invasion, 1941–1942*

Donald J. Young

McFarland & Company, Inc., Publishers
*Jefferson, North Carolina*

LIBRARY OF CONGRESS CATALOGUING-IN-PUBLICATION DATA

Young, Donald J., 1930–
　The fall of the Philippines : the desperate struggle against the Japanese invasion, 1941–1942 / Donald J. Young.
　　p.　cm.
　Includes bibliographical references and index.

　**ISBN 978-0-7864-9820-8** (softcover : acid free paper) ∞
　**ISBN 978-1-4766-2047-3** (ebook)

　1. Bataan, Battle of, Philippines, 1942.　2. World War, 1939–1945—Campaigns—Philippines.　I. Title.

D767.4.Y693 2015
940.54'2599—dc23                                                     2015006191

BRITISH LIBRARY CATALOGUING DATA ARE AVAILABLE

© 2015 Donald J. Young. All rights reserved

*No part of this book may be reproduced or transmitted in any form or by any means, electronic or mechanical, including photocopying or recording, or by any information storage and retrieval system, without permission in writing from the publisher.*

Cover image: Japanese air raid in Barrio, Paranque, in the Philippine Islands, December 13, 1941, U.S. Army Corps Image (Library of Congress)

Printed in the United States of America

*McFarland & Company, Inc., Publishers*
　*Box 611, Jefferson, North Carolina 28640*
　　*www.mcfarlandpub.com*

# Table of Contents

*Introduction*  1

1. "Never even got into the air"  3
2. The Philippines, December 10, 1941: "Where are our fighters?"  14
3. Moon Under Lingayen  30
4. When America Needed Heroes: Wheless and Wagner, December 10–16  38
5. The USS *Canopus*  48
6. A Scary Christmas But a Happy New Year: The Philippines, December 1941  58
7. The Last and the First: Bataan, January 18, 1942  65
8. The First Battle for Bataan: January 18, 1942  75
9. "Think what we could have done with sixty!"  84
10. Biggest Day for the Bataan Air Force: March 3, 1942  91
11. Japanese Blitzkrieg: April 3, 1942  98
12. The Deliberate Bombing of Bataan Hospital No. 1  107
13. The Fighting General of Bataan  119
14. Honorable But Not Easy: The Surrender of Bataan  133

## Table of Contents

| | |
|---|---|
| 15. "P-40 Something": The Last of the Tomahawks | 146 |
| 16. Corregidor Fights Back: May 6, 1942 | 154 |
| 17. "You will, repeat, *will* surrender" | 191 |
| *Chapter Notes* | 203 |
| *Bibliography* | 207 |
| *Index* | 209 |

# Introduction

Along with Pearl Harbor and Wake Island, World War II began for the United States with the same-day Japanese attack on the Philippine Islands. Unlike Pearl Harbor and the quick capture of Wake Island on December 25, 1941, war in the distant Philippines would not officially end until June 1942, seven months later.

During those seven months, the Philippines remained virtually cut off from the friendly outside world, as did interest in its end when overshadowed by the miracle U.S. victory at Midway that same June.

Even to this day, the battle and fall of the Philippines has never attracted interest like other events of the war. Along with its loss went experiences and history of the battle that, compared to those covered in the two and a half years of war to come, have still never been told. While there are many stories lost or unwritten, because of the rapid fall of the distant and isolated islands, I have chosen to write about the 17 I feel best represent that bitter and oft forgotten campaign.

# 1

# "Never even got into the air"

In the 1943 Hollywood movie *Air Force*, a gruff B-17 crew chief, played by actor Harry Carey, when told that his fighter pilot son's plane had taken a direct hit while attempting to take off from Clark Field on December 8, commented, "Never even got into the air." Little did the producer of the movie know just how similar that scenario was to what actually happened at Clark Field that day.

Results of the Japanese attacks on U.S. fighter forces in the Philippines on December 8, 1941, amounted to the staggering loss of 35 of the 86 frontline P-40 fighters in the islands. Of that number, nothing was more tragic or devastating than the loss of fifteen of the 20th Pursuit Squadron's eighteen P-40s within the first minutes of the attack on Clark Field. This is the story of those that never did get into the air.

The story of that fateful moment actually began a little after midnight on December 8, when the only functioning radar on Luzon, located at the northern edge of Iba Field, site of one of the four U.S. fighter bases in the islands, picked up a flight of Japanese planes 115 miles northwest of the field. Based on their line of approach, their assumed target was Manila.

When the news reached 27-year-old 1st Lt. Joe Moore, commander of the 20th Pursuit Squadron at Clark Field, he ordered his entire squadron from their quarters at nearby Fort Stotsenburg to the 24th Pursuit Group operations hanger at the edge of the field.

There they were met by group commander Major Orrin Grover who, after explaining why they had been called out, ordered all thirty-six 20th pilots to remain near their planes until further notice. Two hours later, with news that the anticipated intercept by 3rd Pursuit planes from Iba had drawn a blank, Moore, after ordering the 2nd Section pilots to remain at their planes, sent his own 1st Section back to Stotsenburg for rest.

At 4:30 a.m., however, he was on the phone again, this time telling the duty officer to send the 1st Section back to the flight line, that the Japanese had attacked Pearl Harbor.

Two hours later, after listening to reports of Pearl Harbor from broadcaster Don Bell over radio station KZRH in Manila, Moore told them they would be relieving the 2nd Section at 10:00 a.m. and to go back to their quarters and try to get some sleep.

A little after eight o'clock, less than an hour since returning to Stotsenburg, engine noise from planes taking off from Clark Field had aroused most of the 1st Section pilots. Iba radar, for the second time, had picked up and was tracking a flight of planes that initially appeared heading for Clark Field.

Actually, the noise from the field was not only from the 2nd Section fighters taking off to intercept, but from fourteen 19th Bombardment Group B-17s being scrambled to avoid getting caught on the ground if the raid occurred.

For the second time, however, the attempted intercept turned up nothing. Low on gas after a fruitless three-hour search for the allusive enemy planes, the 20th fighters, along with planes from the 17th Pursuit from Nichols Field that had joined in the hunt, landed at Clark Field.

While pilots of the 17th, from their base five miles south of Manila, taxied their planes to position opposite hangers 1 and 2 for refueling, the 20th fighters were directed to their recently constructed revetted positions on the northwest edge of the field. The 18, V-shaped, blast-proof revetments, actually constructed from stacked, sand-filled, 55-gallon drums, were lined up facing east for quick access to the runway.

As for the second failure to meet the Japanese bombers at the anticipated intercept points, Lt. Joe Moore, under "comments" found in the 5th Interceptor Command diary for that day, wrote, "No interception.... Instead of preceding south from Lingayan Gulf, [Japanese] turned northeast. 20th then out of gas; land at Clark Field to refuel."[1]

While most of the dog-tired 2nd Section pilots headed for their

## 1. "Never even got into the air"

Stotsenburg beds, it was Moore's 1st Section boys' turn. After the refueling was completed, they climbed into the cockpits of their Tomahawks in hopes that their guns which, after 3 months of training, had never been fired, would work when the time came.

Incoming information on approaching enemy planes from Iba radar and other spotters was initially sent to 5th Interceptor Command Headquarters at Nielson Field located on the southern outskirts of Manila. In the Air Warning Service room at the field, it was picked up and continuously tracked on a big 15-square-foot Plotting Table Map, whose size nearly took up the entire floor.

At 11:27, Iba reported a pair of plots that looked to be two 100-plus formations of planes, one heading southeast on a bearing roughly in line with what could be Iba Field or Manila. The second appeared to be headed for Clark Field. Colonel Harold George, Interceptor Command CO, and his aircraft warning officer Colonel Alexander Campbell, who had been monitoring their progress since they first appeared on the Plotting Room map, decided that their objectives were both Clark Field and Manila.

Campbell, at that point, quickly wrote out a message alerting Clark Field and handed it to communications NCO, Sergeant Alfred Eckles, telling him to send it by teletype. When Eckles returned, Campbell asked him if it had been acknowledged. Eckles said it had. Campbell looked at this watch. It was 11:45 a.m.

At the 24th Group operations hanger at Clark Field, 1st Lt. Buzz Wagner, 17th Pursuit commander, who had been anxiously reading the teletype messages coming in from Air Warning, read that one enemy formation was less than 50 miles from the 3rd Pursuit's field at Iba. The decision of what to do was now on the cautious shoulders of one man, Group CO Major Orrin Grover. It was not an easy one. Were the Japanese heading for Iba, or was the target Manila? Deciding it was Manila, at 12:15 he ordered the 17th to join both the 3rd and the 21st Pursuit from Nichols that he had ordered to cover the city 10 minutes earlier.

Meanwhile, as George and Colonel Alexander continued to watch the picture take shape on the Plotting Board, both men began to panic, particularly after following the progress of the flight that appeared headed for Clark Field.

## The Fall of the Philippines

"We watched this particular flight for a considerable length of time," wrote Campbell in his notebook later. "I kept urging them to do something about it, but they insisted on waiting until [it] reached a certain distance from the field."

As the enemy formation continued to move toward that "certain distance," Campbell, rightfully nervous about whether the big airbase had received the 11:45 teletype warning, got a call through to an unknown NCO at 12:20. The man, probably lunch relief for the regular operator, told him that he would give the message about the rapidly approaching enemy formation to "the base commander or operations officer ... at the earliest opportunity." Whether the message was ever delivered is not known.

With the 17th Pursuit now on their way to Manila, at 12:20 Colonel George, who initially had held up ordering the 20th Pursuit into the air until they were finished refueling, sent his operations officer Lt. Bud Sprague to the teletype room with the one-word message "Kickapoo."

"I asked what 'Kickapoo' meant," wrote Campbell in his notebook, "and was told it meant 'Go get 'em.'"[2]

When "Kickapoo" came through to the 24th Pursuit Group communications center, Major Grover, with no other reason than being unsure if it was directed at Clark or Manila, held up ordering the 20th to take off. Sadly, within minutes of the first Japanese bomb that fell on Clark Field, this moment of indecision would literally lead the Army Air Force to write off the 20th Pursuit Squadron as a functioning fighter squadron.

On the field, meanwhile, seventeen anxious 1st Section 20 year olds, sitting in their planes with windscreens back, sweating and cursing from their two-and-a-half hours in the mid-day sun, had no idea the red flag they had anticipated would soon send them up to intercept the approaching enemy would never be run up in time.

The eighteenth pilot, squadron leader Joe Moore, his plane parked a few yards in front of the rest of his 1st Section planes, had remained near the squadron operations shack listening for the phone. He had been told that as soon as reports of what appeared to be two approaching enemy flights had been sorted out, the 20th would be scrambled.

At 12:35, some 15 minutes since Kickapoo and the situation appar-

## 1. "Never even got into the air"

ently still not sorted out, Moore heard a cry that he would remember the rest of his life. It was from one of the crew chiefs standing near the operations shack. "Good God Almighty," he yelled, gesturing toward the sky, "yonder they come!"

Moore, initially thinking like many others that the large number of planes, flying very high and in two V-shaped formations, must be from an American carrier, suddenly realized they had to be the anticipated Japanese. After yelling for the red flag to be run up, he sprinted toward his plane, signaling to the crew chief who was sitting in the cockpit to "wind her up."

In the excitement, Sgt. Bill King, who had also identified the planes as Japanese, after firing his .45 in the air three times as a warning, ran to the phone in the operations shack. Probably hearing the shots, Lt. Benny Putnam, in the Group Headquarters office with Major Grover, grabbed the phone on the first ring. King told him to sound the alarm that Japanese planes were approaching. Putnam passed the word to Grover, who asked, "How does he know they're Japanese planes?" Overhearing the question on the other end of the line, King yelled, "We don't have so goddamn many!"

On the field, in anticipation of the need for a hasty departure, Moore already had the remaining five planes of his A Flight out of their revetments and formed in a loose line behind his P-40. Immediately behind his Tomahawk, wingman Randy Keator, rightly anticipating what the skipper sprinting toward his fighter meant, quickly jumped into his plane and started his engine.

Whether it was the red flag or seeing Moore and Keator turn over their engines, the four remaining A Flight pilots, Edwin Gilmore, Dan Blass, Max Loux, and Harrison Hughes, in quick order, did the same.

In his excitement, Joe Moore actually began his takeoff roll without buckling his parachute—an ironic moment of hesitation that without, may have saved the lives of Keator and Ed Gilmore. For no sooner had the three lifted off the runway, than, as if following them down the field, the first of 636 132-pound Japanese bombs, dropped in clusters of 12 from each plane, blanketed Clark Field. Within seconds, hangers, shops, planes on the ground, headquarters, officers' quarters, mess halls, and an oil storage area were destroyed. Outside of its pockmarked yet partially usable runway, as a functioning U.S. air base, it was finished.

As Moore, Keator, and Gilmore cleared the field, they were, of course, unaware of the tragedy that was unfolding behind them, for not one of the remaining 20th Pursuit fighters would, as Actor Harry Carey said in Air Force, "even get into the air." The three trailing A Flight fighters, like the rest of the squadron that had just began taxiing out of their revetments toward the runway, would all be destroyed by what appeared to be the deadly mix of fragmentation, high-explosive, and incendiary bombs that in moments would rain down on Clark Field.

Lieutenant Dan Blass, immediately behind Gilmore, was the first to feel the effects of what was probably a fragmentation bomb when, in the beginning of his takeoff roll, he suddenly felt the plane shudder and come to a stop. Not waiting to see that both tires had been shredded by shrapnel, he quickly jumped from the plane and sprinted 100 yards to one of the newly dug V-shaped trenches near the squadrons operations shack.

To the left of Blass, Lt. Max Louk's P-40, within a moment of liftoff at the end of the runway, was hit by an incendiary bomb, causing it to burst into flame. Trapped inside and apparently unable to open the canopy that he had just secured, the young 22-year-old Kansan, whose skill a month earlier had led to an early promotion to element leader, was burned alive.

The third A Flight pilot, Lt. Harrison Hughes, barely into his takeoff run, smartly cut the switches and, moments before his plane was hit by a bomb, was able to scramble to the safety of one of the newly dug V trenches near the squadron revetments.

Of the remaining twelve 20th pilots, only seven would be virtually unscathed. Pilots of the last five C Flight P-40s out of their revetments, upon sight of the curtain of bombs blanketing everything around them, with canopies still back, were able to quickly jump from their planes and make it safely to the nearest trench.

For the two B Flight pilots ahead of them who would also survive, it was not so easy. Lt. Parker Geis, in the number-two position behind flight leader Fred Armstrong, had just turned over his engine when two fragmentation bombs exploded 20 feet in front of him, knocking out

## 1. "Never even got into the air"

the engine and riddling his P-40 with shrapnel. Momentarily disoriented by the blast but instinctively remembering to unbuckle his parachute, he was quickly out of the plane and, along with his crew chief, made it safely to a nearby V trench. Despite the excitement of the moment, the extra few seconds he had taken to buckle his chute and safety belt before starting to taxi, probably saved him from being directly under the two bombs that knocked out his engine.

The most adventurous incident involved the other B Flight pilot, Jim Fossey. Not far behind leader Fred Armstrong, Fossey had taxied to the take-off position when a stick of 12 bombs dropped from a single enemy bomber exploded in rapid succession on the runway in front of him. Almost instinctively, by alternately releasing his brakes and kicking his rudder to turn, he was able to zigzag his way to an open area off the runway. At that point, a crew chief who had been watching from a nearby revetment dashed out waving frantically for him to cut the engine while pointing to a spot on the fuselage immediately behind the cockpit. As Fossey climbed out and slid down the wing to the ground, he realized what the man was pointing to—gas gushing out of a shrapnel hole in the side of the ship. Anticipating that the plane would blow up any second, Fossey quickly dove into a patch of tall cagon grass growing a few feet off the edge of the runway. Realizing moments later that the field was on fire, he ran back to the plane, started the engine and taxied it to an open area safely away from the fire before seeking refuge in a nearby ditch.

B Flight leader Fred Armstrong, who had begun his takeoff roll moments ahead of Fossey, may have been victimized by the same string of incendiary bombs. Two bombs in quick succession exploded on either side of his ship, the concussion momentarily knocking him out. Regaining conscious moments before flames totally engulfed the cockpit, he quickly made it onto the wing and slid onto the now-burning, gasoline-soaked ground, scrambling on hands and knees out of the circle of fire that moments later would totally consume his fighter.

The planes of two other pilots, Guy Iverson and Max Halverson, just yards from each other as they taxied out from their revetments, were both caught in a fusillade of fire bombs that actually cloaked the entire area. With canopies fortunately still back, both were able to safely extricate themselves moments before the two fighters burst into flame. Despite receiving second-degree burns about their face and hands, the two young pilots would survive to fly another day.

Possibly unaware of the string of bombs that made Fossey take his evasive action, Lloyd Mulcahy and Jesse Luker may have unavoidably taxied directly into their path. The two young men, who had grown up not far from each other in California's San Joaquin Valley, were killed instantly when both planes took direct hits. (To stress the effectiveness of the attack, it must be remembered that everything, from when the bombs hit the ground behind Moore, Keator, and Gilmore to the deaths of Mulcahy and Luker, actually occurred in what was described as one, almost simultaneous explosion of 636 Japanese bombs.)

Incredibly, from the 15 destroyed 1st Section planes, nine pilots were able to escape relatively unscathed. Two of these, Paul Gies and Jim Drake, after the enemy bombers had passed overhead, were able to find two unassigned P-40s that had survived the attack and attempted to take off.

Unbeknownst to the two men, on the heels of the bombers were 34 Zero fighters, whose job, since there was no real air opposition, was to "clean up" after the raid. Somewhat like the initial reaction to the bombers, when the enemy fighters were first sighted, they, too, were assumed to be American. Gies and Drake would be the first to find out otherwise.

Gies, in his anxiousness to get into the air, and despite his crew chief waving for him to stop before he hit it, taxied his Tomahawk into a bomb crater. Realizing as he climbed out of the plane that the field was being attacked by Zeros, the two men, for the second time, made it safely back to the same trench they just minutes before had jumped into.

Jim Drake, after successfully maneuvering his way through the bomb-cratered field, lost his race to get off the ground when a low-flying strafer caught him just seconds before liftoff. He was the fourth 20th pilot killed, and his burning P-40, the 1st Section's fifteenth and last fighter, was destroyed literally within seconds of the attack.

Of all the comments made about the effectiveness of the bombing, those of Japanese ace Saburo Sakai, initially flying cover for the bombers, was perhaps the most telling: "Their accuracy was phenomenal, in fact

## 1. "Never even got into the air"

was the most accurate bombing I ever witnessed by our planes throughout the war. The entire base seemed to be rising into the air with explosives. Pieces of airplanes, hangers, and other ground installations scattered wildly. Great fires erupted and smoke boiled upward!"[3]

When Joe Moore and Randy Keator returned from their successful run-ins with the Japanese around 1:15, they found the sky clear of enemy planes. The obvious shock they no doubt felt when they first saw what an hour earlier had been the finest U.S. airbase in the Far East, although not recorded, can easily be imagined. Their first concern, however, was locating part of the field that wasn't pockmarked by bomb craters.

It took Keator, who arrived first, no less than three passes to size up the field before negotiating a landing on the 2,000-foot extension strip close to the 19th Bombardment Group area. Moore made it on his third attempt. Ed Gilmore, the third 20th pilot, had opted for the 34th Pursuit's field at nearby Del Carmen, where he landed safely.

Little did the two men know as they were being directed through the smoke-filled field toward what was left of the squadron's operational area, of the 23 P-40s available to the squadron before the attack, they were sitting in two of the only three flyable planes left.

Nor were they equipped to face what was laid out on the ground nearby—the bodies of Max Louk, Jesse Luker, Lloyd Mulcahy, and Jim Drake. Louk, who in his last letter home prophetically wrote to his sister that not only were "our planes ... not good enough to fight with," when the war comes, "we are doomed at the start."

Joe Moore, after being critiqued on what happened on the field during the attack, drove to the hospital at Ft. Stotsenburg to check on his three badly-burned 1st Section pilots. Guy Iverson and Max Halverson, whose burns, as mentioned, would later allow them to return to duty, were not as serious as Fred Armstrong's.

Suffering near third-degree burns of his hands, face, and legs, he was soon transferred from Stotsenburg to Sternburg Hospital in Manila. There, on December 29, he, six other 24th Pursuit pilots, along with 240 other badly wounded men, were loaded onto the converted Inter-Island ship *Mactan* and safely evacuated to Australia.

With the setting of the sun on the evening of December 8, it appeared that the story of the disastrous loss of the entire 20th Pursuit

## The Fall of the Philippines

Squadron within just seconds of the attack on Clark Field had at last ended. However, even with the deaths of four of its pilots and 23 of its 26 P-40Bs destroyed, history could not have written a more tragic ending to the story than that which happened to two more of its pilots on December 10.

Early that morning, a Japanese invasion force as spotted landing troops near the Luzon west coast town of Vigan. By 9:00 a.m., two separate dawn attacks on the landing had been made by P-35s of the 34th Pursuit from Del Carmen and a dozen P-40Es of the 17th, which squadron had been transferred to Clark Field the day before.

Of the 17th's 11 P-40Es that would make the second attack on Vigan, including himself, Joe Moore assigned eleven anxious pilots from the 20th to, for the first time, get a revenge shot at the Japanese. Despite the opportunity, none of his pilots had yet flown the new E model P-40, although they had been warned that the 1,600-pound heavier Kittyhawk, in particular, demanded a lower and faster landing approach than their familiar B model Tomahawks. Sadly, the situation portended a disaster.

It occurred when the planes returned from the first Vigan raid at 11:15 a.m. A handful of pilots from the 20th and 17th had gathered in a stand of woods on the edge of the field to watch the landings. As the third plane, flown by Morgan McCowan, one of the 1st Section pilots who had survived the attack on the eighth, approached the field, it was obvious he was coming in too high.

Watching from the edge of the field, Ed Gilmore, one of the pilots who was scheduled to go on the raid but had inadvertently taxied into a bomb crater, said it looked like McCowan, after first throttling back to drop down, attempted to recover by applying maximum power.

But it was too late—the plane, awkwardly landing on one wheel, careened sharply to the left on a direct line toward the trees and the group of pilots watching from the edge of the field.

One of the men directly in line with the oncoming plane was 1st Lt. Glen Alder of the 20th. Ironically, on December 8, he and McCowan were two of the six men from Alder's C Flight whose fighters were destroyed as they were taxiing out from their revetments.

Although Alder saw the plane in time to hit the ground before it passed over, McCowan's fate was sealed when his Kittyhawk slammed

## 1. "Never even got into the air"

into the trees behind the shocked group of pilots. Despite the efforts of Jim Fossey and Ed Gilmore to pull him from the wreckage before it caught fire, it was too late, his head crushed in by the gun-sight.

Meanwhile, Alder, who had gotten to his feet, asked what had happened. Cy Blanton, one of the 17th's pilots who had been standing near him before the plane hit, noticed blood trickling out of his left ear. Guessing that he had been hit in the head by a tree limb, he led his dazed friend to an ambulance that had rushed to the scene to take any of the injured to the hospital.

Alder was taken to the 19th Bombardment Dispensary to be checked out. When Blanton returned later to see how he was doing, the doctor told him that he had died; the blow to the head, he said, was obviously worse than it initially appeared.

Even though the loss of all but three of the 20th's planes meant the end of the squadron, it was the near-instant deaths of four of its young pilots and the two who were killed on December 10 that hurt the most. Hit particularly hard were Jim Fossey, Randy Keator, and Dan Blass who, along with their dead buddies Jesse Luker, Jim Drake, and Morgan McCowan, as flying cadets at Stockton and Hamilton Field, California, learned to fly together, got their wings together, were commissioned together, came across on the same ship, and ended up members of the same 20th Pursuit Squadron.

One of the unanswered questions about the bombing of Clark Field on December 8 involved the time between when the first of the 636 bombs hit and the last. Most witnesses on the ground agreed that they seemed to explode in one huge simultaneous blast.

The planes, flying side by side in two identical V formations, were made up of 53 Mitsubishi G3M "Nell's" and G4M "Betty's," each carrying 12 132-pound bombs. Flying at the scheduled speed of 132 mph, it is estimated that all 636 bombs were dropped within the 30 seconds it took for the 53 planes to cross the field, supporting witnesses "simultaneous blast" estimates.

# 2

# The Philippines, December 10, 1941

## *"Where are our fighters?"*

Results of the devastating Japanese attacks on December 8, 1941, on the U.S. Army fighter forces in the Philippines led to the loss of 35 of the 24th Pursuit Group's 86 operational P-40s in the islands. Despite this, not counting 18 obsolete P-35s that survived the first day, there were still 51 P-40s left—that is until the afternoon of December 10.

An inventory of the number of American fighters lost that afternoon amounted to 23 more of its best, plus all 18 P-35s. This, along with the loss of six P-40s and two pilots the day before in non–combat-related accidents, amounted to 64 front-line fighters destroyed. Left to defend the entire Philippine archipelago with only 22 fighters on the fourth day of the war, there was little doubt about the outcome.

Primary targets of the Japanese on December 10th was the U.S. Navy's Asiatic Fleet Base at Cavite and Nichols Field, the only remaining Army air base that had so far escaped the wrath unloaded on Clark and Iba air fields two days earlier.

Out in Manila Bay in wait of the anticipated Japanese air attack that day were three PT boats of Motor Torpedo Boat Squadron 3, whose commander, Lieutenant John Bulkeley, had led his little group out into open water following the warning of the raid he had received an hour earlier.

It was 12:45 in the afternoon when the Japanese planes were first spotted. "The first big V had 54 planes in it," said Bulkeley, "and they

## 2. The Philippines, December 10, 1941

came in at about 20,000 feet, with their fighters up above to protect them from ours—only ours didn't show up? We couldn't believe it."

Bulkeley's second-in-command, Lieutenant Robert Kelly, who also saw them, first thought to himself, "when our fighters get up there and start rumpling their hair, their formations won't look so pretty." But, after scanning the sky, he wondered, like many would that day, "…where are our fighters?"[1]

Uninformed of the devastating losses incurred by the Air Force two days earlier, it was hard for the Navy or anyone to fathom what appeared to be the almost total absence of American fighters in the sky above Manila Bay. With no less than 51 P-40s available at dawn that morning, it was unbelievable that anything close to a repetition of the December 8 debacle could be duplicated—but it almost was.

Interestingly, the third day of the war for the Far East Air Force started with great anticipation. There would be no repetition of December 8, this day. This time it would be the Army Air Force that would strike first.

Along with the loss of over one third of its P-40s on December 8, the Air Force also lost 17 B-17s—exactly half of the total bomber force in the Philippines. Despite this, a plan was made to launch a retaliatory strike with what was left on Japanese air and naval bases on Formosa. Fourteen B-17s were to be flown up from Del Monte Field on Mindanao on the ninth in anticipation of launching an attack the next morning.

Sometime during the night, however, information was received that a Japanese invasion force had been spotted approaching Vigan off the Luzon west coast and another off Aparri in the north.

Although the war was entering its third day, information on the whereabouts of the enemy from various sources had been so inaccurate and exaggerated, that no one knew what to believe. It was perhaps best characterized by Admiral Thomas Hart, Asiatic Fleet commander, who said that there were numerous reports of "enemy sightings when nothing was actually sighted; and when a vessel was really seen, she was usually reported in one of two categories: irrespective of size, she was either a transport or a battleship."

If there really was an invasion force off Luzon's west coast, it was vital that accurate information on numbers and types of ships be verified.

## The Fall of the Philippines

To tackle this so far, allusive task, veteran pilot and Nichols Field base operations officer Lieutenant Grant Mahoney was selected to fly the reconnaissance mission. Anxious to finally get into the air, he took off from Nichols a little after 2:00 a.m. for the two-and-a-half hour, round-trip flight to Vigan and back.

It was just getting light in the east when the engine of a plane was heard approaching the field. It was Mahoney's P-40. Suddenly, a trigger-happy Philippine Scout anti-aircraft battery, located at the end of the runway, opened up, hitting the plane and forcing him to bail out over the very field he was trying to land on.

Fortunately, Mahoney survived and was taken back to headquarters, where he phoned the Far East Air Force Headquarters at Nielson Field to report what he had seen. He told them that there were six transports, a cruiser, minesweeper, and approximately ten destroyers standing off the Vigan coast.

With confirmation of the anticipated Japanese invasion, the planned bombing of Formosa was scrubbed. One of the six B-17s that had come in from Del Monte the day before had already taken off on a reconnaissance mission to Formosa and would miss the raid.

Nevertheless, with 13 B-17s, a dozen P-40s, and 13 P-35s still available, the attempt would be made to break up the enemy invasion force before they could land. Although on the surface the plan seemed simple enough, as had already become the rule rather than the exception, it, too, would be one racked by confusion, lack of communication, and mechanical difficulties.

From the beginning, however, with the element of surprise now on the other foot, it appeared that the attack had an excellent chance of succeeding. A little after 6:00 a.m., the five B-17s, each loaded with 20 100-pound bombs, took off for Vigan, escorted by 12 P-40s flown by pilots of the 17th Pursuit Squadron.

A few minutes after takeoff, one of the aforementioned mechanical problems occurred when Lt. John Brownewell, leader of the escorting fighters, decided to test-fire his guns. There was no response. Not a single gun of the six .50s on his Kittyhawk fired. Frustrated, he turned the flight over to Lt. Jack Dale and returned to Clark.

Ironically, Brownewell's problem had already plagued many of the

## 2. The Philippines, December 10, 1941

P-40E Kittyhawks during the first two days. It was eventually traced to an unexplained order received from the Air Force's Material Division a few weeks before the war not to connect the gun-charging system in the newly arrived fighters. No explanation of why or who originated the order was ever discovered. Even more frustrating was that it would often happen after an initial check, when all the guns worked, but failed on subsequent attempts because they could not recharge.

Over Vigan, meanwhile, the first scheduled U.S. Army bombing raid of the war looked like it couldn't miss. Coming in at 12,000 feet, four of the five B-17s found six enemy transports neatly lined up off the beach unloading troops. With little antiaircraft fire and no enemy fighter opposition, they dropped half of their bombs, wheeled out over the sea, turned, dropped the rest of their 100-pounders, and headed for home.

The fifth plane, piloted by Lt. Elliot Vandevanter, could not get its bomb release mechanism to work on his initial pass. Dropping down to 7,000 feet for his return run after being told by his flight engineer that the problem was fixed, all 20 bombs did release as he passed over the transports. A few minutes later, he caught up with the rest of the group, in time to get in on the backslapping chatter over the radio of their success.

Results of the five tons of bombs dropped on the sitting-duck transports, however, appeared disappointing. According to pilots of the fighters who had stayed behind to strafe the ships, only one was burning. As far as the fighters, of the eleven planes that attacked, two were plagued by inoperative guns: none of Lt. Bill Hennon's guns fired, and only one of Walt Coss' six .50s worked. Several of the transports were strafed, as was the cruiser who was attacked by a lone P-40 piloted by Cy Blanton.

Although none of the fighters who took part in the attack was damaged to any degree, there was one late arrival that ran into trouble of a different kind.

The plane was flown by Lt. Bill Sheppard, who, the day before, had been forced to land his slightly damaged Kittyhawk at the 34th Pursuit's base at Del Carmen. With information of the 17th's involvement in the attack but held up by repairs, Sheppard took off for Vigan around 9:00 a.m., hoping to catch up with the rest of his squadron. By the time he reached the landing beach, however, the 17th was already back on the ground at Clark.

While searching for a target, he spotted three twin-engine Japanese bombers approaching the coast. Apparently unaware of his presence, he immediately attacked. "I felt like a ... big game hunter who'd caught up with three tigers," he said later. Although only two of his six .50s worked, he made three successful passes at the enemy planes before taking a hit himself. As he broke off the fight, he glanced back in time to see that two of the bombers had dropped out of the formation, one of which he claimed was going down.

Getting as far away from Vigan as possible before his engine quit, Sheppard bailed out near the barrio of Bangued, where he was later joined by Ed Houseman of the 34th who, on his way to Vigan, had left his P-35 when his engine quit.

Scheduled to resume the attack on the heels of Clark's P-40s were 13 P-35s from Del Carmen. Right away, however, things went badly for the 34th as an engine on one of the planes failed to turn over. Although the remaining 12 got off the ground and assembled for the attack, by the time they reached the coast, five had been forced to return with engine problems. Less than a mile from the target, the engine on a sixth plane quit, forcing pilot Ed Houseman to bail out.

Despite being an hour behind their scheduled arrival time, they gave a good account of themselves. Lieutenant Sam Marett, popular commanding officer of the 34th, immediately went after a minesweeper, at which he made two successful strafing runs on. On what was his third and final attempt to knock out the ship, he again bore in with all guns blazing. As witnessed by his wingman "Shorty" Crosland, just as he pulled up to clear the masthead, the ship blew up, the explosion blowing off the wing of his plane as he passed over. According to Crosland, the minesweeper went straight to the bottom after the explosion, giving Marett credit for what may have been the first Japanese ship to be sunk since Pearl Harbor.

Lieutenants Ben Brown and Jack Hall, meanwhile, had made several successful passes over two of the transports, both of which were left burning as the five remaining P-35s headed back for Del Carmen.

Back at Clark Field, meanwhile, the same 12 P-40s that had escorted

## 2. The Philippines, December 10, 1941

the flight of B-17s over Vigan, flown this time by pilots of the 20th Pursuit Squadron, took off for a third attack on the enemy landing. It would not be without incident.

The first would occur before takeoff. Momentarily blinded by the dust thrown up by the plane ahead of him, Lt. Edwin Gilmore accidentally taxied his P-40 into a bomb crater along the edge of the runway. Between waiting for the dust to settle and an unusual low overcast over the field, not a single plane of the remaining eleven that got off the ground joined up with one another. Because of this, their attacks were piecemeal. Of those, outside of one reported by Lt. Randy Keator, who, with all but one of his guns working, successfully strafed one of the transports, most were without significant results.

Prior to December 8, the 20th Pursuit was made up of older P-40B Tomahawks. But the loss of all but three of their planes on the 8th forced nine of their pilots to fly the newer, less-familiar and heavier P-40Es that morning.

Because of this Lt. Morgan McCowan, while coming in for a landing on his return from Vigan, hit the ground awkwardly, causing the fighter to veer off the runway towards a startled group of 17th pilots who had gathered to watch the flight come in. Crashing into the trees near the scattering observers, McCowan was killed instantly, along with a sergeant. A second 20th pilot, Lt. Glen Alder, died later from injuries incurred from the accident.

With the destruction of the only operating radar on Luzon on December 8, Interceptor Command was blind. With the loss of its early warning system on the first day of the war, the reliability of accurately predicting an enemy attack was based as much on anticipation as on actual knowledge.

Comments by Captain Frank Kurtz, who lost his B-17 at Clark Field on the eighth and worked the control tower on the morning of the tenth, support this.

"Everybody was jumpy. We didn't know what minute the Japs would come back. There was an alert at least once an hour all day long, even though each one was called off fifteen minutes later."[2]

One that wasn't "called off" came in around twelve-thirty, when word came of Japanese bombers heading for Clark Field. When the air raid sirens went off, pilots made a wild scramble for their planes. Chaos reigned. In some cases, two pilots raced to get to the same plane, particularly those of the 17th and 20th Pursuit Squadrons, who had both flown the same fighter over Vigan that morning.

Between the dust created by planes taking off and the numerous bomb craters from the December 8th raid, it was a miracle any got off without incident. One that didn't was the Kittyhawk piloted by Lt. Bob Newman, who crashed his plane into a parked B-17, destroying both ships. Newman was okay.

Lieutenants Ed Dyess and "Buzz" Wagner, squadron leaders of the 21st and 17th Pursuit Squadrons respectively, were eating lunch when the alarm sounded.

"I dropped my food and ran to the edge of the field just as a motorcycle dispatch [rider] chugged up," said Dyess. Climbing on the back, he told him to "hightail it for the line." Dyess didn't see Wagner anywhere. "[I] wondered how Buzz would get to his plane in time." Ironically, Wagner did reach *a* plane in time to take off, but not his.

Luckily avoiding the bomb craters, Dyess was halfway through his takeoff run "flying absolutely blind in the pall left by the other planes, when I realized I had left goggles, helmet, and parachute behind.

"When I shot out of the dust into the dazzling sunlight," he said, "I about jumped out of the cockpit. Right beside me was another P-40, its wingtip almost touching mine. It was Buzz, laughing like a hyena. I laughed too—rather shakily I think—then we pulled apart."[3]

At that point they were told that the destination of the bombers initially reported heading for Clark had changed—it was Manila.

Of the three squadrons of Japanese bombers, one that was scheduled to hit Del Carmen was ordered to join with the main force heading for Cavite and Nichols Field. They weren't needed after the dozen or so Zeros had, for all practical purposes, wiped out the entire squadron of P-35s that had been neatly parked on the edge of the field.

"We were gassing up [when] 12 Zeros came in strafing while we were still on the ground," remembered Lt. Bill Brown, who, since the death of the 34th's commander, Sam Marett, earlier that day, had "inherited" the job. The attack, according to Brown, accounted for "one gasoline truck, one oil truck, 12 P-35s destroyed and six damaged."

## 2. The Philippines, December 10, 1941

"After the strafing," he said, "we were ordered to abandon the field and [walk] to the sugar central at Del Carmen and wait for further orders."[4]

Although five or six of the old Severeskys were repairable, not a single one would ever see combat again.

When the Zeros first hit the field at Del Carmen, five of the Clark Field pilots, who had just taken off after hearing the frantic call for help over their radios, headed for the besieged air base.

First to arrive was Edwin Gilmore and Al Strauss. After Gilmore's first burst at an unsuspecting Zero, all of his guns quit. However, smoke from the enemy plane indicated that the single burst from his six .50s might have been enough.

Al Strauss, who had picked out the wingman of the first Zero, with all guns working, also scored with his initial burst.

Third to arrive was Jack Dale. After successfully clearing his guns on the seven-minute flight from Clark, he was able to close within 50 yards of one of the strafers. However, when he pressed the trigger for the second time, there was no response—not one of his .50s fired. Frustrated, he decided to head for Nichols to have his guns worked on.

Last on the scene were Lieutenants Parker Gies and Henry Rancke. Several ground crewmen and pilots who had taken cover on the edge of the field were to witness a very rare but satisfying spectacle—two P-40s hot on the tails of a pair of Japanese Zeros, one of which had obviously been hit.

Unknown to the men on the ground, the plane that ended up crashing moments later at the end of the runway was the first of two Parker Gies would be credited with.

The second one came when he and Rancke spotted three Zeros swing into position for a head-on attack. Turning into them, Gies kept his finger on the trigger until they had passed. The bold move by the young second lieutenant paid off, as one of enemy planes was on fire as they broke away. Although his Kittyhawk was damaged by return fire from one of the enemy fighters, he was able to nurse it safely back to Clark.

As the three squadrons of enemy bombers and fifty or so escorting

## The Fall of the Philippines

fighters neared Manila, the best the Americans could put up against a force of over 120 Japanese aircraft was so insignificant and piecemeal that the question of "where are our fighters?" asked before the attack would be changed to "where *were* our fighters?"

Of the handful of planes that had hurriedly scrambled to get off Clark Field before the anticipated Japanese attack at 12:30, only four got word that the enemy objective was changed to Manila. As mentioned, because of the chaotic circumstances under which they had raced to get up, all headed for Manila alone. Unfortunately, none would make it.

Ed Dyess was one of them. As he approached the Manila waterfront, he could see enemy bombers "dropping their eggs along the shipping centers." He pulled the trigger to warm up his guns. Nothing happened. "I tried again," he said, "[but] was rewarded by a discouraging click."

Unaware that Del Carmen was under attack, he radioed for the 34th to take off for Manila. Receiving no response, he tried his guns for a third time. "All were useless. [It] was beyond understanding. They had worked perfectly during the morning flight." Picking out a small auxiliary field north of Manila, he landed safely, but was out of the fight.[5]

Another pilot who had trouble with his guns was Milt Woodside. Buzz Wagner, it will be remembered, had grabbed the first P-40 he saw and took off from Clark Field. So had Woodside, who ended up in Wagner's plane. Unfortunately for him, Wagner's Kittyhawk was either out of ammunition or his guns were jammed. Also unfortunate was that he was jumped by Japanese fighters a few miles north of Manila, where, after taking several hits, he was forced to bail out.

Fate of a third American pilot who had responded to Manila's call for help was young Kiefer White. Like Woodside, his P-40, damaged enough by a Zero who had unsuspectedly camped on his tail, he, too, was forced to bail out. Like Woodside, he, too, landed safely.

Unlike Woodside and White, Lt. John Posten had chosen to take on the first Zero he saw but quickly found himself the subject of a pair of enemy fighters who had meanwhile camped on his tail. Although riddled by enemy fire, the rugged Kittyhawk held together enough to allow him to make a run for it. The chase took him clear up the west coast of Bataan to Subic Bay before the dogged Japanese finally gave up.

On paper, it appeared that the best and only chance to answer the

## 2. The Philippines, December 10, 1941

"where-are-our-fighters?" question would come from the planes at Nichols Field.

With the Air Force's early-warning system destroyed two days earlier, pilots of the 3rd, 17th, and 21st Pursuit Squadrons had been alternately patrolling the skies over Manila since dawn in anticipation of a Japanese attack. When it came, however, it would be a surprise.

Although Clark Field had been alerted that the enemy raiders were headed for Manila, it appears that no one bothered to pass the word on to Interceptor Command at Nielson or to Nichols Field. In fact, the first that the just-relieved pilots of the 3rd Pursuit Squadron knew of the attack was when their lunch was interrupted by the sound of antiaircraft fire.

Also taken by surprise was every American fighter in the air. About the time the lead flight of Japanese bombers drew within sight of Manila, the mid-morning patrol was preparing to land at Nichols. Up since 10:00 a.m., all were dangerously low on fuel for having to wait for the seven-plane relief flight to take off before coming in.

Ahead of the bombers, Japanese fighters had arrived first over the area in hopes of catching the Americans on the ground, thus allowing their bombers to go unmolested in their attacks on Cavite and Nichols Field. Fortunately, there were no U.S. planes on the ground. Unfortunately, it didn't make any difference.

As the line of 17th Pursuit fighters were preparing to land, first word of the Japanese presence over Cavite came in over the radio. With probably less than 15 minutes of gas, squadron leader Lt. Willie Feallock found himself faced with a dilemma—to go after the Japanese and face running out of gas, or to land and probably be destroyed on the ground. The choice was obvious—attack.

Feallock's group wasn't the only American fighters in the air. As mentioned, his mid-morning patrol had waited for the relief flight to take off before coming in. That flight of seven P-40Es, led by Grant Mahoney, was climbing for altitude when they were jumped by several Zeros. At that moment, everything the U.S. Air Force could put up was in the air. Although the exact number of American planes is not known, in less than an hour they would be swept from the skies.

The fourth American fatality that day occurred moments after Lt.

## The Fall of the Philippines

Forrest Hobrecht lifted his P-40 off the field. To the dismay of those watching, the young pilot took the fatal hit from the marauding Zero as the two planes passed directly over the runway. His plane went down some three miles east of the field, not far from where his body was found with his unopened parachute.

Lieutenant Ed Erickson, like Hobrecht, was also jumped by Japanese fighters after taking off from Nichols. No less than three Zeros went after him, riddling his plane with bullets.

Too low to bail out, the big American decided to take his chances on landing back at Nichols. Unable to lower his wheels because of a shot-up undercarriage, however, he belly-landed his fighter, causing it to slide off the runway directly into a tanker truck loaded with aviation gasoline. Blown free of the plane by the ensuing explosion, Erickson literally walked away from the burning wreck with only second-degree burns of his hands and face.

On the ground at Nichols, John Coleman, commanding officer of the 27th Material Squadron, on December 9 had deployed one of his platoons on a ridge overlooking the field, from which their antiquated Lewis machine guns could be used in antiaircraft defense of the base. It paid off.

In the middle of the fight, the now-alerted gunners spotted a burning P-40 approaching the field with two Zeros hot on its tail.

"All my men opened fire with rifles and machine guns," said Coleman. "Our P-40 went into Manila Bay about one-half mile from us. One of the Zeros went into the water too ... our coast guard went out to rescue the P-40 pilot [Lt. Gordon Benson]. He was not hurt."[6]

Earlier that morning, three PBYs from the Navy's Patrol Wing 10 (Patwing 10), patrolling the west coast of Luzon, spotted the enemy invasion convoy off Vigan, resulting in a five-plane raid by them later that morning.

At almost the exact time the Japanese launched their attack on Cavite and Nichols, four of the planes had just taken off for a second strike at Vigan. Jumped by two enemy fighters, two of the lumbering Catalinas were forced down with severe damage.

Perhaps unknown to them, an attempt to get the enemy off their tails had been made by Lt. Jim Phillips, who saw the two Zeros take out

## 2. The Philippines, December 10, 1941

after the PBYs. As the three planes crossed over the Navy base toward Sangley Point, they were fired on from the ground by a Marine antiaircraft battalion. Probably unaware of the presence of any American fighters in the sky, to them every plane they saw was considered the enemy.

Unfortunately, it was Phillips' P-40 that turned out to be the victim, not the Japanese. Able to bail out before it crashed into the bay, when picked up by navy patrol boat, he was congratulated for shooting down one of the Japanese. The credit actually belonged to a gunner on one of the Catalinas, who hit the enemy fighter moments before his plane hit the water.

Willie Feallock, meanwhile, had gone after a string of Zeros he spotted working over the Philippine Army Air Corps base at Zablan Field, a few miles north of Manila. Diving on one of the unsuspecting enemy planes, he pressed the trigger. Nothing happened. He pressed it again—still nothing.

By then he had been spotted by one of the Zero pilots. Within seconds, William "Willie" Feallock witnessed one of the numerous maneuvers that would soon astound many a pilot who decided to dogfight a Zero—an abrupt 180-degree turn. Suddenly, instead of being on his tail, he found that the Zero had turned and was coming head on, firing everything he had at him.

Diving for the deck after the enemy passed, seconds later he again found himself unsuccessfully trying to avoid the same plane, which had turned again and was now on his tail.

It was soon all over for the young American. Hit several times and trailing smoke, Feallock bailed out from the burning fighter, his chute opening just feet from the ground. Outside of a couple of sprained ankles and a newly found respect for the Zero, he was okay.

Unknown to Feallock, things were also happening on the ground at Zablan Field. Home of the fledgling Philippine Air Corps, it was made up of a handful of obsolete, open-cockpit, fixed-landing gear P-26s, with two .30-caliber machine guns and top speed of less than 200 barely qualified them as training planes.

After the enemy's first pass at the field, Captain Jesus Villamor, commander of the squadron, and three other pilots made a mad dash for their planes.

Villamor, who was first off, immediately found himself in the sights of a Zero. If nothing else, the little P-26 proved maneuverable enough to keep the Japanese from drawing a bead on it. As a last resort, he dove his pre-war blue-and-yellow fighter under a row of high-tension wires, which, for whatever reason, caused the Japanese pilot to break off the pursuit.

By that time, three more of his comrades had taken off, and together took out after an unsuspecting formation of Japanese bombers who were wheeling north after their bombing run over Cavite.

Villamor, below and from a head-on position, cut loose with his two .30s at the lead bomber. To his surprise, the port engine began belching smoke, and the plane dropped out of the formation.

Another game Filipino pilot, Lt. Jose Gozar, who found his guns jammed, actually tried to ram one of the enemy bombers. Although his tired little P-26 was unable to catch up with the now-alerted Japanese, his suicidal effort was actually responsible for scattering the entire formation of enemy planes.

Andy Keieger, one of the pilots with Feallock's flight, after shooting down a Zero, found himself unable to shake off a second enemy fighter. After taking a .20 mm hit in the tail, he did a half roll, which, as he wrote later "threw the Nip off and when I rolled out, [I] had two of them dead in my sight.

"Just as I was about to pull the trigger, my engine quit—out of gas." Diving for the ground with the two enemy fighters now in hot pursuit, "they hit my tail again as I banked, and the ship rolled onto its back and started to spin. But I got out [of it] somehow...."

Leveling off just feet from the ground, his engine suddenly kicked in. "So I began to run at ground level, wide open, with the two Zeros still on my tail, peppering away. I gave them such a ride as they won't forget," he wrote, "taking them up and down ravines, between houses and trees...."

Despite his effort, he was unable to shake the enemy fighters, who continued to bang away at the rugged Kittyhawk. "The noise of their cannon shells bursting on my armor plate was deafening."

When his engine finally quit, he said, "[I] pulled up until she stalled, then jumped." When he hit the ground in an open field, he was rushed

## 2. The Philippines, December 10, 1941

by several Filipino farmers armed with bolos, pitchforks, and even an antiquated musket. Once they realized he was an American, they celebrated him as a hero, taking him to their village and showering him with gifts and drinks of what he later called "some kind of native rotgut."

Another pilot, Don Steel, like many others, quickly found himself the target of a pair of Zeros. Although his Kittyhawk was hit, he was able to evade the two enemy planes by darting into a cloudbank.

"When I came out," he wrote later in his diary, "[one of the Zero's] was just ahead and below me. He was rocking his wings frantically trying to find me.

"I skidded over onto his tail and gave him one burst; he completely disintegrated. The air was filled with flying wheels, cowling, and scraps of airplane. He rolled over ... on his back and crashed into the shore of Laguna de Bay, just east of Nichols Field."

Of Grant Mahoney's seven-plane relief flight that had just taken off from Nichols as the Japanese attacked, only four had managed to safely escape. It was the same for 15 others, many of which had discovered that the only way for the P-40 to escape the Zero was to dive for the ground and outrun him.

By mid-afternoon on the tenth, the few flyable American P-40s remaining in the Philippines, estimated to be 22, were scattered amongst no less than six different airfields—from Clark Field, 50 miles north of Manila, to Batangas, 55 miles south of the city.

Sadly, in just two days—December 8 and 10, 1941—for all practical purposes, the U.S. fighter force of 86 Curtiss P-40s had ceased to exist as primarily intended—to intercept, disperse, and destroy an attacking enemy force. Never again would the few remaining planes of the 24th Pursuit Group take to the air in the defense of the skies over Luzon.

In critique of the disastrous two days, outside of the frustrating and costly problem of malfunctioning guns, the greatest contributor to the calamity was the absence of an early-warning system. Every single Japanese attack on Clark, Nichols, Iba, and Del Carmen airfields on the 8th and 10th were surprise attacks. Had Interceptor Command been adequately warned, and had there been no malfunctioning gun problems, the question of "where are our fighters?" may never have been asked.

As far as the results of the raid on Cavite, the reaction of Lt. John

## The Fall of the Philippines

Bulkeley, as he led his little PT boat squadron back to the naval base, tells it all. "After the Japs left," he said, "we went to see what happened. They'd flattened it—there isn't any other word for it ... the only American naval base ... beyond Pearl Harbor pounded into bloody rubbish."[7]

Nichols Field, on the other hand, received only minor damage in the raid. Compared to Cavite, whose losses were over 500 killed, casualties at Nichols amounted to 20 dead and 100 wounded.

On the afternoon of December 10, 1941, 14 American B-17s were set to launch a planned retaliatory attack on Japanese bases on Formosa. By the end on the day, only one of the 14 was to be found on the island.

On the morning of December 9, 14 B-17s were flown up from Del Monte Field on Mindanao, six arriving at Clark Field early that afternoon. The remaining eight, leaving later for the 500-mile trip, landed at the nearby auxiliary field of San Marcelino.

Sometime during the night, however, word filtered in that two Japanese invasion forces had been spotted off the coast of Luzon. Acting on this information, the target for the big bombers was changed to the two convoys approaching the coastal towns of Vigan and Aparri.

One of the six Del Monte planes at Clark was lost to the raid earlier that morning, having taken off for Formosa on a reconnaissance flight before the planned attack was scrubbed. One down.

The remaining five B-17s took off for Vigan at 6:00 a.m., returning with little to show for the 5 tons of bombs dropped on the enemy transports.

Without an early-warning system (destroyed on December 8) and living under the constant threat of a surprise enemy air attack, when the leader of the returning flight requested bombs for a follow-up raid, he was ordered to get his planes off the ground and return to Del Monte. Japanese bombers, he was told, were expected any minute. Six down.

Meanwhile, all eight planes from San Marcelino had taken off on the short hop over to Clark. Because of the threat of air attack, however, only five were allowed to land. The remaining three were told to return to San Marcelino, gas up, and head back to Mindanao. Nine down.

Of the five planes from San Marcelino that landed at Clark to get

## 2. The Philippines, December 10, 1941

bombs for their runs at the Japanese, only three got full loads. Operating in constant fear of a Japanese raid "at any minute," one plane was hurried off the field with only one bomb. The fifth, piloted by Captain Colin Kelly, took off with only three out of its capacity of eight 600-pounders.

When two of those planes returned, they were waved off for San Marcelino, where, after refueling, were told to beat it for Del Monte. Eleven down.

Of the three remaining B-17s, one was shot down (Kelly). A second was lost when it was crashed into by a taxing P-40. When the last one returned from raiding Aparri, it was off to Mindanao for him, too. Fourteen down.

Of the 14 flyable Fortresses that were available that morning, only one, the B-17 that had been sent to reconnoiter Formosa, remained at Clark Field that night.

"Like scared rabbits," lamented one of the pilots later, "all 12 of us high-tailed it for the temporary safety of Del Monte; some of us flew over a thousand miles and never even dropped a bomb."

# 3

# Moon Under Lingayen

On the morning of December 22, 1941, U.S. Navy submarine *S-38*, under the command of Lt. W.G. "Moon" Chapple, single-handedly penetrated and later escaped the Japanese protective blockade of its massive near–100-ship Lingayen Gulf invasion force. Much of this story of what happened during the four-day operation comes from Lt. Chapple's official "War Patrol Report for Period 8 December 1941 to 27 December 1941."[1]

In chapter 2 of author Clay Blair's excellent two-volume work, *Silent Victory: The U.S. Submarine War Against Japan*, he listed eight major errors on what he called the "abysmally planned and executed" submarine defense of the Philippines. Of Number 6, "No Defense of Lingayen Gulf," he wrote that although the Navy believed it would be "the logical place for the main landing on Luzon … only one S-boat was placed inside the gulf and no fleet boats [were placed in advance] along its approaches."[2]

This is the story of that one sub, 18-year-old USS *S-38*, which found itself in the midst of 85 Japanese troop ships, two light cruisers, and 16 destroyers, while *S-40* and four newer, faster "fleet boats" vainly attempted to break through the protective screen of destroyers that stretched across the entire Gulf. Four days later, after failing to penetrate the blockade, all five, including *S-38*, were back in Manila.

The story of *S-38*'s single-ship adventure into harm's way goes back to December 9, when four S-boats and 14 fleet boats were ordered by Submarine Asiatic Fleet commander Captain John Wilkins to spread out west, northwest, and east of Luzon in anticipation of Japanese invasion forces approaching the island from any one or more of those directions.

## 3. Moon Under Lingayen

On December 21, *S-38*, under the command of popular Wreford Goss "Moon" Chapple, former Naval Academy heavyweight boxing champion and football player, was patrolling off Verde Passage between Luzon and Mindoro when, along with four other subs, got the order to enter Lingayen Gulf and attack the already arrived Japanese invasion force.

Arriving at the 20-mile-wide entrance before the other subs, Chapple, because of the uncharted reefs that literally blocked a submerged sub from entering, decided to chance it on the surface. In the dark, pre-dawn hours on December 22, he began what would be a three-and-a-half-hour maneuver through the treacherous obstacles, clearing the dangerous area and submerging just before daylight.

It was daybreak by the time *S-38* caught up to the Japanese invaders, who had already begun landing operations. Perhaps overconfident that no subs had challenged the reefs or destroyer screen to get in, it made it relatively easy for Chapple to move about looking for a target. After about an hour or so, he found one that for submariners was a dream shot—four slow-moving transports, all oblivious to the possibility of being a target for an American submarine.

Maneuvering the ship into what he considered a can't-miss position, Chapple launched a four-torpedo spread at the unsuspecting ships. But as clocked-time for impact came and went without a single explosion, how they all could have missed drew puzzled looks from everyone. With no time to speculate on what caused it, he quickly took the ship deep. As anticipated, a Japanese destroyer was quickly on to the tell-tale wakes left by the American tin fish. For the next 45 minutes, after skillfully avoiding their first depth charge attack of the war, the enemy broke off the attack.

While searching for another target, Chapple turned his focus on the new Mark X torpedo as possibly being the culprit for the painful missed opportunity. Heavier than the older Mark series, the chief torpedoman recalled that it had been recommended the run-depth be reset on the new Ten's four feet deeper, from 12 to 8 feet. It was 7:58 a.m. Having meanwhile moved in on an unsuspecting transport in the process of unloading troops, 16 minutes later, after firing two reset torpedoes at the ship, he would know if that was the answer.

Although the first fish missed, through the scope he was close enough to see the expressions on the faces of disembarking Japanese soldiers at the sight of the wake from the number two, which hit amidships, the explosion tearing up and sending them and the 5,445-ton *Mayo Maru* to the bottom.

With 18 Japanese destroyers inside the gulf mothering their over 80 transports, Chapple was not surprised to again see the explosion had immediately drawn unwanted attention. Spotting a pair of destroyers bearing down in his direction, he ordered a crash dive, the ship settling on the bottom at 80 feet. Unknown to the men of the old S-boat, the next 12 hours of their lives would be spent in and out of the soft, muddy bottom of Lingayen Gulf in fear that it was where they would forever remain.

Like sharks at feeding time, until the sun went down that night, there was a seemingly endless parade of destroyers, searching and dropping depth charges on the only U.S. submarine within the 350-square-mile gulf. Absent depth-finding gear on board, maneuvering blindly to escape the seemingly endless "pinging" sound omitted from the enemy destroyers and the depth charges that usually followed, left little time to celebrate the ship's first kill.

After riding out several minutes of attacks, the first of what would be a series of strange, unexplained events occurred when the ship uncontrollably began to rise toward the surface. Quick-thinking Chapple ordered her forward auxiliary tanks be flooded, stopping the rise 47 feet short of what would have surely meant the end had she broken the surface. However, as he angled the ship back toward the bottom, she ran bow-first into what turned out to be a mud bank. Deciding not to chance giving away his position by attempting to free it, he decided to rig for silence, and sit out the attack until it let up. (As a collection point of over hundreds of years of sand and silt from the numerous rivers that fed the huge gulf, for the next 3 days, *S-38*'s hang-ups with the buildup of sticky, glue-like mud would remain as much of a problem as dodging Japanese destroyers.)

After sweating out an hour of off-and-on depth charging, Chapple called a meeting to decide what to do. First on the agenda was to turn off the sound-gear, for every time an enemy ship passed overhead,

## 3. Moon Under Lingayen

whether it dropped depth charges or not, the anticipation was the same. They were stuck on the bottom, so why cringe with the sound of every ship that passed by.

Next on the list was what to do—surface when the sound of enemy ships had gone, or wait until dark. The second alternative was chosen. The question now was, could they survive what would be another 10 hours on the bottom?

It was 8 p.m. Chapple's order to start the engines could not have come at a better time. The thought of fresh air to the 42 men who had suffocatingly lived for hours in the equivalent of a sauna made what might be waiting for them on the surface well worth the chance. Engines started, Chapple, with ballast tanks blown, began to hopefully clear the boat from the mud. Slipping free easier than anticipated, the happy yell by the crew was suddenly cut short as the extra power used to back out sent the ship in a steep, backward angle before Chapple was able to cut the power. Although the backward plunge was only for a few feet, the port propeller was damaged when she hit bottom, causing a scraping or raspy sound as it turned, and all but ending any chance to move without being detected by marauding Japanese destroyers. Although relatively minor in damage, after alternately surfacing to charge batteries and diving to avoid an enemy destroyer, it is doubtful that what was in store for *S-38* and her crew during the next 72 hours would ever by duplicated.

The second of the strange, unexplained events actually happened just after noon on December 24. At 11:27, six, what Chapple described as large, auxiliary-type ships, were spotted some distance away. Thirty minutes later, while moving toward the area at periscope depth, an explosion, the origin of which was never explained, occurred just forward of the conning tower, its impact knocking everyone in that part of the ship off their feet.

Chapple quickly crash-dived to 90 feet, while the chief engineer frantically worked to reset the depth gauges that had also been momentarily knocked out. One thing about the mysterious explosion was clear—it had attracted the unwanted attention of two enemy destroyers who were detected closing in.

With only one American submarine having so far been detected within the entire gulf, there was no doubt that when it came, the attack would be relentless. In fact, between the time the first series of charges bracketed the ship at 12:05 and the last 48 minutes later, 28 separate explosions were counted.

Unscathed after the first series that let up at 12:26, the skipper decided to make a run for it. But, as anticipated, the noisy propeller wouldn't allow his movement to escape detection, for no sooner had the engines started than four more depth charges exploded off the starboard side. Ordering all engines stopped, Chapple "pulled the plug," allowing the ship to silently sink to the bottom. His decision, as it turned out, probably saved the ship, as before settling on the soft muddy bottom, eleven more depth charges shook the ship.

At 5:30 p.m., with no enemy ships detected for over four and a half hours, Chapple's decision to get under way was short lived, as in quick succession a half a dozen more depth charges rocked the ship from seemingly out of nowhere. Unknown to the battered and puzzled crew, what had just happened was only a continuation of mysterious, frightening, bad luck occurrences that, as previously mentioned, probably no American submarine in the two-and-a-half years of war to come would ever equal.

Although the origin of the explosions remained a mystery with still no enemy activity detected, Chapple decided to run submerged away from the area until he determined it safe to surface. However, at 10:30, exactly 11 hours since 18-year-old *S-38* last rode the surface, they ran aground again. Fortunately able to easily to break free from the obstacle, Chapple decided to surface. But again, the anticipated enjoyment of cool night air that they had not breathed for a remarkable day and a half was interrupted by yet another piece of unexplained bad luck—an explosion and fire in the ship's after battery compartment.

Within minutes, Chapple and two crewmen from the engine room, with protective clothing and fire extinguishers, entered the compartment. Finding two men badly burned and one with a broken back, as soon as the fires were put out, they were taken to sickbay. More important than tracing the origin of the explosion was that the damage to the batteries led directly to the loss of 50 percent of the ship's power needed to propel it underwater.

## 3. Moon Under Lingayen

It was near dawn by the time they were seaworthy again. Despite the anticipated difficulties due to the loss of speed, good news came with a pre-dawn radio message ordering them to return to Manila.

With daylight approaching, Chapple decided it was time to submerge. As the ship slowly began its decent, a sudden cry came to stop because they were unable to secure the engine room hatch cover. Old lady bad luck had struck again, this time from word that the gaskets that help seal the hatch cover had partially rotted from exposure to the air.

As work to "batten down the hatch" continued, lookouts, who had been ordered down when the ship began its dive, were ordered back up. It was just in time, as no sooner had they reached their perch than an enemy destroyer was spotted heading their way. Quick work by the engine room crew, however, saved the day, as the hatch was secured just as seawater broached the deck.

For the next hour or so, the cat-and-mouse game with the enemy destroyers and patrol boats continued, with noise from the damaged propeller forcing Chapple ever deeper into the gulf's uncharted depths. In the middle of maneuvering up from the bottom, a sudden, what had become familiar jolt occurred, announcing for the third time that they had hit yet another underwater obstacle.

Chapple's quick attempt to back away from it, found, like with their first encounter with the unfriendly gulf mud, that they were hung up again. Unlike the first one, however, the collision this time had left the bow of the ship dangling an unbelievable 50 feet higher than the stern, making it impossible to stand up or move about without hanging on to something. After several tense minutes of wrestling with the controls, it suddenly broke free from its muddy stranglehold. The jubilation of the crew was soon cut short, however, when it was realized that it was not slowing down. Because of the loss of electrical power from the engine room fire, Chapple was unable to stop or level the ship in what now had rapidly become an uncontrollable slide toward the bottom.

Needless to say, all eyes were glued to the pressure gauges as the boat slid past the 250- and 300-foot mark, with no signs of slowing down. The moment perhaps more frightening than any came at 325 feet, when the walls of the empty ballast tanks were heard buckling under the pressure, a dreaded sign that old '38 couldn't take much more. Moments later at 350 feet, however, the ship almost magically stopped, leveled off, and began to rise to the surface.

Although everyone was celebrating that they had avoided the dreaded "deep six" and would soon be leaving the gulf for home, few realized that the fight had suddenly become one to stop what quickly had become a runaway ascent to the surface. Again, as with its uncontrollable backward slide to the depths, Chapple was unable to stop it. Moments later, with everyone now paralyzed with the fear they would emerge amidst a group of enemy destroyers, old '38 shot bow first to the surface like a harpooned whale. A quick call to battle stations-surface, however, happily found the calm waters completely void of enemy ships.

Having had more than enough of strange, below-the-surface encounters, Chapple decided to chance it on the surface. After about an hour of clear sailing, lookouts reported what appeared to be the silhouette of two Japanese destroyers approximately 12 miles away, and in line with the anticipated escape route. Reluctantly, down they went one more time. Moments after leveling off and reaching maximum underwater speed, the craggy-bottomed gulf got her one last time, the effect of the sudden impact more violent than any of the collisions or depth-charge explosions yet felt on the ship.

As Chapple and his staggered crew struggled to recover, the former Naval Academy football star decided that enough was enough—hell or high water, its escape from the gulf would be on the surface.

Well overdue good fortune was on their side, however, as the "destroyers," which turned out to be two small auxiliary craft, did not see the '38 slip free from its four days and nights in gulf waters and sail safely into Manila Bay that Christmas 1941 night.

In early March 1942, Chapple was assigned to command the USS *Permit*, in which he remained until December 1943. Prior to General MacArthur's evacuation from Corregidor by PT boat on March 11, 1942, he had requested to be taken off by submarine. *Permit*, under new commander Moon Chapple, was assigned the job. When it reached the Rock on March 13 to find MacArthur already gone, Chapple was ordered to

*3. Moon Under Lingayen*

evacuate 47 men from the island, which, when added to his 64 man crew, amounted to a total of 111. Twenty-three days later on April 15, 1942, the sardine-packed ship arrived safely in Australia. Before he was retired from commanding a sub in December 1943, Chapple led *S-38* and *Permit* on eight war patrols and 294 days at sea.[3]

# 4

# When America Needed Heroes

## *Wheless and Wagner, December 10–16*

In between the disaster at Pearl Harbor, the loss of Wake Island, and rout of the American and Filipino army in the Philippines, the country found itself in desperate need of someone or something to indicate that we were fighting back. It needed heroes or heroic deeds to offset the dark headlines that daily dominated every newspaper in the country. Colin Kelly was the first, and later, two other American flyers, Hewitt Wheless and "Buzz" Wagner, who, unlike Kelly, survived to become real-life heroes.

Although the exploits of these three would be matched or surpassed many times over in the three-and-a-half years of war to come, they were just what we needed at the time.

Ironically, when people today are asked, "Who was the first American hero of World War II?" many would still answer, "Colin Kelly." But what of Wheless and Wagner? Few remember them or their exploits. Here are their stories.

Twenty-eight-year-old Hewitt T. "Shorty" Wheless was a Boeing B-17D pilot with the 19th Bombardment Group stationed at Clark Field in the Philippines when the war broke out. Fortunate to have missed the Japanese attack on Clark Field on December 8, he, along with what was left of the original 17 B-17s at Clark, flew south to Del Monte Field on the island of Mindanao two days later.

From temporarily safe Del Monte, some 500 miles out of range of

## 4. When American Needed Heroes

Japanese bombers, six B-17s on the afternoon of December 14 were ordered to attack an enemy invasion force at Legaspi on the southern edge of Luzon. Wheless' B-17 was one of the six.

Although the six Fortresses were scheduled for what would be the biggest single raid against the Japanese in the week-old war, bad luck and mechanical difficulties that had plagued the 19th from the beginning would continue.

It started with the lead B-17, piloted by Lt. Jim Connally. As he began his takeoff run, the plane blew a tire, forcing the big ship off the runway, crumpling the right wing-tip as it skid off the field. The five remaining planes, piloted by Wheless, Lieutenants Lee Coats, Jack Adams, Elliot Vandevanter, and Walter Ford, got off okay, the last plane leaving the runway at 12:14 p.m.

About 200 miles out, they ran into a spot of bad weather. When they broke out of it a few minutes later, Wheless was nowhere to be seen. His Number 3 engine had quit, forcing him to drop out.

From that point on, things went from bad to worse. A half hour out from the target, Walter Ford radioed Lee Coats, who had taken over from Connally, that he was having engine trouble and was returning to Del Monte. At the scheduled rendezvous point, some 35 miles from where the flight was to make its final turn for the target, Coats radioed that his engines were performing so badly that he was unable to make altitude and was turning back.

That left Vandevanter and Adams to go it alone. Forced to drop down to 18,000 feet below the clouds, Adams was the first over the target. After releasing his eight 600-pounders at the line of enemy transports sitting off the Legaspi coast, he was jumped by five Zeroes.

Adams quickly dove for cloud cover, the Zeroes hot after him. By the time he reached its protection, two engines had been knocked out, and two of his crew had been wounded. Despite shooting down two of the enemy planes during the race for the clouds, the remaining three Zeroes were waiting for them when they came out.

At that point, Adams "pulled a cute trick," said Harry Schrieber, his navigator. "He throttled back suddenly and one Zero overshot us to the left, which our side gunner picked off. Another came up under the stabilizer, and our bottom gunner got his second for the day."

# The Fall of the Philippines

Losing altitude while still battling the last enemy fighter, Adams decided to try for a beach landing on the nearby island of Masbate, just south of Luzon. Unfortunately, there wasn't one, "only jagged rocks with white surf wrapped around them," remembered Schrieber.

Desperately looking for a place to land, Adams spotted a rice paddy, "cutting the remaining two motors so we wouldn't have to climb out of her in flames," said a relieved navigator. After a couple of unsuccessful passes at the downed bomber, the lone enemy plane turned for home.[1]

Vandevanter in the other B-17 arrived over the target three minutes behind Adams, who, fortunately, had drawn all the Zeroes to him. This allowed three uncontested runs over the target before being discovered and chased into a cloudbank, from which he was able to escape and return safely to Del Monte.

Unknown to Adams and Vandevanter, the engine trouble on "Shorty" Wheless' B-17 that had forced him to drop out of the formation as they passed through the storm clouds had been corrected. Although well behind what he thought were the other four planes, Wheless chose to continue on to the target, despite knowing that he would be flying into a well-alerted enemy whose defenses would no doubt, include fighters.

Unknown to him, when it was over, the results of his decision would vault his name into every major newspaper and magazine in the country, with the story of the flight read to the nation over the radio by President Roosevelt. It would also appear in a 20-minute film narrated by Ronald Reagan.

The story the President told and the actual events of that afternoon, except in a few places, was quite accurate.

> ROOSEVELT: "By the time [Wheless] arrived over the target, the other Flying Fortresses had dropped their bombs and stirred up the hornet's nest of Japanese Zero planes. Eighteen of these Zero fighters attacked our lone Flying Fortress. Despite this mess, our plane proceeded on its mission."
>
> FACT: Although Wheless didn't find out until two days later, as noted, only two planes made it to the target ahead of him. Although the number of enemy planes that jumped him was said to be 18, the number was never known. While the running battle with the enemy fighters

## 4. When American Needed Heroes

was going on, Wheless headed straight for six transports neatly lined up off Legaspi. After bombardier R.W. Schlotte released his eight 600-pounders, his attention was entirely focused on taking evasive action and giving his gunners a crack at the Japanese.

ROOSEVELT: "As it turned back on its homeward journey, a running fight between the bomber and the 18 Japanese pursuit planes continued for 75 miles. Four pursuit planes of the Japs attacked simultaneously at each side; four were shot down with the side guns. During this fight, the bomber's radio operator was killed, the engineer's right hand was shot off, and one gunner was crippled, leaving only one man available to operate both side guns. Although wounded in one hand, this gunner alternately manned both side guns, bringing down three more Japanese Zero planes."

FACT: W.G. Killin, radio operator and belly gunner in what was called the "bathtub" position in the old D-model B-17, had the top of his head blown off and his gun put out of commission. Gunners Russell Brown and W.W. Williams each claimed a Zero before being wounded. Williams, who was hit by a 20mm slug from one of the enemy planes, had his leg ripped open from knee to thigh, knocking him out of the fight. Brown, his right hand nearly shot off, was able to operate his gun. The job of firing both waist guns went to Sgt. John Gootee who, although wounded in the right wrist, alternately kept firing both guns until helped by bombardier Schlotte.

(The seven enemy planes claimed by Wheless and the other four by Adams, by later World War II standards, may seem hard to believe. However, this was the first time the Japanese had tangled with the B-17. Being unfamiliar with the Fortresses' fire power and location of its guns may account for the claim of that many. On the other side of the coin, the system of authenticating a kill by a witness had not yet been put in place by the air force. Had it been, the count may have been reduced to five or less. Also, despite how it might sound, it was apparently impossible for a large number of planes to literally swarm all over a B-17. Said Saburo Sakai, the famous Japanese ace, after his experience of shooting down Colin Kelly, "It was impossible for [a large number of Zeroes] to make a concerted attack against the bomber, for in the rarefied air we could easily over control and collide with each other. Instead we swung out in a long file, and made our firing passes one after another, each plane making its run alone." This was particularly easy against the D-model B-17, since it had no tail-gun, relying instead on the gun from the "bathtub" position to help cover the tail.[2])

# The Fall of the Philippines

ROOSEVELT: "While this was going on, one engine in the American bomber was shot out. Out of eleven control cables, all but four were shot away. The rear landing wheel was blown off entirely, and the two front wheels were both shot out."

FACT: As far as it went, the President's assessment of the damage was correct. The diminutive five-foot-six, 138-pound Wheless was struggling for all he was worth to keep the big plane in the air while it was literally being shot to pieces by 7.7 machine gun and 20mm cannon fire from the Zeroes. The running battle with the Japanese fighters, which began the minute the plane appeared over the target, would last, as the President said, "for 75 miles." The first to go was No. 1 engine, its throttle cable shot in two. Then, in rapid succession, the radio, oxygen system, a six-inch hole in the right wing fuel tank, and seven of the eleven control cables of the big plane shot out. Both wheels were shot flat, and the tail wheel was blown completely out of its mount. This, not to mention the three wounded and one dead crewmen, the three machine guns out of commission, and the loss of gas, which would cause a second engine to quit just miles from the Mindanao coast.

ROOSEVELT: "The flight continued until the remaining Japanese pursuit ships exhausted their ammunition and turned back. With one engine gone and the plane practically out of control, the American bomber returned to base after dark. The mission had been accomplished. The name of that pilot was Captain Hewitt T. Wheless."

FACT: Not quite that simple. Looking for protection from the gang of Zeroes on his tail, Wheless, as he left the Luzon coast, ducked into a cloudbank. When he broke out minutes later, not a Japanese plane was to be seen. Either low on ammunition, fuel, or sure the battered B-17, trailing smoke and limping along on three engines, was finished, the enemy had abandoned the chase. But Wheless' exhausting battle, which would last close to 6 hours, was a long way from being over. As he neared the Mindanao coast, it started to rain, and it was getting dark. After fighting to keep the plane in the air for over 300 miles, he knew chances were slim of them reaching Del Monte. When the second engine ran out of gas, and with nothing but jungle between the Mindanao coast and Del Monte, Wheless decided for an auxiliary strip at Cagayan on the northern coast of the island. Afraid to fly anything but in a straight line because of the damaged control cables, there would be no checking the field first before coming in. As he gingerly banked the plane toward the field and started in, he was aghast to see it had been barricaded in anticipation of it being used by the Japanese. Past the point of no return and unaware that the tires had both been shot flat, he lowered his wheels. After ripping through several barricades, some 200 yards down the runway, the big bomber's brakes suddenly locked up, causing the 39,000-pound plane to momentarily stand on its nose

## 4. When American Needed Heroes

before crashing back down on its tail. They were down, even though it was far from the "return-to-base" landing to which the President referred. After getting the wounded crewmen to a small hospital at Cagayan, they found that among the 1,200 or so bullet holes they counted in the plane, even the propeller blades had been hit several times.

For his gallant effort in bringing the shot-up Fortress safely through, Hewitt. T. Wheless received the Distinguished Service Cross and was promoted to captain.

On the island of Saipan on the morning of March 9, 1945, B-29 aircrews were shocked to learn that henceforth they would abandon the high-altitude bombing they had been using and instead bomb Japanese targets from the unprecedented altitude of 5,000 to 8,000 feet. The attacks would be carried out at night with incendiary bombs. That night, 300 B-29s bombed Tokyo, resulting in over one fourth of the city being consumed by fire. From that night on, the strategic bombing of Japan was changed forever. Although credit for implementing this strategy went to General Curtis LeMay, the idea actually originated with Brigadier General Thomas Power and then Colonel Hewitt Wheless. The two men got the idea after studying an earlier strike photo of Tokyo, where several blocks of the city had been burned from a previous high-altitude raid. LeMay listened intently to their idea, then gave them 24 hours to get ready. The rest is history.

In the six months between Pearl Harbor and Midway in June 1942, U.S. Army fighter activity against the Japanese was pretty much confined to the Philippine and Dutch East Indies.

Of the few recorded incidents where the U.S. bested the Japanese, one man's name stands out above all others—26-year-old First Lieutenant Boyd D. "Buzz" Wagner. Few who knew of his exploits were not quick to say that he was the best pursuit pilot they had ever seen, comments that encompassed not only his flying skills, but his daring as a combat pilot as well.

Wagner was commanding officer of the 17th Pursuit Squadron stationed at Iba airfield when the Japanese struck the Philippines on December 8. By the end of the day, only five of eighteen Curtiss P-40s of his squadron were left, and Iba, as a functioning base, was destroyed.

Early on the morning of December 12, Wagner, who, up to that time had not seen any action, took off on a lone reconnaissance mission to observe the number of enemy ships off Aparri, where the Japanese had landed a few days earlier.

Because of the devastating losses suffered by U.S. fighter forces between December 8 and 10, orders had come down from air force headquarters restricting its use to reconnaissance only. Confrontation with enemy fighters was to be avoided at all possible.

The morning was overcast, forcing Wagner to rely on his compass to lead him to Aparri. Estimating that he was close to his objective after approximately 200 miles, he let down through the overcast, only to find himself practically on top of two enemy destroyers. Sight of the American fighter brought quick response from Japanese antiaircraft gunners on the two ships, forcing him to, as he said, "turn nose-down and dive within a few feet of water" to avoid the heavy barrage.

Flying inland directly into the morning sun, moments later he was startled by tracer fire zipping over his canopy. Looking back, he spotted a pair of Japanese fighters on his tail and three more above. Surprised by how quick they responded to his presence, he said, "I pulled nose-up directly into the sun at full throttle. The two Nippos lost me, and I went into a half-barrel role onto their tails. They were in close formation, and both burst into flames almost simultaneously when I fired."

Looking down, he found himself directly over Aparri airfield with twelve enemy fighters neatly lined up on the edge of the runway. "I made two passes at the field," he said, "and saw five of them burst into flames."

As he pulled up from his second pass, he spotted the three remaining enemy fighters boring down on him. "I dropped my empty belly tank and dived close to the ground, then gave it the needle and easily out distanced them. The last I saw of the field was two columns of black smoke."[3]

It didn't take long for word of Wagner's foray to reach the news-hungry correspondents hanging around General MacArthur's headquarters in Manila. Although perhaps unaware at the time, they had found

## 4. When American Needed Heroes

the fighter pilot hero for whom they'd been hoping. Four days later he would more than prove them right.

On the morning of December 10, the same day the Japanese invaded Aparri, a second landing force came ashore on the northwest coast of Luzon at Vigan. As at Aparri, they had flown in a squadron of fighters to the Vigan airfield, which, along with several troop ships, had been spotted by Lt. Russell Church on a reconnaissance mission over the area on December 15.

At 6:00 a.m. on the morning of December 16, Wagner and Church, with each plane carrying half a dozen 30-pound fragmentation bombs, took off for Vigan. A third P-40, piloted by Lt. Al Strauss, assigned to fly cover for them, also joined the flight.

As at Aparri, Japanese antiaircraft gunners were quick to open up on the unwelcomed visitors. Undaunted, Wagner, with Church a few hundred yards behind, headed for the row of enemy ships off the coast. Coming in at 2,500 feet, Wagner unloaded all six of his 30-pounders. As he pulled up, he looked back in time to see Church take a direct hit, flames shooting out from the belly of his P-40.

At that point, Church, still in control, banked his burning fighter toward the Vigan airfield. Leveling off at treetop level, the young pilot dropped all six of his bombs on the line of enemy fighters at the edge of the field. It was a "perfectly executed attack," said Wagner, "and for seconds it seemed that he would be able to regain control, but the plane suddenly rocked wildly and plunged sideways to earth."[4]

There was no doubt in Wagner's mind that the courageous 17th Pursuit pilot knew he was facing certain death when he chose to attack rather than gain altitude and bail out. "The Medal of Honor has been given for less," he told a correspondent later.

Joined now by Strauss, the two angry Americans decided to make the enemy pay for the loss of their comrade. As the two started their run on the field, Japanese pilots and ground personnel were seen running for their planes.

As Wagner began his final pass, he spotted a single enemy fighter take off from the opposite end of the field. Blocked from view by his own wing, Buzz calmly rolled his Kittyhawk over on its back to get a clear view of the enemy plane, then righted the ship, throttled back to let the unsuspecting pilot pull away to a comfortable shooting distance, then shot him down.

Amazing as this feat was, the nickname "Buzz," although of his own making, was not of his own choosing. It was one given by fellow pilots before the war. The name related to his penchant for "buzzing" private and commercial planes in the pre-war skies above Luzon in order to sharpen his skills for, if and when, the war started.

When the two Americans turned for Clark Field, ammunition exhausted and fuel tanks near empty, they left behind an estimated 17 Japanese planes destroyed and numerous "Sons of Nippon" dead among them.

Despite recording the most devastating results of the air war to date, air force headquarters was not happy with the "unauthorized" use and exposure of the precious fighters. However, when the news-hungry correspondents got wind of the second "Wagner foray" in four days, it was out of their hands.

Ironically and perhaps sadly, Wagner may have been too good a pilot too early in the war. His exploits at Aparri and Vigan, the latter earning him the Distinguished Flying Cross, were, for all practical purposes, to be his last as a fighter pilot. On January 2, he, along with 16 other pilots, was flown out of Bataan for Australia, in hopes of ferrying fighters back to the Philippines. They did not return.

By January, Lieutenant Wagner became Captain Wagner, and by April, he was jumped one full rank to lieutenant colonel, becoming the youngest pilot in the Army Air Force to wear the silver leaves. Along with it, except for one occasion, went his combat flying days.

That "one occasion" occurred when, on April 30, 1942, Buzz accompanied a group of his "students" on a raid over Lae, New Guinea. Flying a Bell P-39 Airacobra, Wagner shot down three enemy fighters, at the time making him top ace in the Pacific Theater.

Tragically, Boyd D. "Buzz" Wagner lost his life in an aircraft accident back in the U.S. in 1943.


On December 29, 1941, *Life* magazine published "Boyd Wagner's Story: America's First Ace Tells How He Shot Down First Two Planes."

## 4. When American Needed Heroes

On February 16, 1942, the magazine initiated what they called their "Roll of Honor." It contained the names and photographs of American servicemen honored by *Life* for their acts of heroism in the young war. Interestingly, of the 18 men honored in the initial February 16 issue, nine were pilots, including Colin Kelly. Hewitt Wheless was honored in the March 16 issue, and "Buzz" Wagner on April 20, following his becoming the first "official" American ace of the war.

# 5

# The USS *Canopus*

Of the many stories to come out of the battle of Bataan, perhaps the most unusual involved a 23-year-old U.S. Navy submarine-tender named the *Canopus*. At first glance, it is hard to believe that a Navy ship, too old and too slow to escape the Philippines with the rest of the 16th Naval District's ships on December 16, could, in any conceivable way, contribute to U.S. efforts during the battle. This is the story of the "Old Lady," as she was affectionately referred to, and of her 90-day contribution to the story of the battle.

Perhaps the best way to get to know the ship is to read what her skipper, Captain Earl L. Sackett, wrote about her after the war in his 24-page, "History of the USS *Canopus*."[1]

> Built in 1921 as a combination freight and passenger carrier for the Grace Line, she was shortly taken over by the Navy and converted to a submarine tender. She was given extensive machine shops, foundries, storerooms, cabins, living spaces for the comfort of their submarine crews when off duty, and a few guns as a concession that she was now a man of war.
> 
> In the fateful first week of December, the *Canopus* had just finished an extensive overhaul at Cavite Naval Yard and emerged looking more like a war vessel than ever before. Many antiaircraft guns had been added to her armament, and light armor had been fitted around exposed positions, which later proved immense value in warding off bomb fragments.
> 
> With the ship as ready as the men could make her, the grim question as to whether the value of her services in the time left would be worth the expected sacrifices was all that remained to be decided.
> 
> Although *Canopus* was still intact, the harbor, by December 23, could no longer be used as a submarine base. It was, therefore, decided on Christmas Eve to get underway for what proved to be our last journey, and steamed out of the bay toward Corregidor.
> 
> We set up shop in Mariveles Bay on the southern tip of Bataan peninsula. With hopes that Mariveles, being close to the guns of Corregidor,

## 5. The USS Canopus

would keep us immune from air attacks, we moored the ship to the shoreline in a protective cove named Lilimbon, again spreading our camouflage nets overhead.

And so, with the spreading of the net, the story of the first of what would be the old ship's final 90 days began. But it was not one that after the first seven days, any of its crew, short of a miracle, would have believed possible.

For the first three days, to blend the old ship in with the anticipated jungled Bataan shoreline, the crew worked diligently at painting it to match. Unfortunately, green was far from the right color for her moorings in Lilimbon. Just behind the road that bordered the eastern edge of the bay was a huge white-faced cliff from which most of the rock used for road repair and construction on Bataan was quarried. When finished, *Canopus* stuck out like a big, green thumb, or as one of the crew more accurately put it, "like a cruiser" against the chalky white background of the quarry.

He was right. *Canopus*' ploy would, in fact, last through just two enemy air attacks. Of the Japanese planes involved in the three raids launched against Corregidor and southern Bataan on the 29th, those in the last one went after the *Canopus*. Although it wouldn't be the last, except for a true miracle, it could have been.

Of the attack, Earl Sackett wrote that the planes "wheeling in from the fatally exposed direction over the bay ... blanketed the *Canopus* with a perfectly placed pattern of bombs. Only one actually struck the ship, but that one nearly ended our career then and there. It was an armor-piercing type which went through all the ship's decks and exploded on top of the propeller shaft under the magazines, blowing them open and starting fires which threatened to explode the ammunition.

"Meanwhile, below decks," he continued, "Lieutenant Commander Al Hede had organized [a] fire party which tackled the problems by carrying their hoses through choking smoke in the compartments near the magazines, pulling wounded and dying away from ... where they had fallen. Chaplain McManus then led a rescue group into the engine room, where bomb fragments and escaping steam had caused the most casualties, administering last rites to dying men and helping to evacuate the injured...."

With both officers in charge of the engine room badly wounded by the blast, the Chief Machinist's Mate shut off the steam at the boilers until the severed steam pipes could be isolated. By his action, said Sackett, "he saved more of his men from being scalded to death. He then helped the wounded to safety and was later found wandering around dazed, having no recollection of what happened after the blast."

When the fires were finally put out and the magazines inspected, several exploded powder bags were discovered. "Evidence," said Sackett, "how close to complete destruction the ship and all on board had been. Nothing less than a miracle could have prevented a general explosion at the time the bomb set off those powder charges, but miracles do happen—the engine of destruction had carried its own antidote. Its fragments, which severed pipes near the magazines, had released floods of steam and water at the danger point, automatically keeping fire away from the rest of the powder."[2]

Although the loss of life and wounds that occurred from the attack was both sad and tragic, "the damage suffered by the fire actually provided," wrote Sackett, "a silver lining for our Supply Officer and crew." It seems that the fire, which had damaged Lt. Gus Johnson's office, had destroyed all of his records, forcing him to "put an end to the accounting system for the duration. "What we had," said the ship's captain, "we could use without the usual red tape. There was nothing for the men to spend money on, so there were no more paydays. All clothing became community property, doled out to [those] who only appeared in a nearly naked condition. This Utopian state, inevitably welded us into a great family, working and fighting in common cause—to do our damndest to lick the Japs. Even punishment became unnecessary, as this spirit of community would not tolerate shirkers, the men themselves seeing to it that no one was derelict in his duty."

Although the ship had survived the bombing, all knew it was just a matter of time before they were hit again. It came on January 5. Could another miracle be in waiting with this one?

Despite being totally bracketed by a series of high-explosive bombs, the concussion of which literally lifted the *Canopus* out of the water, only one actually found its mark. This one, a fragmentation bomb, exploded against the smokestack, raining shrapnel down on the decks.

## 5. The USS Canopus

Although several of the crew were wounded in the explosion, damage to the ship was only superficial. Superficial or not, "inspection below decks," said Sackett, "disclosed that the several near-misses had taken their toll. Each side had been pierced a few feet above the water by ... fragments of bombs exploded in the water alongside. Another bomb had exploded deeper in the water, cracking the plating and loosening rivets, which were leaking steadily."

After suffering its second bombing within the last six days, it had become sadly apparent that under the existing circumstances, her days were numbered. Or were they? After inspecting the damage above decks, which appeared far worse than it actually was, Sackett had an idea: Why not make use of the existing damage, along with a little added "makeup" of their own, to fool the Japanese into believing that the ship was foundering and abandoned? They had to work fast in order to trick the daily Japanese "Photo Joe" reconnaissance plane when he came over the next morning, into believing the last attack had finished her.

"The next morning when 'Joe' came over," remembered Sackett, "his picture showed what looked like an abandoned hulk, listed over on her side, with cargo booms askew and blackened areas around the bomb holes, from which wisps of smoke floated up for two or three days. The smoke actually came from oily rags in strategically placed smudge pots. Our antiaircraft guns were taken off and mounted on the hill nearby so as not to draw further retaliation to the ship."

Machine guns and light antiaircraft guns that had been removed from the ship were manned, wrote Sackett, "by our alert sailors with itchy trigger fingers, just living for the day when [one] would venture close enough to give them one good crack at him."

Weeks before the war broke out on December 8, army engineers had successfully dug four large tunnels into the face of the cliffs that paralleled the shoreline along which the *Canopus* was tied. What was called Tunnel No. 1, or Navy Tunnel, was taken over as living quarters by off-duty *Canopus* crewmen to allow the on-duty crews to continue to provide what was the ship's main function—a 24-hour repair shop. Wrote Commander Sackett of it: "More than a hundred men not having repair duties lived underground with reasonable comfort, at least after the water dripping from bare rocks overhead had been tapped and piped to a shower...."

On January 15, just as the ship's crews were getting used to their new routine, Naval Commander Frank Bridgett, popular operations officer of the now planeless Patrol Wing Ten, was ordered to establish a Naval Battalion defense force. Its job was to protect the undefended 2-mile southwest corner of Bataan shoreline against a possible enemy invasion. Not only did the former Patwing executive have no planes, he also had no men to man his Naval Battalion.

Starting with 150 Patwing sailors of his own, he got 130 volunteers from the *Canopus*, another 100 from the Cavite naval yard, and 100 veteran Marines from Corregidor. *Canopus* executive officer Lt. Commander "Hap" Goodall was named second-in-command.

Outside of the ready-equipped Marines, the problem of equipping the sailors was top priority. Rifles, from 1903 Springfields to 1917 Enfields, were somehow scrounged up. With many of the sailor-recruits uniforms either duty light blue or dress white, it was decided to dye the whites a khaki color to blend in with the anticipated terrain. Unfortunately, the whites dyed with boiled coffee grounds came out what was described as a "sickly mustard yellow."

It was not until about January 20 that training of the sailors under the guidance of the Marines began. Unbeknownst, of course, to the anxious bluejackets, their very first training hike actually became the first day of what would be called the battle of Longaskawayan Point.

Also unbeknownst to them until then was the landing that night of some 250 soldiers of the Japanese 20th Infantry Regiment who, separated from the main body of 900 during the night, had unknowingly landed on Longaskawayan Point, some 7 miles south of their intended invasion point.

The ensuing battle for Longaskawayan and the surrounding jungle terrain against the lost, yet resilient Japanese lasted a total of 7 days. Reported losses to the Naval Battalion included 11 dead and 26 wounded. Not reported was the effect the sailors had on the outcome. Although their contributions were recorded by the Marines as exemplary, it was not until Army Intelligence Sergeant Russell Sakakida read from a diary taken from a dead Japanese officer of the surprising effect the mustard-

## 5. *The USS* Canopus

yellow-clad sailors had on them. "This new type of suicide squad," he wrote, "thrashed about in the jungle wearing bright colored uniforms and making plenty of noise. When they reached a clearing, they would attempt to draw our fire by sitting down, talking loudly and lighting cigarettes."[3]

Although the sailors' role in the ground fighting was over, the battle to destroy the few remaining Japanese, who had taken to the caves and rough terrain along the sea cliffs, kept the *Canopus* in the picture. It became obvious that, after failing to dislodge the enemy from their well-hidden positions, it would take an assault from the sea. But with no ships available for the duty, Commander Bridgett asked if a couple of modified 40-foot motor launches from the *Canopus* could be used. The answer came some 12 hours later when he was told that the first of two, what would later be called "Mickey Mouse Battleships," were ready to go. Converted, it looked like this: three-eighths-inch-thick armor plating bolted to the bow and over the engines; sandbags stacked around the gas tank; a captured Japanese 37 mm antitank gun lashed to the bow; two .50-caliber machine guns set up just behind the bow plating; and two .30-caliber machine guns positioned at the waists.

The next morning, Saturday, January 31, the first miniature "battleship," amid shouts of encouragement and envy from the group of well-wishers from the ship, pushed off for Longaskawayan. Under the command of "Hap" Goodall, the little boat was to make two round trips to the cliffs and back before the day was over. "It was a seven- or eight-mile cruise by water to the point," said Goodall. "We made two trips the first day, blasting scores of Japs out of their caves with gunfire. As evidence of our success, we brought in two prisoners, alive but dazed, among others which had not survived the return voyage."

A somewhat humorous incident occurred on the way back from the first foray, when one of the two thought-to-be dead enemy soldiers regained consciousness. At that point, a Philippine Scout on board gave the man a cigarette, then bent down and said something to him in Tagalog. Later, when an interpreter was asked what he said, he smiled and said, "When I get ashore, I cut your God-damned throat."

With the immediate threat to southern Bataan ended, it was decided to incorporate the Naval Battalion into the 4th Marine Regiment on

Corregidor. The reluctance of the *Canopus* crewmen among them, however, was rife with threats of what they would do if the ship tried to leave without them. Wrote Earl Sackett of them: "They swore that the big guns they were about to man would be kept trained on the channel leading out of the harbor, ready to blow the ship out of the water at the first sign of a treacherous attempt to abandon them."

On the same January 20 night the 200 Japanese were discovered on Longoskawayan Point, the main body of 700 successfully landed some 8 miles north on Quinauan Point. Their discovery, like with Longaskawayan, opened what would be called "the battle for the points." It would last 16 days, and would be one of the bloodiest and agonizing battles of the campaign.

On the morning of February 5, after two weeks of brutal and difficult no-holds-barred fighting, the remaining Japanese, pushed to the very cliffs they had ascended earlier, had taken refuge in the caves and rocks below the point. Despite their efforts, the Americans and Filipinos found it difficult to make headway from above, bringing General Wainwright to place a call to "Hap" Goodall on the *Canopus*, requesting that he standby with his armored motor launches in case he was needed to help mop up on Quinauan.

Later that afternoon, Captain Ed Dyess, commander of the Air Force's 20th Pursuit Squadron, whose men had been "drafted" into the point battle, got a call from "Hap" Goodall. He was to report with a dozen of his men to the *Canopus* that evening. Arriving by truck, he and his men were treated to a hot meal, after which Goodall told of the upcoming operation scheduled for early the next morning. Among other things, Dyess mentioned that the Scouts would have white sheets lowered to a point just above the known enemy positions on the cliff.

The two "Mickey Mouse Battleships," each towing a motorized whaleboat with Dyess and six men in one and the rest in the other, shoved off at 6:00 a.m.

Arriving of Quinauan at 8:00, the 37mm's and twin .50s on the "battleships" were immediately put to work, blasting the white-sheet-marked caves and ravines the Scouts had pinpointed the day before.

"I opened fire with the 37mm gun," recalled Goodall, "and on the second shot at about 300 yards ... the whole cave collapsed. We contin-

## 5. *The USS* Canopus

ued firing at selected areas until [we were] about 75 yards from the beach [then] shifted to the .50s."[4]

Meanwhile, the two whaleboats, which had been cut loose, headed for the beach. Each group, armed with grenades, submachine guns, and a couple of Lewis guns, made quick work of the few remaining Japanese once they reached shore.

As they began working their way around the point, three Japanese dive-bombers, who had spotted the tiny flotilla of boats off Quinauan, dropped sticks of bombs near Dyess, killing one of his men.

In the meantime, the two "battleships," leaving the beached whaleboats behind, started back for Mariveles. Probably alerted of their presence off Quinauan by one of the planes attacking the point, they were soon jumped by four enemy planes.

In the one-sided running gun battle that followed, both motor launches were damaged. "In the fight," wrote Earl Sackett later, "Commander Goodall and three navy crewmen were wounded. One of the planes was shot down by Gunner's Mate Charles Kramb, who was killed at his gun. Goodall was badly wound in both feet, but ordered the beaching of the little boats to save the lives of the men still unhurt. Three men were killed and four others wounded, but the survivors made crude stretchers for the wounded men and laboriously cut their way through the jungle to the road, where they were taken by truck back to the ship." This was a sad, but in a way, glorious end to the two "Mickey Mousers" as they were called by the ever-envious crewmen who had been left behind on the ship.

Although her adventurous contributions to the army on Bataan were over, to the end the "Old Lady" continued to engender herself to those lucky enough to take advantage of her presence. Wrote Commander Sackett of it:

> Nearly every evening, Army officers and nurses who were able to stretch a few hours of leave from their duties gathered on board the *Canopus*. We had refrigeration, excellent cooking facilities, and decent living quarters, which seemed heaven to them compared to their hardships afield. To enjoy a real shower, well cooked meals served on white linen with civilized tableware, and the greatest luxury of all, real butter ... topped off with ice cream and chocolate sauce, seemed too much for them to believe.
> Our visitors repaid us in full for any hospitality with tales of their own

adventures. Captain Arthur Wermuth, famous "one man army of Bataan," often regaled us with graphic, even gruesome accounts of his many encounters. Lt. John Bulkeley and other Torpedo Squadron 3 officers particularly enjoyed our ice cream desserts.[5]

Army nurse Lt. Juanita Redmond, who, along with all the nurses, had a standing invitation for dinner on board the old ship, summarized as well as anyone what a visit to the *Canopus* meant: "We were almost overcome by nostalgia at the sight of the silver and table linens. They gave us wonderful food and lots of cigarettes, and after dinner we played bridge.... When the Chaplain said good night, he handed us each a lollypop; we could hardly believe our eyes."[6]

By the first week of April, it was obvious that the end was near. Commander Sackett's narrative covering their last hours before the surrender in part tells it best:

"It was scarcely a surprise when we heard reports on April 6 that the front lines were in serious trouble. On April 8 came news that the Army forces on the eastern flank were retreating toward Mariveles, leaving us with the grim duty of destroying everything that might be of value to the Japanese. Early in the day, the Commandant told us that no Army or Navy forces would be evacuated to Corregidor, since the island was already overcrowded. However, at 10:30 that night, he telephoned that General Wainwright had decided to accept ... the naval forces at Mariveles.

"That wild and horrible night must be imprinted forever in the memories of all who lived through it. Roads were choked with retreating troops. Around the shores of Mariveles Bay, Navy men blew up the old Dewey Dry Dock. The *Canopus* seemed reluctant to go, but her crew still took pride in the fact that the Japs were unable to knock her out."[7]

At 4:00 a.m., *Canopus* backed out of her berth to a spot some 400 yards off Lilimbon Cove, where anchors were dropped and flood valves opened. As the sentimental pride of what could be called the Bataan navy slowly slipped into her 12-fathom-deep grave, few officers, men, nurses, and PT boat skippers who had partaken of her generous supply of long-forgotten favors would not have paused in salute to her memory.

As the old ship began to settle into her watery grave, an explosion

## 5. *The USS* Canopus

of the first of the four navy tunnels on the eastern edge of the bay momentarily illuminated the sky. Forty minutes later, all tasks completed, a small fleet of motor boats filled with the last of the naval personnel shoved off for Corregidor. As the last three boats, loaded mostly with exhausted *Canopus* crewmen, cast off, a tremendous explosion erupted from the northernmost of the four tunnels.

"The last three boats had just left the dock when the tortured earth struck back at us," wrote Sackett, who was in the lead boat.

> The whole hillside erupted in a tremendous burst of orange flame, hurling huge boulders half a mile out into the bay. Evidently, gasoline drums stored in the tunnel had broken open when the entrance was dynamited closed, and fumes in the corked-up passage had built up a gigantic charge. Our three boats were squarely in the path of that deluge of destruction. Two were struck by massive boulders, one of them sinking instantly under the impact that sheared off the whole stern and leaving its three occupants struggling in the water. Fortunately unhurt, they were soon picked up by shipmates in the undamaged boat. The third boat did not sink, but boulders crashing down through its canopy killed an officer and three men. Nine other men were wounded by the rain of heavy rocks. Fortunately, the battered boat was still able to make it to Corregidor, whose arrival announced the informal end to the story of the "Old Lady."[8]

# 6

# A Scary Christmas But a Happy New Year

## *The Philippines, December 1941*

This is a story that began on Christmas Day, 1941, involving Company C of the U.S. Army's 194th Tank Battalion. It originally appeared in the 1949 book *Bataan Uncensored,* written by its commander, Lt. Colonel Ernest B. Miller.[1] While in prison camp at Cabanatuan, he actually got the story secondhand from men who had heard it from the survivors. Part of the story was also told to Navy Lieutenant Robert Kelly of Motor Torpedo Squadron 3, who, while recovering from a wounded arm in the hospital on Corregidor, heard it from two of the survivors.[2] Since the names of only two of the four tank crewmen appeared in his account but were not on the list of prisoners at the camp, no evidence of their fate has ever been found. It is possible that they died in the prison in Manila.

In the 15 days between the 8th and 22nd of December 1941, the Japanese invaded the island of Luzon at four different locations. On December 24, a fifth enemy force made a surprise landing at Lamon Bay, 60 miles southeast of Manila.

Ordered to defend this particular area was part of what was called the South Luzon Force, partially composed of troops of the Philippine Army's 1st Infantry Regiment and C Company of the U.S. Army's 194th Tank Battalion.

After landing unopposed, the northernmost arm of the two-pronged Japanese invasion force, having moved some 10 miles inland

## 6. A Scary Christmas But a Happy New Year

from the beach, was surprised by an advanced party of Americans looking for a suitable location to make a stand the next day.

Coming under heavy enemy machine gun and small arms fire, the Americans beat a hasty retreat back to the 1st Infantry outpost line. There, Major Ralph Rumbold, senior U.S. advisor with the regiment, ordered five C Company tanks to fight a delaying action battle on the road the next morning to allow the 1st Infantry time to dig in. Despite platoon leader Lt. Robert Needham's protest against going without a reconnaissance of the road and possible enemy strength, the order was not rescinded.

And so, a little after 9:00 a.m. on Christmas day, as ordered, five Stuart M-3 light tanks started single file down the narrow mountainous road toward the Japanese. All was quiet for the first mile or so. However, as Lt. Needham in the lead Stuart rounded a blind curve several hundred yards in front of the second tank, he took a direct hit from a Japanese .75mm gun, the impact of which killed all four crewmen and knocked the tank off the road into a rice paddy. Evidently, the run-in with the Americans the night before had brought the Japanese to anticipate a U.S. counterattack the next day, prompting them to set up a roadblock and bring up the anti-tank gun.

Back on the road, meanwhile, Sgt. Robert Mitchell, driver of the second tank, having lost sight of Needham after he disappeared around the bend, had hurried to catch up. Seconds after rounding the curve, an enemy shell from the .75 exploded in the road behind, prompting him to speed up to catch up with the lead tank.

While expecting to run into Needham's Stuart when they came around the bend, they unexpectedly ran into a roadblock of burning logs which, without hesitation, was easily smashed through. After breaking out of the smoke and debris from the scattered logs, they came face to face with the Japanese .75mm set up in the middle of the road. Again, without hesitation, Mitchell sped head-on into the gun, knocking it off the road and scattering its startled crew.

Continuing on and firing at enemy troops as they moved, with the remaining three tanks following behind, they soon came to a wide spot in the road. Realizing that their only hope was to turn around and fight their way out, they started back. As they neared the curve in the road,

Needham's tank was spotted lying on its side in the rice paddy, its smoldering wreckage leaving little doubt as to the fate of its crew. One crewman said it had taken a direct hit in front, which had knocked off both front doors.

Moments after reaching a point where they believed they were safe, Mitchell's tank, still in the lead, was hit by an enemy shell that sent it tumbling off the narrow road and into a rice paddy, where it fortunately came to rest upright.

Realizing that in moments they could be surrounded by enemy troops pressing the attack on the three remaining Stuarts, the four men decided that their only chance was to secure everything and play dead when enemy soldiers came to investigate, which they were sure to do.

Their instincts, of course, soon proved correct, when a group of Japanese were heard climbing over the outside, peering through the slits and trying unsuccessfully to force the doors. After a few minutes they were surprised and relieved when in English, they heard someone say "Americans all dead," after which everything became quiet.

One thing that may have helped convince the Japanese when they peered through the slits that "Americans all dead," was the site of blood splattered against the white interior of the tank. It had come from crewmen Pvt. Edmond de Beneditti and driver Mitchell. Impact from the direct hit by the enemy had caused several rivets to pop loose inside the tank and fly missile-like about the interior, one striking de Beneditti in the neck and Mitchell in the throat.

Unknown to the four trapped Americans, the game of having to play dead was only the beginning. An hour or so later, a second group of enemy soldiers came to check it out. After also deciding that the crew was dead, they, too, went to work on forcing their way inside. After about 30 minutes, they gave up and left.

As time went on, playing dead became the easy part. By noon, after baking in the hot Philippine sun for over three hours, temperatures inside had climbed to well over 100 degrees, the armor plate becoming too hot to touch. In fact, given a four-hour respite before yet another group of enemy soldiers became curious, the temptation to open the hatch and surrender just to escape the oven-like confines of the tank were quietly discussed but never seriously considered.

## 6. A Scary Christmas But a Happy New Year

Despite the unbearable heat and ever-curious enemy, even darkness offered no let up or chances to escape. Around midnight the Japanese set up a field kitchen a few feet away from the tank, bringing with it an unending stream of soldiers to nose around and sit on while eating what the Americans quietly joked was their daily ration of fish heads and rice.

Suddenly around 3:00 a.m., after playing dead for over 17 hours, the four tankers heard the explosion of the first round of what would be a two-hour U.S. artillery interdiction of the area.

The Americans, having brought up a battery of .75mm guns from the south, continued to blast the area off and on for two hours. An hour or so after the shelling let up, the Japanese, apparently convinced that the bombardment had not precluded a U.S. counterattack, started up the road. By 7:00 a.m., all was quiet.

Satisfied that the Japanese had pulled out after their twenty-first hour inside the steamy, oven-like confines of the tank, the four men, uniforms soaked with sweat, cautiously climbed out and into the bright morning sunshine. "It had been hotter than hell in the tank," said one of the survivors, "so we decided to cool off in a creek just across the rice paddy. Having to go through mud to get there, we took off our shoes and hid them in the tall grass. However, when we got back we couldn't find them, so we started on, barefoot."

There for the first time, they were able to see the effects of the two-hour U.S. bombardment. The field kitchen that had been set up next to the tank had taken a direct hit, as had three Japanese trucks parked on the road. Sadly, they also found two of the three remaining C Company Stuarts that had been knocked out, along with the bodies of six crewmen—bodies of men like them, from Salinas, California—men who had been their neighbors, school chums, and had served together in the Salinas National Guard when they were integrated into the regular Army in November 1940.

After scavenging food and water from the two tanks, the four men started out, apparently unconcerned that they were following the Japanese up the road. That is until nearly blundering into a nipa hut of chattering enemy soldiers busy loading machine gun belts. After quietly slipping past, they still continued to stick to the road until chased off by what sounded like approaching enemy trucks. "Resting in the bushes by the roadside," said one of the men, "we scooted low and saw some go by on bicycles. Then came trucks and guns and infantry, going by so close we could have reached out and touched them. They kept it up most of the night. One group stopped and ate chow on the road bank opposite us. It was especially hard for our tank driver with the rivet stuck in his throat. Every time he took a drink, the water would come leaking out. The rest of us were okay, but our feet were getting goddamned sore."

For the next three days, with help from local Filipinos, they stayed to jungle trails. On the morning of December 29, one of their guides led them to two survivors from one of the other tanks, who had been able to escape capture. Both had been wounded and were in very bad shape.

After several hours on the torturous mountain trails carrying and sometimes dragging the two wounded men, they reached the tiny barrio of Lilio, where a Filipino doctor treated them and Pvt. de Beneditti. "The tank driver with the hole in his throat said for us to leave him behind. However, he changed his mind, and decided to come. He made it too. It took plenty of guts."

Unknown to the six tankers, who had expected to catch up with the South Luzon Force, on December 23, with the Japanese virtually unimpeded in their drive to capture Manila, General MacArthur had ordered a systematic delaying action withdrawal of the army into the confines of Bataan Peninsula. In fact, by the morning of December 30, the entire South Luzon Force was in full flight to their next position north of Manila on the road leading to Bataan.

With no friendly troops between them and Manila, some 50 miles away, their only hope was to somehow out-race the advancing Japanese. For the next two days and nights, they were led through and around no less than seven villages, all the while warned that the Japanese were both in front and behind them.

On the night of December 31, they at last reached the edge of Manila Bay, 20 miles south of the city, from where they were taken by banca to the coastal village of Cardona. There they were given food and a safe place to sleep.

## 6. A Scary Christmas But a Happy New Year

The next morning, January 1, they hiked up the coast to the village of Binangonan, where they got a boat to take them to Manila. As they approached the usually bustling Manila waterfront, they were dismayed to see it almost abandoned. Where had all the ships and small boats gone, and where was the army? They were told it had withdrawn to Bataan Peninsula.

Also unknown to them, on the same day General MacArthur ordered the withdrawal, he declared Manila an open city, telling the Japanese that the army was evacuating and it was theirs for the taking.

After turning de Beneditti, tank driver Mitchell, and the other two wounded men over to the Philippine General Hospital, they were informed that the Japanese army, at that moment less than 10 miles from the city, was expected to arrive sometime that afternoon.

Still not out of harm's way, the hospital put them in touch with the Philippine Red Cross, who drove them to the dock area just in time to catch one of the last boats to Corregidor. Arriving in the middle of the night, dirty, unshaven, half-starved and totally exhausted, they happily spent the next three days in the hospital ward.

Unable to get any information on the whereabouts of the 194th on Bataan, on the morning of January 5, they were taken by boat across to Mariveles, where, with the withdrawal still under way, they found the situation chaotic. No matter who they asked, they were told there was no information yet available on where specific units had or would be bivouacked.

Believing they would eventually run into the battalion somewhere up the peninsula's East Road, the two men walked and hitchhiked their way north, until finally, on January 7, they spotted the one thing that left no doubt they had found their outfit—a lone Stuart tank. They had made it.

That night they told their story: Lost behind enemy lines for 11 days; 21 hours spent playing dead inside their tank while surrounded by the Japanese; a harrowing 50-mile march through enemy-controlled territory until reaching Manila by boat on New Year's Day, just hours before the Japanese entered the city.

When asked how they survived inside the tank when their water ran out, they said that when the inside cooled during the night, they were able to get a little moisture by licking the condensation off the sides of the steel plates.

(Because of the occurrence of "flying rivets" as described in this story, riveted construction was discontinued in later models of the Stuart.)

# 7

# The Last and the First

## *Bataan, January 18, 1942*

## The Last

Following the successful Japanese invasion of the island of Luzon in early December 1941, General Douglas MacArthur, commander of U.S. and Philippine forces, on December 23 ordered a general withdrawal of his army to Bataan Peninsula. From there, it was felt that a successful defense of Bataan and the island fortress of Corregidor would give his army the best opportunity for reinforcements, which, if they arrived, all were confident Manila Bay could be held indefinitely.

Part of the make-up of his woefully unprepared army on Bataan was one of the most storied units in the American Army—the 26th Cavalry, made up of perhaps the most well-known and respected soldiers in it—the Philippine Scouts.

Although Philippine Scouts, the men of the 26th Cavalry actually remained separate from the two Scout infantry regiments—the 45th and 57th. What separated them was the horse—the 26th Cavalry was the last horse-mounted cavalry unit in the United States Army, and one that would be involved in not only the last horse-mounted cavalry charge in its history, but the last since the Indian War. This is the story of that charge.

What could be called the opening battle for Bataan began on the night of January 11, 1942, with a Japanese Banzai attack against the eastern or II Corps half of the pre-established U.S. line on the peninsula.

On the western half of the peninsula, Japanese assault on what was the U.S. I Corps line did not occur until January 16. As the main line across the corps area near the barrio of Mauban was in the process of being established, Japanese troops, detected by a horse-mounted patrol of the 26th Cavalry, were spotted moving south from Olongapo and Port Binanga on the eastern edge of Subic Bay. Their movements brought I Corps commander General Jonathan Wainwright to order troops from the 26th Cavalry and the Philippine Army's First Regular Division to form defensive positions along the southern bank of the Batalan River near the coastal village of Morong, northernmost road-connected barrio on the west coast. They were also assigned to cover the 2 miles of accessible sandy beaches between Morong and Mauban to guard against a possible seaward invasion of the area. Wainwright felt that the natural obstacle the Batalan presented and adequate defense of the beaches below gave them the best chance to prevent what would be the main Japanese advance down the west coast.

Despite the general's hopes, however, word came down on the morning of the sixteenth that the Japanese had successfully crossed the Batalan and moved through the burned-out, deserted village of Morong before being stopped by units of the 1st Division.

It was early afternoon when Wainwright arrived at the 26th's bivouac a mile south of the village. Angered that the 1st Division had failed to push the Japanese back across the river, he ordered E and F Troop of 26th Cavalry Scouts, that had been combined into a single, undermanned unit, to attack and hold the village until the balance of the 1st could come up to secure it.

In command of the Scouts was Captain John Wheeler, who, splitting his command, ordered Lt. Edwin Ramsey to lead off with his platoon of, as he said, "27 worn and weary Filipino Scouts." Wheeler would follow with the remainder of the troop.

Ordering four men to take the point, Ramsey, with the balance formed into a staggered column of two's, moved out. As he approached the village and saw his point riders enter and then disappear around the Catholic church, there was an explosion.

"In a moment," said Ramsey, "the point came galloping back…. An advance guard of Japanese … had crossed the river and was passing near the church when we entered the village…." Unaware, of course, of their presence, they had run headlong into lead elements of the Japanese

## 7. The Last and the First

122nd Infantry, who had just crossed the river and were entering the village.

Ramsey, believing that a mounted charge would not only be their only hope to survive but their best chance to drive the enemy back across the river, quickly deployed his platoon as foragers—a cavalry formation similar to an infantry skirmish line—and charged. Suddenly, as the unsuspecting Japanese moved forward toward the center of the village, over two dozen mounted horsemen, guns blazing, came charging around the corner of the church. "Bent nearly prone across the horses' necks," remembered Ramsey, "we flung ourselves at the Japanese ... pistols firing full into their faces. A few returned our fire, but most fled in confusion, some wading back across the river, others running madly for the swamps."[1]

The impetus of the unexpected assault took them clear through the village to the edge of the river, where they quickly dismounted. Leaving a squad to block the Japanese from fighting their way back across, the young lieutenant led the rest of his men back into Morong to search for stragglers. Finding themselves under heavy sniper fire from both sides of the street as they worked their way back through the village, Ramsey sent a rider back to Captain Wheeler for help. It wasn't long in coming as Wheeler, at the unmistakable sound of machine gun fire, was already moving up.

It was not only machine-gun fire that attracted Wheeler. The Japanese had begun lobbing mortar shells into the village from across the river, some bursting amongst the horses that had broken loose from the troopers. Moments later, Wheeler, leading the two platoons of his anxious Scouts, came charging around the corner of the church, where, dismounting, he directed the lead platoon to reinforce the men at the bridge, then joined what Ramsey said had quickly become "a full-pitched battle."

An interesting event occurred as Wheeler reached the wall of the church. Unbeknownst to Ramsey, General Wainwright had sent his trusted chief of staff, Col. William Mahar, to ride in with E Troop to report the results of the assault. Under heavy fire, Ramsey spotted what he said was an unidentified American officer "taking cover against the wall of the church."

"Hey, you yellow son of a bitch, get over here and fight!" he yelled, at which the man quickly disappeared behind the building.[2]

Although Ramsey had unknowingly yelled at Mahar, there only as an observer, Wheeler, crouching nearby, thought it was directed at him. "This prompted me," he said later, "to try to get myself shot just to prove him wrong."[3]

At this point, the story of what followed is from the official "Action Report" filed the next day by Capt. Wheeler himself who, by the way, would not only get the wound he wanted, but the Distinguished Service Cross as well:

> Ramsey had taken cover in a ditch behind some coconut trees. One man was dead and three wounded. At that point, Pvt. Pedro Euperio, a 19-year old Scout, spotted three soldiers wearing Philippine army uniforms. He moved forward until they saw him and fired, and then he shot, quickly killing them. They were Japanese disguised as Philippine officers. Euperio was shot in the arm. The last time I saw him he was drenched with blood, propped against a house, pistol in his good hand, directing us how to move up, indicating points under enemy fire.
>
> We attacked straight through to the beach. We fired where we heard fire and were happy to see when we went through the bushes that there were dead Japanese. We got straight through to the water, reorganized, and attacked around Ramsey, using him as a pivot, sweeping south and killing them under houses, in trees, and under bushes. About 20 broke, throwing down all equipment, even guns, in the high grass. I was surprised to see two of my men with bullet holes through their helmets, yet unscratched. I had Pvt. Gonzales behind me, and as I went along, grabbed the Jap maps, compasses, and so forth, handing them to Gonzales. Then there was a lull.
>
> Ramsey and I saw three inert Japanese. Two were dead—the third had been hit in thigh and shoulder. He would make a begging sign, pull open his shirt and pull his bayonet point toward his chest. He may have been told we killed all Japanese by torture, but I think he was just in terrible pain. We tried to give him water, and I left him my canteen.
>
> Suddenly we heard a machine gun from the river and all hell broke loose again. We realized that we had been fighting an advance group and that a battalion was forming across the river. We fought in small groups, every man for himself. Sergeant Tolentino ran forward under heavy fire and threw a grenade into a house that had been giving us lots of trouble. Later he grabbed a light machine gun and began chasing a squad of Japanese down the road, moving in on them alone and without fear. I grabbed a rifle and followed him. We had no cover, but it seemed to me, if you run

around and fight hard, you don't get hurt—you keep moving aggressively, and it's the best defense.

I hit one Jap who was trying to shoot Tolentino. He twisted, squirmed, and finally ended up hanging over a fence. Sergeant Tolentino closed in on one flank while I went around another, shooting another Jap. Just then, his companion leaned around behind a tree and shot me in the leg. Sergeant Tolentino had been shot, too. About that leg wound of mine, have you ever been kicked in the leg by a horse? It felt just like that. Knowing how it feels is a great satisfaction—doesn't leave anything unknown to fear.

Morong became a hail of bullets that never stopped. There were so many in the air that if you put out a sheet, in five minutes it would have been riddled. We were outshooting them and could, any day. We fought all day. I can remember running through fire behind some little houses trying to get a drink but all the pumps were dry. Our lips were so swollen we could hardly talk. The Scouts were loyal to the nth degree. All they said were things like: "Don't go there, sir; I will go," and "They are shooting from that, sir; be careful." Late that afternoon my mission had been accomplished—the town was held adequately, and I was to fall back again in reserve.

We slipped out on a trail south along the beach. Morong was held for 24 hours after our withdrawal, and the final withdrawal was by order, not by Japanese action.[4]

## The First

As significant as the Scout's "last charge" was to U.S. Army history that day, so was there the first naval action of its kind in World War II, that ironically occurred at the same time a mile or so north of Morong, in Japanese-controlled Subic Bay.

On January 1, Navy Lieutenant John D. Bulkeley, at that time commanding officer of Motor Torpedo Squadron Three, was placed in charge of establishing a PT boat patrol of the west coast of Bataan. Using the six boats of his squadron, he began the official operation the next night.

For that and the subsequent 15 nights, patrols remained uneventfully routine. But the 18th promised something different. On the afternoon of the 17th, observers from General Wainwright's I Corps reported seeing two Japanese ships, one thought to be a destroyer, in Binanga Bay near the eastern entrance to Subic Bay. With the presence of Japanese war ships a real threat to U.S. I Corps positions along the vital west coast, Wainwright requested the enemy ships be attacked.

Later that afternoon, Bulkeley received the following message from naval headquarters on Corregidor: "Army reports four enemy ships lying off Binanga Bay. Force may include one destroyer, one large transport. Send two boats to attack between dusk and dawn." It was action at last.

The two boats selected for the raid were PTs-31 and -34, the latter skippered by young Ensign Barron Chandler, who was joined at the last minute by Bulkeley, who had decided to go along "for the hell of it." The 31 boat was skippered by Lieutenant (jg) Edward DeLong.

The plan was for the two boats to separate one mile outside the entrance to Subuc at 11:30 p.m., then rejoin at 1:00 in preparation of launching a simultaneous attack from the opposite sides of Binanga.

All went well according to plan until the two boats split up at 11:30. Fifteen minutes after separating, both wing engines on PT-31 stalled from fouled carburetors. Still intent on making the 1:00 a.m. rendezvous, DeLong continued running on his center engine, while the engine room worked feverishly to unclear the clogged carburetor jets.

"While steaming at idling speed," wrote DeLong in his Combat Report two days later, "I was about to turn south past Mayagao Point for rendezvous with PT-34 when my fresh water cooling system became air bound and quit."[5]

Dead in the water, the boat began drifting south while work on the engines continued. A few minutes later, however, the center propeller touched bottom, followed by the agonizing sound of the boat scrapping against rock—they had drifted hopelessly onto the rocks a few yards off Mayagao Point.

The problems with the fouled carburetors were soon fixed, and the engines restarted. Moments later, a gun from Ilinin Point opened fire in the general direction of the sound of the big motors.

"Despite the gunfire, I continued attempting to clear the hang-up by walking out the anchor and backing off the rocks, until all reverse gears were burned out," wrote DeLong, "at which time preparations were made for abandoning ship."[6]

Meanwhile, no sooner had PT-34 entered the big bay than it was challenged. "Pt-34 was challenged with a signal, dash-dash-dash," wrote Bulkeley later. "Ignored. Course changed to 060 degrees, speed slowed to 10 knots."

## 7. The Last and the First

A few minutes later, a second challenge, "Course changed to 110 degrees and reduced to 8 knots to be at northern entrance of Port Binanga at 0100, at which time PT-31 would join and attack would be made." It was sometime between the two challenges that shore battery fire was heard originating from the eastern shoreline "between," as Bulkeley remembered, "Mayagao and Ilinin Points.... This could have been fired at PT-31, as no splashes were seen around PT-34."

He was right. The gunfire was directed toward the stranded 31 boat. Fortunately, it was sporadic and wild. On board the little ship, a makeshift life raft had been prepared by tying several floating mattresses to the engine room canopy. Despite the probing enemy fire, DeLong was determined not to destroy the boat until PT-34 had completed its attack.

In the meantime, PT-34 had arrived at the rendezvous point off the northern entrance to the little bay at 1:00 a.m. A half hour later, with the 31 boat still not there, there was nothing to do but go in alone. "Entering the bay on two engines at idling speed," wrote Bulkeley; "at 500 yards, spotted two-masted frigate.... Preparations made to fire. The enemy vessel then challenged with "option, interrogatory" at 0140.

"We answered ... with two torpedoes.... One hit home with a hell of a thud.... Looking back, we saw red fire rising, and presently two more explosions which might have been her magazines."

Suddenly, somebody yelled, "Port torpedo didn't fire, sir!" It hadn't. "It failed to clear its tube," said Bulkeley, "and was there making what we call a 'hot run,' its propellers buzzing like hell, compressed air hissing so you couldn't hear yourself think.

"We were in plenty of trouble. A torpedo is adjusted so that it won't fire until its propeller has made a certain number of revolutions, [after which] an eighty-pound blow on its nose would set it off, blowing us all to glory."

With the torpedo hanging out of its tube like a half-extracted tooth, torpedoman John Martino ran to the head and came back with a roll of toilet paper. Jumping astride it "like it was a horse, he quickly jammed the vanes with toilet paper, stopping it," said the relieved skipper.

Having stopped while Martino worked on the torpedo, fire from the burning ship, in the meantime, had lit up the sky behind them. "Suddenly, all over Subic" said Bulkeley, "all hell broke loose. So we started up, gave her everything we had, [and] got the hell out of there."[7]

Meanwhile, back on PT-31, Lt. DeLong had held up destroying the boat until Bulkeley had made his attack. "At about 0140," he wrote, "I heard an explosion in the vicinity of Port Binanga, followed by the engine roar of PT-34."

With enemy attention now focused on PT-34, final preparations were made for abandoning the ship. Finally, at 3:00 a.m., the makeshift life raft with all twelve crewmen shoved off, with the 31's second officer, Ensign William Plant, in charge. They were to proceed 100 yards or so out to the edge of the reef to wait while DeLong set fire to the boat.

"Finally, after chopping holes in the gasoline tanks and blowing holes in the boat with grenades, [she] was burning sufficiently, and I took to the water at 0340," wrote the skipper later. By that time, however, there was no sign of the crew, the tide having drifted them south out of voice range.[8]

After searching for the crew for over an hour, DeLong gave up and swam for shore. As soon as it was light enough to see, he started down the beach. A few yards below Mayagao Point, he came across footprints of several men leading from the water's edge to a clump of bushes a few feet off the beach. There he found nine members of his crew, who had decided to abandon the raft rather than face being spotted in broad daylight by the Japanese. He was told that Ensign Plant and two men who could not swim had decided to take their chances on the raft.

Not long after he was reunited with his crew, a firefight erupted near the village of Morong, a few hundred yards to the south. "The greatest firing was about a mile from us in the vicinity of the mouth of the Batalan River."

Of course, had he known, it was the previously mentioned all-out effort by Filipinos and Americans to stop the Japanese from gaining a foothold on the south bank of the river. In noting in his Combat Report later that most of the firing had come from the vicinity of the mouth of the river, the 31 boat skipper had unknowingly made reference to the last horse cavalry charge in U.S. Army history.

As the battle raged, DeLong decided that if it appeared the Japanese been pushed out of the village, "I was determined to make a run for our

## 7. The Last and the First

lines around the beach at about 1500." On the other hand, in case the battle went the other way, the young lieutenant, who had spotted a large banca a half mile down the beach near Morong, had put together an alternate plan—to wait until dark and make an escape by banca around U.S. lines to Napo Point, some four miles down the coast.

By three o'clock, signs had mistakenly indicated that the battle had gone against the Americans and Filipinos, prompting DeLong to decide for the alternate plan.

Six men were sent to look for bancas. Four, who had gone to investigate one spotted on the beach a half mile north, nearly ran into a Japanese patrol but were able to return unnoticed.

When told of the presence of the Japanese patrol, Delong told his men, who between them had only six pistols and one rifle, that unless they were rushed by a superior force, they were not to shoot, as that would draw attention. "They were to allow any small patrol to come into the bushes, then club them with the butts of their pistols."

Around five, the two men who had gone to investigate the large banca on the beach to the south returned to report that they had found a second, smaller boat and that both appeared seaworthy.

At twilight, the ten men left their hiding place and headed for the bancas. In anticipation of having to jury-rig sails for the boats, men had gathered pieces of canvas and stripped beach defenses of barbed wire to be used for rigging. Sturdy bamboo poles were cut down for masts.

Finding two paddles, a board, and two shovels for paddling, they loaded the two boats and pushed off from the beach at eight o'clock. Safely clearing the breakers, sails were rigged, and the two boats headed south.

Things went well for the first three hours, until a sudden gust of wind capsized both boats. "…practically all equipment was lost," wrote the skipper. "After righting the boats, we had two bailers and two paddles left between us. With this we managed to become more or less seaworthy and set a course southeast toward Napo Point, with the small banca towing the larger one."

Two agonizing hours later they were off Napo Point. Trying to round the familiar headland, they ran into a strong headwind and stubborn current. For over an hour the exhausted crewmen, alternating paddlers, fought what seemed a losing battle with the two elements until, finally at 3:00 a.m., they "reached the lee ... and picked the point for landing."

"We landed at about 0300," wrote DeLong, "beached the bancas, crossed barbed wire entanglements, and found ourselves against a steep cliff. At that point I decided to stay hidden until daylight to avoid being mistaken for the enemy by Philippine army troops in position above the bluffs."[9]

In wait of daylight, within minutes most of the spent crewmen fell into an exhaustive sleep. It had been eight and a half hours since they shoved off from the beach near Morong, 32 hours since they pulled away from the docks back at Sisiman Bay, and nearly 48 hours since they last slept.

Filipino soldiers of the 2nd Battalion of the 92nd Infantry Regiment, who had moved into position on Napo Point seven days earlier, had just finished their slim morning ration of rice and salmon gravy when two bancas were spotted on the beach below, and a small group of men were seen working their way up the cliff face.

A few minutes later when the exhausted 31 crewmen reached the top of the trail, they were greeted by a grinning Filipino soldier, whose first words were, "Hey, Joe—got a cigarette?" They'd made it. An hour later, as guests of the 2nd Battalion, they sat down to their first meal in almost two days.

Of the original six boats of the squadron, only PT-31 was lost during the Bataan campaign. Of the three men who opted to stay with the makeshift raft that night, two were lost, becoming the only men of Motor Torpedo Boat Squadron Three to lose their lives during the battle.

Most of the comments and information on the Binanga raid are taken from the official "Combat Reports" written by John Bulkeley on January 19 and DeLong when he returned on the twentieth. Along with John Wheeler's "Action Report," Ed Ramsey's comments come from his book, *Lieutenant Ramsey's War*.

# 8

# The First Battle for Bataan

## *January 11, 1942*

### *Historic in More Ways Than One*

Early on the morning of January 12, 1942, the opening Japanese attack in the 90-day battle for Bataan took place against U.S. positions on what was called the Abucay line. The incidents of that and the subsequent 3 days would provide several firsts in the young Pacific war, including an insight on Japanese tactics the Americans would face throughout the balance of the fighting to come.

When the war broke out on December 7/8, 1941, the Philippine Division consisted of nine Philippine Army divisions and a regiment of horse-mounted 25th Cavalry that would participate in the battle for Bataan. It was composed of the only all-American combat regiment in the islands—the 31st and two regiments of Philippine Scouts, the 45th and 57th.

In the long history of the United States Army, no soldiers were more respected for their courage and dedication to duty by Americans who fought beside them than were the Philippine Scouts.

Two young Americans, Lt. John E. Olson and Captain Ernest L. Brown, attached to the Scout 57th Infantry at the time, survived both the Bataan and Japanese prison camps. As career officers, after the war they attended the Army's Infantry Officers Advanced Course at Ft. Benning. There, an assignment led them to write a paper relating to their Bataan experiences. Although attending at different times, both chose to write of the opening battle. Because of the surrender of Bataan and capture of 75,000 men, few, if any official records or diaries detailing specific events of the battle survived. The following story, taken from the monographs of eyewitnesses John Olson and Ernest Brown, however, offers a rare, detailed look at what occurred in that first crucial engagement with the Japanese.

In the opening of his monograph, Captain Brown described the background and history of the Scouts. "The Scout soldier," he wrote, "was a product of a highly selective recruiting system, as it was considered an honor to belong to this organization. As such, they were well known to the rest of the United States Army for their proficiency in marksmanship and love of soldiering. Court-martials were rare and venereals unheard of. Retirement was the rule rather than the exception. Their standard of discipline was among the highest in the Army. Their willing and immediate obedience to orders provided inspiration to their American officers in combat."[1]

While five Philippine Army divisions and the 26th Cavalry were carrying out General MacArthur's strategic delaying-action withdrawal into Bataan, on December 30, the entire unexposed Philippine Division was ordered to move into the peninsula. Once there, the 57th was directed, as Lieutenant Olson, regimental personnel officer wrote: "... to organize and be prepared to defend the right flank of the Abucay position from Manila Bay to a point some 2,000 yards west of the barrio of Mabatang" (the village of Abucay, after which the position was named, was one mile south of Mabatang).[2]

The U.S. line at Mabatang was laid out parallel to an east-west road on the northern edge of the little barrio. The reason for its establishment at that point, remembered Olson, "was that the area to the front lacked cover for an approaching enemy." On the right of the main or East Road leading down the peninsula, there were "several hundred yards of artificial fish ponds that were formed by steep-sided dikes, 6- to 8-feet high and filled with water. An advance from there could not only be easily detected but made in single file. The area west of the road was made up of rice fields, which were dry and hard at this time of year. Only on the extreme left was there any cover for an advancing enemy."

Based on tendencies learned from several days of delaying action fighting, "it was felt," wrote Captain Brown, "that the Japanese would attempt to come through our position. We knew they liked to stick to

## 8. The First Battle for Bataan

roads whenever possible. To block them from using the main road, 14th Engineers set off three huge dynamite charges whose craters closed it off to possible use by enemy tanks. If attacks failed, they would slide to the flank in repeated attacks until they found a weak spot."[3]

Accordingly, the area across the 57th front west of the main road was secured by both double-apron barbed wire and some 2,000 homemade antitank mines. Since few, if any, mines had been shipped to the Philippines before the war, Army engineers, whose creativity did as much to keep the Japanese at bay during the 3-month-long battle as anyone, built the mines out of wooden boxes. Stuffed with 10 pounds of dynamite, a flashlight battery and appropriate wiring, they were designed to take a minimum of 500 pounds to explode.

In anticipation of the Japanese attack, the 57th's 1st Battalion was given the role of defending the barrio of Mabatang and the fish-pond-lined area east of the main road. The job of covering the remaining 2,000 yards up to the Philippine Army's 41st Division sector on its immediate left went to the 3rd Battalion. Lt. Colonel Philip Fry, the battalion commander, deployed K Company on the right along a front that ran from Mabatang to an east-west "Back Road" that split the sector in half. To its left, Fry gave I Company the responsibility of defending the remainder of the area up to the line defining the 57th-41st Division area.

For artillery support in the 3rd Battalion area, Brown, commanding officer of the battalion's Company L, wrote that they had "a battery of 24th Field Artillery 75mm's on the immediate MLR (Main Line of Resistance) of the battalion ... dug in directly on line with the riflemen of the two companies. On the left flank of the battalion area," he continued, "was a large sugar cane field approximately one hundred and fifty yards in front of the MLR. Tactically speaking, we felt it would be neutralized as an approach by our artillery. We were to learn a bitter lesson for failing to cut it, however."[4]

John Olson also noted it. After writing that "Fields of fire [had been] cut in front of the 3rd Battalion [and that] automatic weapons were sighted in to cover the whole front," he wrote that "Nothing was forgotten, except to cut the cane field."[5]

So did another American officer, Major William E. Webb, with the 41st Infantry of the Philippine Army's 41st Division. In a monograph

77

also written for the Infantry officers Advanced course at Ft. Benning in 1950, he wrote that "In front of the 3rd Battalion 57th Infantry on our immediate right was a heavy sugar cane field approximately seven acres in area. It was 150 yards in front of MLR positions. This gave the enemy a superior route of approach to attack positions in front of the 3rd Battalion and the 1st Battalion 41st Infantry Regiment."[6]

A day or so after the 57th moved into positions on the Abucay, Ernest Brown made note of a Japanese tactic that, until figured out, was successful in unnerving the troops, particularly those in the rear areas. "For several days before the attack," he wrote, "the Japanese would fly over at night and drop firecrackers. Since they sounded exactly like Japanese .25-caliber rifles, the troops thought snipers had infiltrated through our lines. It took several days to discover the phantom rifle shots were firecrackers, but they had served the purpose of keeping the troops on edge."[7]

Later, after examining the bodies of dead Japanese soldiers, along with finding packages of firecrackers, a third explanation as to how they were set off behind the lines was discovered, when bullets from the cartridges of their .25-caliber rifles had been replaced with firecrackers.

On January 10, some 36 hours before the initial Japanese attack against the Abucay line, word from a patrol returning from the barrio of Samal, 2 miles north of the MLR, indicated that the Japanese had moved into the tiny nipa hut village. Wrote Lt. Olson of what followed, "It was decided that the village offered an excellent assembly area for forces planning to attack the U.S. lines. The decision was made to burn it. But since enemy patrols were already in the area, it presented a difficult problem. A request was made to have the artillery fire on the village with incendiary shells, but they had no incendiary ammunition. Lt. Arthur Wermuth of D Company of the 1st Battalion volunteered to enter the village to attempt to burn it with gasoline. This he did. Exactly at 1700 on the 10th, a thin curl of smoke was seen ascending from the vicinity of Samal. In accordance with a prearranged plan, two batteries of the 24th Field Artillery lowered a box barrage on the barrio, thus preventing the Nipponese from following Lt. Wermuth. Inside of a few hours, the majority of the buildings had burned to the ground."[8]

For his action, Wermuth received the Distinguished Service Cross.

## 8. The First Battle for Bataan

This was not the first nor the last time his name would surface during the battle, however. In fact, because of his many exploits involving behind-enemy-lines forays, Associated Press correspondent Clark Lee, whose stories of Wermuth sent from Bataan and appearing in most major U.S. newspapers, would dub him "The One Man Army of Bataan."

The Army's definition for the initials OPLR, or Outpost Line of Resistance, is "a line selected to be held in case of attack until the main body can prepare for it."

"Around 1800, by sheer weight of numbers, the Japanese forced the OPLR to withdraw." So wrote John Olson of the night of January 11. "Night," he continued,

> found the troops on the MLR alerted and ready for an attack. They did not have to wait long. About 2300 the enemy opened up with a heavy barrage of artillery and mortars, which was followed soon by small arms fire from the cane field. Upon request of Col. Fry, the 24th Field Artillery fired several concentrations into the area. No sooner had this begun than the Japanese burst from the cane field. Screaming 'Banzai!' in a frenzied charge, the leading men hurled themselves on the barbed wire, making bridges of their bodies over which the remainder climbed. All weapons on the American front opened up. The battery of the 2nd Battalion, 24th Field Artillery, with trails propped up, fired shrapnel at point-blank range into the charging enemy. Though dozens of them dropped, the others by their very ferocity, forced the men of I Company out of their foxholes and back several hundred yards. The left flank of K company was also forced back. Col. Fry then threw in Reserve Company L and succeeded in restoring the line. Gradually the firing subsided until there were only sporadic bursts. The weary men of the 3rd Battalion dug in and anxiously awaited the coming of dawn.[9]

Captain Ernest Brown, who personally led his L Company in the counterattack, said that

> when the Japs got among us, they ceased to yell. The only sound we heard was their officers and noncommissioned officers shouting. However, soon there were no more officers or sword wavers to shout as their drawn Samurai swords made them most conspicuous. They seemed to lose organization when they were among us.
>
> The Japanese failed to press their advantage, and as daylight arrived, we were awed by the great numbers of enemy dead in our position. They were everywhere, in our gun positions, trenches, in the open ground to our front, and hanging on our barbed wire. Estimates varied between 200 and

300 killed. The shields of the battery of 75s had dozens of bullet marks fired from both front and behind. I Company commander was seriously wounded and did not return to the regiment. His executive officer was killed. Other than that, our casualties were amazingly light. We had driven off a battalion.

The next day found us unable to perform many of the things we deemed necessary, however, as we were being constantly harassed by snipers who seemed to realize our every move.[10]

John Olson gave a detailed explanation of what happened. "Though the enemy had failed to dislodge our troops," he wrote, "they had not all been ejected." He continued:

Many had filtered through our lines and taken up camouflaged positions in the bushes and trees. During the day these snipers fired with devastating accuracy at the men moving around behind our lines. After two officers and several enlisted men were killed, a systematic attempt was made to clear the area. First Lieutenant Arthur R. Nininger of A Company, which had remained uninvolved in the fighting that night, volunteered to lead a party of 6 or 8 Scout volunteers through the I and K Company sectors to eliminate this menace. Periodic bursts of heavy fire were heard as they combed the rear areas. In the ensuing two trips, they killed a large number of the enemy but suffered so heavily that the 1st Battalion commander ordered them to desist. Lt. Nininger, realizing the gravity of this menace, armed with grenades and a BAR, rushed back alone for a third try. He succeeded in killing a few more before he himself fell mortally wounded.[11]

Upon his failing to return, a Scout patrol was sent the next morning to try to locate him. His body was found in a clearing where nearby were found three dead Japanese. An examination showed that he had been wounded three times, the third, a fatal wound to the head, was believed to have come as he launched a grenade into the enemy position. For his heroic action, Nininger was awarded the first Medal of Honor voted by Congress in World War II. (His body, thought to have been buried in the courtyard of the Abucay Church, has never been found.)

According to Ernest Brown,

About 2400 the next night, our position was struck again, "But this time we kept our automatic weapons and machine guns quiet so they could not be plotted and focused on as they had the night before. We called for concentrations on the cane field as soon as their fire drew close, but initially it yielded no Japanese. Then, moments later, out they came. Yelling "Banzai!,"

## 8. The First Battle for Bataan

they closed on our wire, but this time most of them were killed before they reached it. With help from our artillery, they were driven off.

But it was not over. At approximately 0430, they resumed the attack with great fury. Mines started going off by the dozens to our front. The Japanese had stampeded a large herd of carabao in front of them. Behind them, they poured out of the cane field again in a combined flank-and-frontal attack. Again they overran the position, massing the attack on I Company.

The new company commander was killed with two of his officers and the first sergeant. The men were in utter confusion and were literally pushed out of the position by force of numbers and their emplacements occupied.

The reserve company was then committed as well as all available men in battalion headquarters. Fortunately, the men from I Company ran into my L Company and were quickly reorganized and forced to participate in the counter-attack. It was just turning light when they reached the main line where the Japanese were driven back and most of the gap closed.

Later that morning, a patrol found the bodies of several members of our outpost whose positions had been overrun two days before. Their hands were tied behind their backs, they were gagged, and lying face down in a shallow creek. This was our first of many experiences with Japanese atrocities. Several days later, one of my men was captured while on patrol. The Japanese had tortured him then hung his bloodied body from a mango tree for us to find.[12]

The Japanese, after twice failing to succeed against the 57th, did what Captain Brown said they would: "slide to the flank (west) until they found a weak spot." A day or so later, after patrols found evidence that, outside of a few of snipers and infiltrators, it appeared that the enemy had moved out of the cane field, a decision was made to burn it. A request was made to support a patrol into the area with tanks.

"The Tank Group commander came up, but after a brief reconnaissance decided that the ground was not suited for tank employment," wrote John Olson. "This decision was protested by the 57th command and by officers within the tank regiment, but to no avail. (Later, through trial-and-error jungle fighting, the successful use of the tank on Bataan supplied valuable lessons for what was to come.)

"Failing to get the tanks, the regimental operations officer, Major Harold K. Johnson, requested the Air Corps drop incendiary bombs. Again, the answer was 'no.' The Air Corps at this time had approximately ten P-40s which were used for reconnaissance only. Furthermore, all

# The Fall of the Philippines

incendiary bombs had been abandoned at Clark and Nichols Fields. The Air Corps did deliver two white phosphorous parachute flare containers to use to burn the field.

"Captain Wermuth offered to take a group of men into the cane field and set off the flares, but the Japanese surprised the raiding party just as the first flare was ignited. Before it could be properly set afire, the enemy brought such heavy fire to bear that Captain Wermuth withdrew his men, leaving two dead behind. This ended the attempts to burn the field." (The above-mentioned Major Harold K. Johnson, after the war became four-star General Harold K. Johnson, U.S. Army Chief of Staff.)

After writing about the unmolested Japanese reconnaissance plane that had been successfully directing enemy counter-battery fire against friendly artillery every time they went into action, Olson wrote that "another extremely annoying feature was the renewal of enemy sniper activity. They had penetrated several hundred yards behind the MLR and kept the troops constantly harassed. An anti-sniper organization was employed and kept busy eliminating the snipers."[13]

The anti-sniper organization he referred to was put together by now Captain Arthur Wermuth. Angered after being shot in the leg by a sniper, with permission from his battalion commander, he personally led 84 anxious Scout volunteers after the Japanese. The snipers Wermuth was hunting were not the same Arthur Nininger had faced. These were trained snipers who, after concealing themselves in densely topped mango trees, fired their hard-to-detect, smokeless powder .25-caliber rifles at unsuspecting officers and rear area troops.

Evidence that this was more than meaningless harassment was indicated by examining the equipment found on dead snipers. Most had enough food to last five days, including hardtack, a small sack of rice, a package of dehydrated or concentrated foods, rock candy, water, and vitamin pills. Items of equipment included a water purifier, quinine tablets, first aid kit, mosquito netting, a climbing rope, extra socks, toothbrush, gloves, and a flashlight with rotating, multicolored lenses for signaling. A sniper's helmet, face, and gloves were usually camouflaged to blend in with the branches of the tree into which he customarily tied himself.

Although the number of enemy snipers killed, estimated to be over

## 8. The First Battle for Bataan

100, was never verified, thanks to what was called Wermuth's "anti-sniper society," life behind the 57th line until the withdrawal on January 23 remained virtually free of sniper activity.

Before he was through, to go along with his Distinguished Service Cross, Arthur Wermuth would earn the Silver Star and two more Purple Hearts. Like Lt. Olson and Ernest Brown, after living through the battle and Japanese prison camps, he, too, would live to return home. Thanks to Clark Lee, if not the most decorated, Wermuth certainly was the most famous soldier on Bataan.

As for the results of the defense of the Abucay line, John Olson wrote that "While the 57th Infantry had been enjoying relative quiet on its front since the Japanese had given up attempting to crack the Abucay front, units on the left had come under fierce attack. The Philippine Army's 51st Division on the extreme left, after taking a terrific pounding, began to withdraw. On January 11, the commanding officer of the II Corps threw in the U.S. 31st Infantry to try to stem the tide. This proved insufficient, so the 45th Infantry was committed. For four days, desperate fighting went on around a tiny village known as the Abucay Hacienda, but to no avail. A general withdrawal of all units was ordered.

"Early on the 23rd the order came for the regiment to move out at dark to an intermediate position west of the town of Balanga. By midnight all units cleared Abucay. The battle of Abucay was over."[14]

Ernest Brown, under the heading, "Analysis and Criticism" in his paper for the Advanced Infantry Course, wrote that

> In making a study of this operation, it is concluded that if the Japanese had been successful in breaking the line at Abucay, the fall of Bataan would have been in January instead of April. Had the Japanese broken through and reached the Reserve Battle Line before the U.S., there would not have been sufficient time to organize a new line of defense.
>
> As a criticism, the failure to cut the cane field on the left flank of the battalion provided a perfect approach to the Main Line of Resistance. Had it been cut, it is unlikely the Japanese would have been able to storm our position, as the rest of the regiment's positions proved to be tactically sound for the situation.
>
> To sum up the results, the 57th Infantry repulsed three attacks by an enemy of superior numbers and defeated the Japanese for the first time in World War II. This was demonstrated by the fact that they abandoned the plan of securing the East Road, which was their primary mission.[15]

# 9

# "Think what we could have done with sixty"

In January 1942, perhaps the darkest month for Americans in the history of the Pacific war to come, a surprise air attack on two enemy airfields outside of Manila was made by Army Air Force planes the shocked Japanese did not know even existed. This is the story of that raid.

On the morning of December 8, 1941, the 24th Pursuit Group in the Philippines had four squadrons of P-40s and a fifth of P-35s spread out amongst four airfields on Luzon. To fly the 112 fighters available that morning was a cadre of 195 pilots.

One month later, on January 7, 1942, what was left of the 24th found itself operating off of a recently graded, dried-up rice field on the southeast coast of Bataan. Appropriately called "Bataan Field," over the 30-day period since the devastating Japanese attack on December 8, the group, now called the Bataan Flying Field Detachment, had been whittled down to just eight pilots and six P-40s. Although the number of available pilots on January 7 was only two more than the number of planes, it wasn't so earlier that morning.

General Douglas MacArthur, in assessing his troop strengths after the withdrawal into the peninsula, decided to use the personnel from the now-planeless 24th Pursuit Group as infantry to beef up the lightly defended Bataan west coast. Consequently, that morning 86 officers, most of them pilots, and 955 24th Pursuit ground personnel, left to take up positions on the bluffs overlooking the South China Sea.

Six days later the detachment's numbers increased, when three planes were ferried up from Del Monte Field on Mindanao. Ironically,

## 9. "Think what we could have done with sixty!"

they were from a group of nine that had been prematurely ordered out of Bataan and harm's way back on January 4.

Of the transfer, one of the pilots, Lieutenant David Obert, wrote in his diary that "none of us Mindanao plots wanted to return to Bataan. There were eight of us available ... so it was decided to draw cards to see which would be the unlucky ones. Lieutenants Woolery, Ibold, Benson, and I drew the low cards [and] started getting ready for the trip everyone agreed there [would be] no returning from." (Lt. Benson's plane incurred engine trouble on the way, forcing him to safely bail out near Panay Island.)

"The morning after our arrival back at Bataan," continued Obert, "Colonel [Harold] George [24th Pursuit commander] called us in and said we could either stay here and fly the planes [we] brought in or go down to the beach and join our units. We all, without a second thought, said that we wanted to keep on flying."[1]

With nine serviceable fighters now available, George, on the twenty-third, recalled three pilots from the west coast, bringing the number of available to fourteen.

"These pilots were all picked by George who, like with us," said Obert, "told them they could quit flying anytime they wished. None quit, although a foxhole looked much more inviting than some of the missions that were flown. Later that day, information that the Japanese had landed on the west coast made all of us happy we'd decided to stay."

Obert's next entry, probably written a couple days later, began, "About the 25th of January, the recently promoted Brigadier General George said he thought it would be a good idea to attack the Japs on Nichols and Nielson Fields, which they were now using for fighter bases."

Up to that time, most of the Japanese planes involved in attacking Bataan and Corregidor originated from Clark Field, some 60 air miles to the north. On January 24, however, intelligence reports gathered from agents working near Manila indicated that the Japanese had concentrated large numbers of fighters at Nichols Field, 10 miles south of the city, and a few at nearby Nielson, site of the original Far East Air Force Headquarters.

Assuming that the large number of planes on the two fields meant that they had moved there to take advantage of the 10-minute, 30-mile flight across Manila Bay to Bataan and Corregidor, it was decided that something had to be done to discourage the enemy plan. But how?

It was a perfect job for B-17s, but there wasn't a B-17 left in the islands. That left it up to George's fighters. But again how, and when? To the small handful of American pilots, imagining the reaction of the Japanese, if it could be pulled off, far outweighed the risk. Since this would be the first offensive fighter attack on the Japanese since the second day of the war, the element of surprise would certainly be with them. Also, who would expect that planes the Japanese weren't sure even existed would even think about attacking the two fields.

To do the job, along with the firepower of the P-40s' .50-caliber machine guns, each was equipped with bomb racks capable of carrying six 30-pound bombs, three under each wing.

The question of when was next. It was a simple decision. A daylight raid was out of the question. Even if successful, any daylight contact with the superior number of enemy fighters reported to be concentrated on the two fields would leave the tiny Far East Air Force open to an immediate retaliatory strike by the Japanese.

With the decision for a night raid made, the question of who would fly it and how it would be carried out, wrote Dave Obert, "was made by the pilots themselves. Lt. Woolery was to lead a flight of three planes to frag bomb and strafe Nielson airfield, while [I] was to lead the other flight of three to make the same type of attack on Nichols...."

Planning for the attack itself was much more complicated, however. Three things had to happen. As an aid to the pilots, the first was a full moon, which would ironically occur for the next three nights. The second was to notify Corregidor to alert their antiaircraft and searchlight crews that the planes that would rendezvous over the Rock at 8:00 p.m. on the night chosen would be friendlies and not to sound the alarm.

The third problem involved making sure the raid, until the actual moment of takeoff, remained a close-kept secret to anyone outside of flying field personnel and pilots. The fear was that a group of anti–American, pro–Japanese Filipinos, known as Sakdalistas, that were known to be operating near the airfield, might alert the Japanese that something was up by firing off flares when planes were being prepared for a night

## 9. "Think what we could have done with sixty!"

mission. It had happened a few days earlier when they made a scheduled night-supply drop to Philippine guerrillas in northern Luzon.

Captain Allison Ind, General George's intelligence officer, who had a run-in with them at Nichols Field back on December 10, wrote that they "had been welded into a malignant anti–American force, a keen-edged, utterly willing tool [of the Japanese]. They were everywhere," he said, "but we knew not just where or how many."

In anticipation of the local spies finding out that something was up because of the usual pre-attack preparations, Ind wrote that "there was no testing of aircraft radio equipment. Even the bombs were not brought out until after dark. Not a light showed. Even the improvised field running lights were left off.

"There would be no warm-up time to warn the Sakdalistas inevitably stationed someplace in the concealing jungle, nor did we dare risk our plans by applying the usual anti-dust treatment to the field that day."[2]

Unbeknownst to the planners, however, the threat posed by the local Sakdalistas would indirectly cost the Americans one of their precious fighters and nearly the life of its pilot.

General George, after talking to his pilots, decided to go after them on the night of January 26. All the pre-launch preparations had gone smoothly and quietly. Everything was ready. First off were the planes scheduled to attack Nielson, led by lieutenants Jack Hall, Bill Baker, and Bob Ibold.

Third off behind Baker, Bob Ibold was making his first takeoff from Bataan Field. Blinded by dust and the absence of running lights, he unconsciously veered off the narrow strip, his right wing striking a large boulder part way down the darkened runway. "…the death-loaded machine spun, half recovered, then whipped around in a great cascade of dust causing the plane to ground loop," witnessed Allison Ind. "Suddenly, there was a blinding stab of flame, then the triple explosion of the three fragmentation bombs slung under the wing of the P-40."[3]

As the men rushed to the crash site, few had any hope that Ibold would be alive. Miraculously, although burned and in shock, he had survived. In fact, two weeks later he was back at Bataan Field appealing to be put back on flying status.

## The Fall of the Philippines

Because of the accident, and to the disappointment of the three pilots scheduled to go next, George decided to call off the attack on Nichols Field.

Meanwhile, Hall and Baker, who were unaware of what had happened to Ibold, circled over Corregidor for several minutes waiting for him to show up. Fearing that something had happened, they decided to head for Nielson on their own.

Nielson, on the outskirts of the lit-up city, would be easy to find, but not as easy as they expected. The Japanese, upon hearing the sound of approaching aircraft, actually turned on the landing lights for what they thought were their own planes. The two young American couldn't believe it.

Three times the two men crossed over the target, dropping their bombs on the first pass, then making two low-level strafing runs before heading for home. It wasn't until the third run that they received any ground fire from the shocked Japanese, which, even then, was wildly probing and inaccurate.

Although there are no recorded comments from Hall or Baker when they returned, an ecstatic General George not only re-scheduled the Nichols attack, but decided to go after Nielson again.

As Dave Obert mentioned in his diary, it was now his and Ed Woolery's turn to lead an attack. George assigned Woolery and Lieutenants Sam Grashio and Lloyd Stinson to the second strike on Nielson. Obert, Bill Baker, and Earl Stone got the Nichols Field assignment.

Both groups cleared Bataan Field without incident, joined up over Corregidor, and took off for their assigned targets. Unknown to them, however, their presence over the island barely missed causing an air raid alarm and an unfortunate incident.

Alerted only of the 8:00 p.m. raid, according to Allison Ind, "Our warnings of the second 11:00 p.m. attack to the antiaircraft officer at Corregidor had never been delivered.... Fortunately, recognizing the distinct sound of P-40 engines, [he] warned them not to switch on the searchlights...."[4]

Woolery, a veteran air corps pilot who had been flying in the islands for 2 years, anticipated that it would be no problem finding the now-blacked-out Nielson. He was wrong. Only after circling over the north-

## 9. "Think what we could have done with sixty!"

ern edge of the city for several minutes was the target finally spotted. Since their presence could have alerted the Japanese to launch some of their fighters, Woolery assigned a disappointed Sam Grashio to fly cover while he and Stinson hit the field.

While Woolery was straining to find the field, Stinson came on the radio. "There it is!" he yelled, and peeled off with Woolery close behind. Despite help from the few remaining fires from the first raid, they were unable to pick out a specific target. Because of this, they agreed instead to make one all-guns-blazing pass over the field, unload their bombs, and head for home.[5]

Meanwhile, 10 miles to the south, Dave Obert, who had no trouble finding Nichols with Baker and Earl Stone close behind, dropped down to 2,000 feet and headed in. Unlike Nielson, intelligence had indicated exactly where the Japanese planes would be parked on the field. Also unlike Nielson, the Japanese were waiting. "Big, fiery red balls" came floating up, said Obert, as the apparently alerted enemy opened up with everything they had. It was, he said, "the biggest, prettiest, and most thrilling fireworks show I'd ever seen."

After dropping his six 30-pounders, Obert had pulled up and glanced back to access the damage when one of his wingman zipped past, missing him by a few feet. Deciding at that point to leave Baker and Stone on their own because "things were getting too dangerous," he decided to circle north along the Manila Bay shoreline in hopes of finding an unsuspecting Japanese truck convoy that might be heading for Bataan. His instinct proved correct.

"On the route back," he wrote, "…I saw a long motor convoy with all lights on driving towards Bataan. It was a wonderful target. Carefully lining up with the front of the unsuspecting target, I raked the entire column with the six .50s … a couple of times, and was so intense on shooting out the disappearing lights that I almost flew into the ground at the end of the convoy. With all bombs and ammunition expended, I returned to Bataan Field."[6]

Guided by a row of dimly lit lights that he later said made the field look "just about two-feet wide," like a blind man, he had to literally "feel" for the ground until he hit the runway. With the other five planes already back, when he climbed out of his plane, he was told that everyone was worried that something had happened. Upon the story of his strafing of the enemy convoy, General George broke out a quart of bourbon he had kept for such an occasion, all six pilots and their commander toasting the success of the mission and rapid recovery of Bob Ibold.

As to the psychological effects of being attacked by six American planes, Ind wrote, "So complete was the surprise, so disproportionately extensive the casualties and damage, and so great the joy of the people the following day," that the Japanese "ordered a general dispersal of all planes in the Manila area in order to reduce the possibility of a repetition."

As far as specific damages, intelligence reports varied. One claimed that between 14 and 17 planes were destroyed and 70 Japanese killed. Ind wrote, "Thirty-seven grounded aircraft ... were riddled with bombs or by machine-gun strafing" and that "others were damaged by resulting fires." He also said that "more than 300 casualties were listed by the Japanese, who claimed in the Manila newspaper that numerous Filipinos had also been struck."[7]

Sam Grashio, who attacked Nichols, in his book *Return to Freedom* written 40 years later, wrote of the six-plane raid that night. "Think what we could have done with sixty." Ind concluded his story with "Sixty.... The United States was going to make fifty thousand in 1942."[8]

# 10

# Biggest Day for the Bataan Air Force

## *March 3, 1942*

By March 3, 1942, the Japanese siege of Bataan was entering its third and final month. The American and Filipino defenders were hanging on by the skin of their teeth. Included was the tiny remnant of the Army Air Force that, on the morning of December 8, had started out with 98 operational P-40 fighters, but by March 3 had been whittled down to just five planes.

But on that day, those five American P-40s would launch a raid against Japanese shipping in Subic Bay that brought Tokyo Radio to announce that they had been attacked by over 40 four-engined bombers. In truth, American losses to Japanese antiaircraft fire were one P-40 and one pilot. This is the story of that raid.

On the evening of March 3, with the sun about 40 minutes behind the South China Sea horizon, the air raid sirens on Corregidor wailed at the approach of unidentified planes. Fifteen minutes later, the all-clear sounded, a false alarm. It didn't take General MacArthur's chief of staff, General Richard Sutherland, long to trace the planes picked up on Corregidor's radar to the Bataan air force.

Upset, he called air force commander General Harold George at his headquarters shack behind Bataan Field. For the second time in six weeks, said Sutherland, the air corps had failed to notify Corregidor of pending night operations. And for the second time in six weeks, they had avoided being blasted by Rock guns by the mere skin of their teeth.

## The Fall of the Philippines

George told him that the air raid alarm incident was caused by his planes returning from their last raid on the Japanese convoy in Subic Bay.

"What were your losses?" Sutherland asked.

"Four planes and one pilot," George answered, quickly adding that one plane could probably be salvaged.

"What did we do to them?"

George told him that the losses were one 12,000-ton transport sunk, one 6,000-ton ship beached and burning, two 100-ton motor transport vessels sunk, several barges and lighters destroyed, an unknown but vast amount of supplies and equipment destroyed on Grande Island and Olongapo docks, and a large but undeterminable number of the enemy killed.

Before the attack, the five remaining P-40s involved in the raid were spread amongst three airfields on Bataan: two were at Bataan Field, one at nearby Cabcaben, and two at Mariveles near the southern tip of the peninsula.

After receiving information of a large number of enemy ships in Subic, George contacted Capt. Joe Moore at Mariveles and told him to have his two planes "take off when ready, and hit and hit 'em hard."[1]

Next, he contacted Captain Ed Dyess, leader of the 21st Pursuit Squadron and senior pilot currently on flying status. Fortuitously, the day before, the ground crew had put the finishing touches on a homemade 500-pound bomb rack for Dyess' fighter that had been put together from cannibalized parts of automobiles and wrecked planes.

George told Dyess that the largest concentration of enemy ships ever reported had been spotted in Subic Bay and asked if he thought the bomb back was ready for a practice test.

"There never was a better day, General," answered the tall, slender Texan. "I'll be ready in an hour."[2]

While waiting for the "big, green 500-pounder" to be loaded onto Dyess' fighter, Lt. John Posten took off from Bataan Field for Subic. Loaded with half a dozen 30-pound fragmentaries, he found the bay full of ships and the docks at Olangapo crammed with newly arrived supplies. Knowing his 30 pounders were useless against the big ships,

## 10. Biggest Day for Bataan Air Force

he chose the docks, but couldn't stay around long enough to find out the results.

Meanwhile, the two Mariveles fighters, flown by Erwin Crellen and Kiefer White, also loaded the 30-pound fragmentaries and arrived over the big bay. They, too, headed for Olongapo, choosing what appeared to be a large warship near the docks. "Judging from the volume of antiaircraft fire from the ships," said White, "it had to have been a cruiser." The two Americans dove down. White, who was in the lead, dropped his bombs and pulled up. When he looked back for Crellen, he was nowhere to be seen, apparently having been hit by antiaircraft fire.

It was now Dyess' turn. At 12:30, loaded with the 500-pound bomb hanging on its homemade rack, Dyess gunned his Kittyhawk, nicknamed "Kibosh," down the gently sloped Bataan Field runway, barely lifting his overloaded fighter over the East Road before pulling up over the bay. Lt. "Shorty" Crosland took off at the same time from Cabcaben.

As the two reached the mouth of Subic, the following scene unfolded before their eyes: there were four transports already in the bay, two unloading on the north side of Grande Island; a fifth, just arriving, was at that moment passing between Grande and the western shore; further inside there were two cruisers, two destroyers, and several smaller vessels scattered about. Dyess also noted at least a dozen ships of various sizes unloading at Grande Island.

Picking the late-arriving transport as his target, Dyess began his run from 10,000 feet. At 5,000, all hell broke loose when the previously alerted Japanese antiaircraft batteries opened up. At 2,000 feet he released his bomb, but it overshot the target by several feet. Angered, he turned to strafe, raking the ship "three times from stern to bow, bow to stem, and from bow again. It stopped dead and didn't move again that day."

Next, he and Crosland ripped a row of warehouses on Grande Island, then jumped a 100-ton motor vessel near the damaged transport that was heading for shore.

"I caught it well out in the open," remembered Dyess, "and concentrated on its two forward guns, then started firing amidships into the hull.

"The Japs aboard her were putting on quite an act. Those astern were running forward and those forward were rushing astern.... They met amidships where my bullets were striking. When I was 100 yards from the ship, I veered off, banked around, and went in again the same way. The fire from my six .50s literally knocked the sides out of her."

A second pass started her sinking, and after a final "short burst at her sister ship," Dyess signaled to Crosland, and the two headed for home.[3]

While the two planes were being rearmed, Lt. Sam Grashio took off from Cabcaben in Poston's P-40 for a run on the string of enemy barges that were reported in the bay. Finding his targets where he was told they would be, he lined up his Kittyhawk and headed in. After pulling the bomb-release lever, he looked over his shoulder to see the results. But there was none, no explosions were seen.

Angered by the thought that all six bombs had badly missed his target, he headed back for Cabcaben.

Unbeknownst to the young lieutenant, he had not seen his bombs explode because they were still on his plane. This wasn't realized until Capt. Ozzie Lund in the Cabcaben tower screamed at him over the radio as he was approaching to land, "Don't land! Your bombs are hanging! Bail out!"

"To say that I was unpleasantly startled would be a gross understatement," said Grashio. "If even one of the bombs should drop while I was attempting to land, the war would be over for me. Yet the last thing I wanted was to bail out."[4]

The choices left to him raced through his mind. Of the three airfields he had to choose from, Mariveles was the longest. The additional space it offered would be needed to hopefully avoid a possible rough, three-point landing, which could jar one of the bombs loose.

Meanwhile back at air corps headquarters behind Bataan Field, General George and his intelligence officer Captain Allison Ind, who had been listening to the radio, heard someone announce, "That plane over Bataan seems to be having trouble; the bombs are still on its wings, but he has decided to land at Mariveles." After several seconds of silence, they heard, "Landed OK ... Palafox" (Palafox was the call sign for Mariveles). Relief. He'd made it.

It was nearing five o'clock when Dyess and Crosland took off on

## 10. Biggest Day for Bataan Air Force

their second run. Again Kibosh was loaded with a 500 pounder. Making the same approach to the bay, Dyess said, "I picked two unloading freighters as my target and went into a dive from 10,000 feet, releasing my bomb at 2,000. It passed just over the freighter but exploded among a concentration of barges and lighters that were receiving cargo from the ships. They went up in a glorious cloud of smoke, water, and debris. I felt better."

"As I pulled up, swarms of Japs began running from the two ships and stampeding along the dock toward shore. I pulled around and cleaned off the dock with my machine guns, [then] sprayed the four warehouses again with everything I had."

With plenty of ammunition still left, he then went after the remaining 100-ton ship he had fired at in the first attack. "This time I gave it a long burst and it caught fire from end to end," he said. "It soon sank."

Dyess then gave Crosland, who had also strafed the docks, the "high sign," and the two headed for home. It was now a little before six o'clock when they landed. Shadows covered the entire length of the runways, and the wind was picking up off the bay. Was there enough time for one more strike? Dyess contacted General George.

"He eventually granted permission," said Dyess. "If he hadn't, I'd missed the best shooting of the day."

Thirty minutes later, Dyess gunned old Kibosh down Bataan's red-dust runway for the third time. Over at Cabcaben, John Burns, in Crosland's P-40, took off at the same time.

Coming in over Subic again from the same direction, Dyess said, "I saw that my two freighters had shoved out from the dock and were running around like mad. I therefore aimed my bomb at the enormous supply dumps that had been built along the northern shore of Grande Island.

Waiting a little longer this time, he released the 500 pounder at 1,800 feet. Seconds later, a tremendous blast shook the island—a direct hit. "Soon," he said, "huge fires erupted, continuously punctuated by explosions."

By now, the sun had dropped down behind the South China Sea. It was almost too dark to see anything, and it was becoming dangerous to be in the air. "Cruisers, destroyers and shore batteries had all cut loose," he said. "They really were filling the sky."

His day appearing to be over, Dyess had just turned for home when he received a message that said army observers on Signal Hill below Mt. Mariveles had picked up a large transport towing landing barges that was trying to slip out of the bay just south of Grande Island.

Dyess quickly banked Kibosh northeast across the bay until he saw the ship's silhouette against the western horizon, then turned and headed in, all guns blazing. A second pass had "fires started all over the bow and in the well deck," said Dyess. "Then it blew up."

"The glow in the west now served me well for the second time. Silhouetted against it was yet another fairly large ship that had been reported as a cruiser, destroyer, tanker, and troop transport.

"I first struck it from the southwest, raking it from bow to stem. Two more passes had all antiaircraft guns silenced and small fires blazing on both bow and stem." Although unable to "make it blow up," the Japanese were forced to beach it, where it was still burning the next day.[5]

It was dark when the two men headed back to Bataan. As Dyess began his over-water approach to the field, he had to fight "a terrific tailwind" but was able to set old Kibosh down safely.

Just over the ridge at Cabcaben, however, John Burns, fighting with the same down-wind conditions, had come in too fast. In order to save himself and the plane, he purposely ground looped his P-40 at the end of the runway. The crash, which caused the inadvertent firing of his guns, sent, remembered Dyess, "a stream of tracers over the ridge," making him think for a moment that "we had drawn some flies (Japanese planes) after all."

At about the same time the two men had taken off for their last attack on Subic, Lloyd Stinson and Jim Fossey left Mariveles for the big bay. Although not able to reap the success Dyess had, they did strafe a 100-ton ship that was trying to get out of the bay, causing it to blow up.

In the communications shack behind Bataan Field, General George and Captain Ind had just finished sweating out Burn's landing, when word came over the radio that one of the Mariveles fighters was in trouble. It was Stinson's. "Heavy tail wind. He overshot and cracked up at far end. We don't know how he is."

## 10. Biggest Day for Bataan Air Force

Waiting anxiously for an answer as to how he was, word was flashed that Jim Fossey also "overshot field because of the heavy tail wind." Minutes later, "Both pilots okay, but planes wrecked beyond repair."

The day was at last over. Allison Ind, who, along with General George, had sweated it out sitting next to the radio, probably summarized the results as well as anyone. "At least the death of our little air force was one of unmitigated glory. It delivered a gigantic blow out of all proportions to its size—then literally collapsed."

The next night, in response to the attack made by nine pilots flying twelve sorties in five P-40s, Tokyo Radio announced that "fifty-five heavy bombers, mostly four engined," had attacked their shipping in Subic Bay, "with some tonnage sunk." Four U.S. bombers were reported to have been shot down.

Although nine different pilots took part in the day's activities, the bulk of the credit, of course, went to Ed Dyess. As for old Kibosh, now the only flyable P-40 in the Bataan air force, it was a virtual sieve. "You could hardly see it for the patches over the bullet holes," said Dyess. "The plane was olive drab, and the patches were bright blue. There were 60 or 70 of them."[6]

# 11
# Japanese Blitzkrieg
## *April 3, 1942*

In examining the Japanese side of offensive operations in World War II, outside of early victories against Malaya, Hong Kong, Burma, the Dutch East Indies, and initial operations against the Philippines, what could be considered a blitzkrieg-type offensive operation had never or would never again present itself—that is until mid–March 1942, when faced with an anticipated one-month campaign to capture Bataan.

Initial Japanese belief that it would take a major offensive to overwhelm the Americans and Filipinos on Bataan actually forced them to design and successfully launch what could be called a near-textbook version of German blitzkrieg: to surprise, cutoff, isolate, and bypass enemy strong points. So effective was the campaign that twice during what turned out to be a 6-day battle, offensive operations actually had to be halted to allow tanks and vital supplies to catch up.

The fact that the starving, emaciated, poorly equipped U.S. troops on Bataan were in such dire straits that they would never been able to stop the Japanese, blitzkrieg or not, is not pertinent to the story. Nor is the fact that Japanese General Masaharu Homma anticipated it would take a month to take Bataan and that his decision to attack Mt. Samat, the strongest position on the U.S. line, was a bold one. It was the plan behind the attack, one that would have made German "Panzer" General Hans Guderian, accepted designer of blitzkrieg, proud.

The physical layout of the U.S. line on Bataan left little doubt, on both sides, of what the focal point of the Japanese attack would be. Ninety-percent of the western half of the line, manned by troops of the

U.S. I Corps, was composed of jungle so dense that it would not only neutralize the effects of Japanese air superiority, but likewise swallow up an invading army within its roadless confines.

In contrast, the II Corps eastern half, outside of its most dominating feature—300-foot Mt. Samat—initially offered a wide-open, jungle-free approach to its gentle rising northern slopes and was accessible to the important engineer-built trails that flanked both the eastern and western sides of the mountain.

General Homma, by choosing to launch his attack against Mt. Samat, which he wrongly anticipated would take one week to capture, did so for two reasons: First, the initial element of blitzkrieg—surprise. The Americans would least expect a frontal assault against the high-ground advantage the 300-foot mountain gave them. Second, if successful, artillery observers from its commanding heights would be in position to direct fire for the important main assault down Bataan's east coast. With the primary objective to cut off and isolate the mountain, it was first necessary to gain control of the three key trails—429, 6, and 4—that together encircled the entire objective.

## The Preparation Phase

Because the Japanese had complete air superiority over the Americans since the start of the battle in early January, the air phase of the plan, outside of a noted increase in the number of planes and seemingly endless daylight attacks, gave little indication of exactly where or when the offensive would be launched.

To beef up the already existing squadrons of light bombers and fighters, the Japanese brought in two heavy, 60-plane bombardment regiments from Malaya and Indo-China, plus two squadrons of Betties and a squadron each of carrier-based bombers and Zeke fighters.

On March 25, on what could be called the opening day of the pre-attack phase of the battle, Japanese bombers and fighters, absent their usual three-hour "lunch break," were literally in the air from dawn to sunset, bombing U.S. front lines and suspected artillery positions.

For the next eight days, it would be the same. On April 2, the day before the scheduled opening of the attack, 82 Japanese bombers pounded the forward slopes of Mt. Samat, while fighters and dive-bombers, directed by ever-present spotter planes, made life miserable for everyone else.

As with the German blitzkrieg, one of the major contributors to the success of the air phase was the use of spotter planes, whose use almost totally neutralized the effectiveness of U.S. artillery. Every time a 1.55- or .75-mm gun fired, coordinates from their smoke trail were radioed to either a patrolling fighter or bomber, who usually made a quick and deadly response to the message.

Their presence not only played havoc with artillery positions. One American officer wrote, "Every few minutes a plane would drop down, lift up a tree branch, and lay one or two eggs. Every vehicle that tried to move, every wire-laying detail, infantry patrol, even individuals moving in the open were subject to these spot bombings."[1]

Captain Alvin Poweleit, a medical officer with the 194th Tank Battalion, of his experience with marauding Japanese fighters, wrote, "We hit an open stretch of road just as Japanese strafers came over. Fortunately, we jumped out of the jeep in time to get out of the rain of machine-gun fire, but several soldiers were killed and many wounded. While dressing the wounded, the planes returned and laid another round of fire on us, killing more. We tried to move the wounded to the side of the road, but again the bastards came back and bombed and strafed us. They continued strafing back and forth for about an hour."[2]

For the artillery phase of the attack, the Japanese had close to 200 artillery weapons, of which nearly half were 150 to 240 mm in caliber. Outside of smaller field pieces, the bulk was set up within a rectangular, four-and-a-half-square-mile area west of Balanga, a mere 3 miles from U.S. lines and the forward slopes of Mt. Samat.

With U.S. artillery nearly neutralized by efforts of the ever-present Japanese air force, anticipated big-gun duels between American 155s and Japanese 240mm's never occurred. Add to that depressing fact was the launching of an observation balloon some 3 miles north of Balanga, well out of 155 range. Interestingly, the effects of the balloon were best noted in the diary of Major Achille Tisdale, an officer under Bataan commander General Edward P. King. In his entry for March 16, he routinely noted that "the Japanese now have an observation balloon." Fifteen

## 11. Japanese Blitzkrieg

days later, however, he frustratingly wrote, "Nip artillery raising hell. If we could only get that damned balloon."[3]

To help conceal their planned D-day assault on Mt. Samat, the Japanese limited their pre-attack artillery concentrations to eliminating U.S. artillery positions and general disrupting of troop movements and destroying enemy command posts, communications, and defensive positions.

The third and perhaps most important pre-attack phase was to secure both flanks of the operation from possible counterattacks against the center or main focal point of the assault. Threats to both the east and west sides of the mountain would also force the U.S. to direct their attention away from the main objective, thereby weakening and perhaps relaxing the possibility of an attack against the relatively quiet center.

It began on March 31, three days before the main effort, when the Japanese 16th Division, on the west and what was called the Nagano Detachment on the east, began their operations. The 16th Division's job was to engage the I Corps from its eastern boundary with the II Corps across its entire front all the way to the west coast. At the same time, to further tie down and decoy the defenders, Japanese warships began shelling U.S. positions from the South China Sea.

While the 16th was busy keeping the I Corps occupied, the Negano Detachment, made up of some 4,000 men from the 21st Division, began pushing down the East Road while at the same time creating a false impression of an invasion from Manila Bay south of the U.S. line.

## *Plans for the Main Attack*

With D-day scheduled for Friday, April 3, it was decided that the planned 5-hour-long artillery phase would open at 10:00 a.m. and continue nonstop until three in the afternoon, on the heels of which the tank and infantry assault would begin.

An hour earlier at 9 o'clock, an estimated 196 Japanese artillery weapons, including 29 mortar and heavy-gun batteries, plus every close-support field piece, would begin to register their guns on preselected targets.

At the same time, the Japanese air force, which at the end of the day would fly 150 sorties and unload an estimated 60 tons of bombs, would begin their assault on the chosen three-mile-wide U.S. front defended by the Philippine Army's 21st and 41st Division's.

## *The Attack*

Captain Paul Ashton, a doctor with the 51st Division hospital high on the east slope of Mt. Samat, that morning had climbed to the brow of the mountain to view the "sweeping panorama of flat farmlands ... and the towns of Pilar and Balanga [from which] it [had been] possible to discern a great increase in the number of gun emplacements ... around those two towns."

"On this day," he wrote, "a large number of guns were zeroing in on us, and the muzzle flashes were plain to see....

> Then at 10:00 a.m., a greatly increased bombardment [came] in waves, steadily creeping up the brow and along the top of Mt. Samat. It continued for five hours and surpassed anything of the like we had ever seen. At the same time, the Nips sent over fleets of bombers ... the explosions [of bombs along] with the whine of smaller strafing planes ... was almost deafening. Communication lines and artillery positions were destroyed. Several acres of brush caught fire and burned fiercely.
>
> It became worse with each hour.... I climbed the hill to the top of Samat for the last time to see what happened. I was amazed to see that the topography had changed. The trees were a jumbled mass of foliage; fire was burning the dry brush at the base and creeping up the front of the hill. A few bodies could be seen scattered along Trail 4, the main [withdrawal] route from the front, and groups of Japanese were fanned out everywhere.
>
> The extensive denuding of the area must have meant that most had withdrawn in units as the barrage crept upward and across the mountain. I found the answer later [when] I drove our only ambulance over trails leading southward from the 51st and 21st Division areas. I was greatly hampered by roads full of aimless stragglers pouring toward the south.[4]

Recorded effects of the bombardment were consistent throughout the command. Captain Carlos Quirino, of the Philippine Constabulary's 2nd Division remembered it as "the most devastating concentration of [enemy] fire seen during the Philippine campaign." Had he known, he could have added "and the entire Pacific war to come."[5]

Although it may have seemed to those men along the II Corps front

## 11. Japanese Blitzkrieg

as though the entire line was being blasted simultaneously, the Japanese were actually directing the bulk of their air and artillery bombardments toward one point in particular.

Sector D, westernmost portion of the II Corps' area of responsibility and widest of the four sectors, stretched some three miles across the lower slopes of Mt. Samat. Divided roughly in half, defense of the sector was shared by two Philippine army divisions: General Mateo Capinpin's 21st Division on the east and General Vicente Lim's 41st Division on the west. Both generals had assigned all three of their regiments to the line. General Lim had his in numerical order from left to right.

It was the 41st Division, and more specifically, the 1,000-yard-wide corridor defended by the 42nd Infantry, at which the main Japanese assault was aimed on April 3.

If the combination of enemy air and artillery bombardments was devastating to those along the II Corps front, there may not be a word left in the dictionary to adequately describe what happened in the 42nd Infantry sector.

Despite the initial pounding of 42nd frontline positions by the Japanese artillery and air force, the Filipino soldiers of perhaps the toughest of the Philippine army divisions on Bataan didn't budge.

After riding out over two hours of steady bombardment, little attention was paid at first to the next squadron of enemy bombers that came over until the usual "freight train" roar of falling high explosive bombs didn't occur.

As the Filipino soldiers cautiously looked up from their holes to see what was happening, they saw what looked like hundreds of stick-like objects falling from the sky. When they hit, they burst into flame. They were firebombs, incendiaries.

It was the tail end of the Philippine dry season. Situated where it was—in the flat, open, lower slopes of Mt. Samat, an area devoid of lush tropical jungle but overgrown by brush and tinder-dry clumps of bamboo and uncut sugar cane—it wasn't long before the hundreds of small fires started by the incendiaries along the line, fanned now by an afternoon breeze, united to prairie-fire dimension.

Gradually as the heat grew in intensity, men were flushed out of their frontline positions back across what had become a churned-up, cratered, lunar-like landscape toward their regimental reserve line. Although it was possible to outrun the fire, continued heavy interdiction of the 42nd's corridor by Japanese artillery forced the Filipino soldiers to seek refuge in shell holes or abandoned foxholes along the way.

Soon, perhaps as with horses when the barn is burning, no matter where men went there appeared no escape. Panic stricken, those who tried to outrun the fire were killed by enemy artillery. And just as many of those who stayed to avoid the artillery burned to death.

Sergeant Silvestro Tagarao of the 42nd Infantry, whose Company K occupied the outpost line on the leading edge of the regiment's defensive positions, recalled the deadly effect of the attack and firebombing:

> The enemy [opened] up with a mortar barrage. We knew that the much-awaited assault was on. We dashed into our foxholes and waited eagerly. Violent explosions came rapidly, blowing up the trees around us. The merciless barrage went on, but there was no reply from our guns.
>
> At the height of the intense fire, incendiary bombs [were dropped]. They came unannounced, going up with a silent blast that became hot, blinding fire that burned the woods and rendered our position insecure. [Soon] the fire was all around us, and we couldn't hold there anymore. We waited for an order from our C.P., but none came.
>
> Soon flames were very close to us. We came out of our foxholes and withdrew. One of the men told me that our left flank had been consumed by flames several minutes before. Again we had to move back because of the flames, moving further until we reached our command post. It was also burning, and nobody was there except a corpse lying on a stretcher.[6]

At three o'clock, the line, masked in dense smoke, already racked by steel and fire, was hit again, only this time by men and more steel—men from General Akira Nara's 65th Brigade and steel from the 7th Tank Regiment.

The objective of Nara's thrust was Trail 29, the feeder trail to 429 which, along with Trails 6 on the west and 4 on the east side of Samat, would together complete the encirclement of the mountain.

The rout of the panicked 42nd, acting like a rampaging river at flood tide, overflowed onto the bulk of the 43rd Infantry on its right, carrying most of it with it. General Nara, who at best had expected to get only as far as the U.S. main line that day, surprisingly found a 1,600-yard-wide corridor completely abandoned to him when he arrived later that afternoon.

## 11. Japanese Blitzkrieg

At the same time, one mile to the east, the 4th Division's 61 Infantry, supported by a dozen tanks, launched its attack against what it found to be nothing but empty 43rd Infantry foxholes. When the battle subsided around 6:00 p.m., nearly two thirds of the enemy's initial objective—the capture of the junction of Trail 6 and 429—had all but been accomplished. At the point where superimposed Trails 6 and 429 reached the backside of Samat, 429 turned east where, upon its capture and linkup with Trail 4, the main objective to cut off and isolate would be considered accomplished.

Buoyed by their unexpected success on the third, beginning at 6:30 a.m. the next morning, the Japanese air force and artillery resumed their attacks with the same intensity as the day before.

Along with keeping the pressure on Samat's west slope, the main focal point of what was called the Left Wing was General Mateo Capinpin's 21st Division.

After the two-hour concentration of air and artillery bombardments, the 21st Infantry, westernmost of the three regiments, was hit by infantry and tanks of the 7th Tank Battalion that together ran rampant over and through the helpless Filipinos. In fact, by 9:00 a.m., less than three hours since the first bomb dropped, outside of the 22nd Infantry, who had sat relatively unchallenged astride the access to Trail 4, the 21st and 23rd along with it were driven back off the main line. An hour later, with the situation now untenable, the 22nd, too, pulled back, signaling, in less than a day and a half, the complete abandonment of the three-mile-wide Sector D fronting Mt. Samat.

April 5. Day 3 of General Homma's anticipated 30-day-long offensive to capture Bataan. However, thanks to the effective blitzkrieg of Mt. Samat and unknown to them at the moment, they were halfway home—the battle for Bataan would be over on day 6, not day 30.

The objectives of the Japanese this Easter Sunday was to capture Trail 4, thus completing the encirclement and isolation of the mountain and to secure its heights, together allowing the main objective of the entire offensive to proceed.

When Japanese Right Wing forces, after consolidating their capture of Trails 6–429, began their assault on the western slope of the mountain, they found the going relatively easy. In fact, by 1:00 p.m. that afternoon, less than 3 hours since it began, they had reached the heights of the mountain.

Before it could be consolidated, however, the stoutest defense so far put up by U.S. artillery came from guns of the 41st Field Artillery, located on the south or reverse slope of the mountain. Until their forward observers were forced from their positions on the heights, they were able to direct fire from their 1917 British wooden-wheeled 75s, and old Vickers 2.95-inch pack howitzers, whose accuracy literally held up the Left Wing's assault on Trail 4 until help came from Right Wing forces later that afternoon.

And so, by roughly four-thirty on the afternoon of April 5, with the capture of the Mt. Samat itself and control of encircling Trails 429, 6, and 4, the Japanese had successfully and perfectly executed what those who had faced the Germans in Europe knew as blitzkrieg. Fortunately, as mentioned earlier, they would never again launch or be presented with the opportunity to mount anything resembling it against the Allies in the Pacific.

General Homma was never credited for the design and strategy of the attack. Nor, with his assignment to command the army in Formosa in December 1940, did he have the opportunity to learn anything from the Germans about blitzkrieg. His accomplishment was unfortunately overlooked by his failure to take the Philippines according to the timeline established by the Imperial High Command following their quick, three-month victory over Malaya and Singapore. The six months it took to take the Philippines resulted in him being relieved of command in June 1942, and he was brought home in disgrace.

# 12

# The Deliberate Bombing of Bataan Hospital No. 1

The battle for Bataan peninsula in early 1942 was tragic, not only because of the Bataan Death March that followed, but because the rag-tag American and Filipino army that found itself hopelessly trapped was forced to fight without an air force, with little food and medicine, with World War I weapons, and against an enemy whose fanaticism and barbarity had never been seen or imagined in the history of modern war.

An example of the latter can be found in the specifications of charges against General Masaharu Homma, commander of the Japanese Army during the Bataan campaign, who was put on trial in Manila in 1946.

Of the 42 "Charges of Atrocities" that led to his being put to death by firing squad on April 3, 1946, Number 2 of the specifications read:

> About 7 April 1942, units of the Imperial Japanese air forces, unlawfully bombed General Hospital Number 1, "Little Baquio," Bataan, Philippines, resulting in the death and wounding of sixty-nine Americans and fifty-two Filipinos, as well as the destruction of portions of said hospital.
> 
> (Omitted from the charges was the first bombing of the hospital on the morning of March 30, for which the Japanese apologized over the radio that night.)

The story of the bombing of the hospital begins back on December 23, 1941. It was on that day that General Douglas MacArthur, with the Japanese army bearing down on Manila from two different directions, ordered his army withdrawn into the Bataan peninsula, hoping it, along with the island fortress of Corregidor, could hold off the Japanese until help arrived.

With less than 20 days to prepare the army on Bataan for the inevitable Japanese attack, little, outside of a few roads and a hastily prepared main line of defense, would be ready for the 90-day siege to come.

Along with the army, the Medical Corps was also hastily preparing itself for the role it would have to play once the shooting started. First on the list was finding a suitable general hospital location. The site, located on the Bataan east coast near the barrio of Limay, was in a group of abandoned barracks used before the war by a Philippine Scout regiment.

Located less than eight miles from the front, as long as the line held, the hospital could exist. However, when the Americans and Filipinos were forced to withdraw back to what would be the final line of defense on January 25, its three-and-half mile proximity to the new main line placed it dangerously close to the battle.

Forced for the second time to find a new site, one was located near the southern tip of the peninsula in an area known as Little Baguio. Taking its name from the physical similarities of the summer capital of the Philippines, surrounded by giant trees, Little Baguio was reasonably cool, breezy, and pretty much mosquito free.

A few months before the war started, army engineers had constructed a cluster of buildings and sheds just off the road in Little Baguio, for use as a motor pool and repair shop during maneuvers. It became the site of General Hospital No. 1. With the anticipated increase in casualties as the battle progressed, it was decided at the same time to establish a second general hospital. Called Hospital No. 2, it was located in the jungle a couple of miles east of No. 1. Unlike No. 1, whose buildings were out in the open, there were no buildings at the No. 2 site. In fact, the entire hospital was established and functioned without a single permanent structure throughout the entire battle, its only advantage being its concealment from the air by the surrounding jungle.

Of that problem, wide-open Hospital No. 1 was liberally marked with red crosses if, for no other reason than to distinguish it from the huge II Corps ammunition dump on one side, an antiaircraft battery

## 12. The Deliberate Bombing of Bataan Hospital No. 1

behind it, and a large quartermaster supply depot on the road in front. "We were petrified," remembered Dr. Alfred Weinstein, one of Hospital No. 1's surgeons, "that on some of their runs, loads of bombs aimed at these installations might be short or long and land in our tiny area, plainly marked as it was by Red Cross flags and signs painted on roofs of the wards."

Another problem with the location was its proximity to a series of switchbacks the road followed as it climbed up from the barrio of Mariveles, four miles west. "To make matters worse for us," remembered Weinstein, "the road swung in a wide curve behind the hospital to climb a slope we called Zigzag. From within the operating rooms, heavily laden trucks grinding up this steep grade sounded exactly like Nip bombers. Standing tense at the operating tables, we paused ... listening to the grind of the motor, praying for the sound of when the driver shifted gears. If it didn't, we waited for the scream of falling bombs –a noise we had to hear only once to remember for life."[1]

In late March, as the end of the battle drew near, enemy air activity over Bataan intensified, as did the chances, as Dr. Weinstein feared, that bombs aimed at one of the neighboring installations might land on the hospital.

It happened on March 27. Incendiary bombs meant for one of the "neighboring installations" fell on the enlisted men's barracks, causing it to partially burn. One man, PFC David Burks, had his upper jaw blown off. "Although we didn't believe the raid was aimed at the hospital," said Weinstein, "that didn't put Burks' jaw back on his face."[2]

Three days later, on March 30, Dr. Alvin Poweleit and another surgeon were waiting for their 7:00 a.m. relief, when Poweleit, reacting to the increasing sound of an approaching plane, half-seriously said, "I'll bet those S.O.B.s drop them on the hospital. Seconds later, I heard the shriek of falling bombs."[3]

Outside, Navy nurse Ensign Ann Bernatitus, who was crossing the compound on her way toward the operating shack, also heard the thunder of approaching motors. The increased presence of Japanese planes over the peninsula since the launch of their final offensive two weeks earlier had everyone looking for cover whenever one came close.

Thinking that "they'll see the Red Crosses on the roof and not bomb the hospital," no sooner had she reached a nearby foxhole than the first tomb hit followed by two more.

In the brief lull between bombs, Bernatitus peeked over the edge of her foxhole, expecting to see nothing but total devastation. Surprisingly, things didn't look too bad. The wards and operating rooms hadn't been hit, but other buildings and a few vehicles were on fire. And somewhere men were screaming.

Thinking it was over, she climbed out of her foxhole and ran for the operating room. As she entered the building, Navy doctor Charles Smith, the surgeon she was on her way to assist with a patient on the operating table, grinningly said, "Bernatitus, where were you?"

Ann looked at the soldier on the table. "He was gravely wounded," she said, "but was conscious."

All at once, the shack swayed as a bomb exploded close by. "You two get under cover," the wounded man said. "There's no sense letting the bastards get you."

"If they get me," responded Dr. Smith, "They'll get me while I'm working."

Ann Bernatitus vowed she'd be right next to him if it did.[4]

Army nurse Lieutenant Juanita Redmond had just come on duty in one of the ten open-sided, tin-roofed garages that had been converted into hospital wards. "The day seemed like any other," she remembered, "until I heard the sharp whizzing of a bomb. It sounded closer than any I had heard before. The next one was nearer and threw me on the floor, several of the patients with me."[5]

Asleep nearby in the officers nipa hut quarters was an exhausted Alfred Weinstein. After operating almost continuously for the previous 24 hours, it would, as he said before he went to sleep, take nothing less than a bomb to wake him. And a bomb it was, as "panic stricken," he sat up to "the roar of exploding bombs and the pungent odor of smoke."

"Walls and floor heaved and tossed, beams groaned, cracked, and fell apart," he said, "and there was a trickle of blood coming from a wound on my forehead."

Back in the wooden-framed operating pavilion, Dr. Poweleit, who had dropped to the floor after the first bomb, thought at first he had

## 12. The Deliberate Bombing of Bataan Hospital No. 1

been wounded, but, as he said, "it turned out to be from a bottle of Lysol, which I thought at first was blood."

Poweleit took quick stock of the damage. "Practically all of the windows were shattered, and the sides of the room were splintered with bomb fragments."[6]

When the bombing stopped and Juanita Redmond got up from, what she described was her "cringing position on the floor," the first thing she saw were flames "shooting in every direction from other buildings and cars and trucks. But none of the wards appeared to have been hit."[7]

D. Weinstein, startled out of his sleep by the first explosion, stumbled out into the compound. "Bombs were still falling throughout the hospital area, sending up showers of dirt and clouds of earth. Clouds of smoke filled the air as smaller incendiary bombs exploded and sent their burning contents in all directions."

From the shallow drainage ditch he had quickly jumped into, he glanced back at the officers hut he had moments before been sleeping in. "The wing where I had been sleeping was still intact, but a bomb had demolished the left wing." Fortunately, the only officer occupying that wing, who had been recovering from a bout of malaria, was out walking when the attack came.[8]

Once the planes had left, results of the bombing were made. A direct hit on a large slit trench near the kitchen area had killed 14 Filipino civilians and one corpsman, PFC Fred Lang. Examining the scene, Al Poweliet wrote in his diary that night, "Legs, arms, heads, and bodies were strewn all over the area," and body parts "were suspended from a nearby tree."

Juanita Redmond, who at first was reluctant to leave her ward fearing what she would find outside, remembered seeing several sheeted figures on the ground. "Most of them were hospital personnel," she said, "men we'd been working with a long time, men we knew and liked."

Near the entrance to the compound, a truck that had taken a direct hit and was still burning presented a ghastly scene. It was on its way to deliver the bodies of men who had died the day before to the cemetery near Mariveles. "Loaded with dead, charred bodies, a burning truck was lying on its side in the road," recalled Dr. Weinstein. "The odor of burning flesh lingered for hours."

When the final count was made, 23 men had been killed and 78 wounded. Outside of two medical corpsmen, not one of the doctors, nurses, or hospital personnel had been killed or wounded.

"That night, " remembered one of the nurses, "someone heard the Jap radio in Manila announce that the bombing had been an accident and wouldn't happen again. Even the Jap prisoners from their guarded compound were positive it had been a mistake."[9]

"They assured us that all pilots were instructed not to fly over hospitals, much less bomb them," said Juanita Redmond. "We really believed it must have been a mistake."

One man who didn't was Al Weinstein. "We knew it was deliberate," he said. "We knew we were living on borrowed time."[10]

Weinstein was right. Eight days later on the morning of April 7, the "borrowed time" the hospital had been living on ran out.

The situation for the exhausted American and Filipino army on Bataan by the seventh was hopeless. In fact, unknown to everyone in the hospital, the white flag of surrender was less than 48 hours away from being presented to the Imperial Japanese Army.

Outside of a continued increase in wounded and malaria and dysentery cases, life at Hospital No. 1 that day was much the same as it had been for the past month. By ten that morning, the medical staff, who had come on at 7:00 a.m., had settled into their usual routine.

About that time, a truck loaded with ammunition destined for the rapidly reeling Bataan front had pulled out from the nearby II Corps ammunition dump.

At 10:15, as it was laboring past the entrance to the hospital, a bomb from a diving Japanese plane scored a direct hit on it. Judging by what followed, it was most likely the first of a stick of several bombs aimed purposely at the well-marked hospital.

On duty in one of the open-sided, tin-roofed wards was Juanita Redmond. Moments before the bomb hit, someone yelled, "Planes overhead!" But those words had become so familiar that most of them paid them little attention. "Suddenly," she said, "the drone of planes was lost

## 12. The Deliberate Bombing of Bataan Hospital No. 1

in the ... roar of a crashing bomb. The concussion threw me to the floor."[11]

Two men, Al Weinstein and Army chaplain Father William Cummings, were crossing the hospital compound when they spotted the Japanese plane bearing down directly on the hospital.

"There was no shelter available, no time to run," said Weinstein. "We hit the dirt and waited, but not for long. The world exploded."

Both men were momentarily knocked unconscious by the blast. "I don't know how long we were out," he continued. "Bleeding from the nose and ears, drums shattered, concussed, and holding on to each other, we stumbled toward the wards...."[12]

Ann Bernatitus was on her way to the operating shack when the ammunition truck was hit. Although she didn't know the blast was from the truck blowing up, she instinctively knew the hospital was the target.

Lying flat on the ground, she was frightened to look up until the sound of shrapnel and rocks falling on the tin roofs of the sheds stopped. When it did, and, as she said, "I dared open my eyes, the entire hospital seemed to be in ruins."

Getting to her feet, she began to run toward the operating shack. Despite the smoke and dust, it was easy to find. "The cries of the injured led me right to the building, " she said. Inside she found glass from the windows and broken antiseptic bottles all over the floor. "Dust and debris were everywhere, and in the midst of chaos the wounded were already waitin...."[13]

Unlike the single plane raid of March 30, the silence following the ammunition truck explosion was only a momentary lull between two more attacks that were still to come.

"They're coming back!" someone yelled. Bombs from the second plane hit the mess hall and the doctors' and nurses' quarters. Although none of the hospital buildings was hit, panic spread, particularly in the open-sided wards.

"When the roar of tire explosions diminished from the near misses," remembered Juanita Redmond, "I could hear shrieks of pain, the helpless sobbing of men in the wards. Debris, dust and tree limbs came flying through the open sides of the sheds.

In the Orthopedic Ward, men with arms and legs suspended in traction were screaming with pain as they were tossed about from the concussion. Nurses and corpsmen had rushed in and begun cutting traction ropes. Those who could stand the pain were gently lowered to the floor for protection against flying debris.

In Juanita Redmond's ward, several of the men had become hysterical. "I would have joined them if I could," she said, "but it was all I could do to go on acting as if I had everything under control."[14]

Fortunately, help was already on the way in the form of Father Cummings.

Hearing the panicked cries of men in Lt. Redmond's ward as he and Dr. Weinstein reached the area, Cummings ran directly into the open-sided building. Patients, even amputation cases who had fallen or rolled out of their double- or triple-decker beds, were attempting to get out of the ward when he arrived.

Mounting a small wooden box, with arms outstretched, in a calm voice he said, "All right boys, everything's all right. Just stay quietly in bed or lie still on the floor. Let us pray together. You know the Lord's Prayer. I'll start in and you follow."

As he began, the third plane dropped its load on the hospital. "This time they scored a direct hit on my ward," said Lt. Redmond. "A (huge) bomb smashed the tin roof into flying pieces, iron beds doubled and broke like paper."

Mesmerized momentarily by the sound of falling bombs, a quick-thinking corpsman grabbed Redmond and pulled her under a desk.

"But the desk was blown into the air when the bomb hit, Sergeant Mays and me with it," she said. "When I fell back on the floor, the desk landed on top of me. Sgt. Mays lifted it off. Gasping for breath … my eyes feeling like they had been gouged out of their sockets and sick from smelling smoke from the explosion, I dragged myself to my feet."

Looking up, she was astonished to see Father Cummings still on his little wooden box. "All through the attack, we could hear his voice repeating the Lord's Prayer," one of the patients told Lt. Redmond later. "He never faltered and never fell to the ground." Despite the bombing, none of the patients panicked; all remained quiet as if realizing that

## 12. The Deliberate Bombing of Bataan Hospital No. 1

through Father Cummings' courage, God really was looking out for them.

As things quieted, the brave priest stepped down from his box, walked calmly over to Lt. Redmond and said, "Put a tourniquet on my arm, will you? I've been wounded."

Looking around, Juanita saw that only one small part of the ward was still intact. "Part of the roof had been blown into the jungle. There were mangled bodies under the ruins; a bloodstained hand stuck up through a pile of debris; arms and legs had been ripped off and flung among the rubbish. Some mangled torsos were impossible to identify. One of the corpsmen who had survived climbed a nearby tree to bring down a body that had been blown into the top branches. Blankets, mattresses, pajama tops hung in the shattered trees."[15]

Dr. Poweleit had just left the operating pavilion and was crossing the compound when he "heard the swish of bombs. I dropped to the ground," he said. "I was slightly lower than where the bomb struck. The crater it created was about 45 feet across and 71 feet deep. I was 40 feet away from its edge. I got a small splinter of steel in my left eye, which caused a slight ... hemorrhage.

"Ward 5 took a direct hit, killing 45 to 75 patients and wounding about 100 more. Arms, legs, bodies, heads were all over the place. Two nurses were there, Rosemary Hogan and Rita Palmer, who both had been slightly wounded. We placed tourniquets and dressings on as many ... as we could."[16]

The wounds to both nurses were more than slight. Rosemary Hogan sustained three shrapnel wounds, and Rita Palmer, according to Juanita Redmond, had her face and arms cut and her skirt and G.I. shirt blown off by the concussion. Both were sent to Corregidor that night.

The bombing finally ended. Although it was over, the heart-rending work around the hospital, which had been over 25 percent destroyed, was just beginning.

In Juanita Redmond's ward, of which two-thirds had been destroyed, she remembered that "the air was rent by the awful screams of new-wounded and the dying. We worked [frantically] to get the men who might be buried, still alive, under the mass of wreckage, tearing apart the smashed beds and debris to reach the wounded and the dead."

One of the men uncovered was an American soldier named Freeman. "Our boy with no legs, " remembered Juanita. When found, the first thing he wanted to know was if "Miss Redmond [was] alive."[17]

Not far away in another ward, Nurse Willa Hook was knocked down by a falling bed. "You all right, Miss Hook?" she heard. Dazed but okay, she raised her head and looked into the concerned face of a young Filipino soldier who, ironically, was another "boy with no legs."[18]

In the middle of the search for victims, a terrible crash momentarily froze everyone in the compound. One of the giant trees near Lt. Redmond's ward, the roots of which had apparently been weakened by a bomb, fell crashing onto the tin roof of what was left of the building. "It sounded like shell fire, and left us shaking," said the startled young nurse.

The busiest place on the hospital grounds was the operating pavilion. "Through the portals of the operating room, the medics carried in unrecognizable masses of human wreckage still pulsating with life," remembered Dr. Weinstein.

One of the men littered in was Father Cummings. "I checked him over hastily," said Weinstein. "Not bad, Father. Your left arm is torn up a little, but everything else is O.K."[19]

While Al Poweleit and Weinstein were working on the courageous priest, a curious religious service took place. Father Cummings, his eyes shut, began saying a Hail, Mary ... to which Filipino nurse Belinda Casteneda made the response.

"While they were praying," said Weinstein, "Al and I swore steadily: 'The yellow bastards ... the slit-eyed lice ... the mother-loving sons-abitches...'"

"Prayers and imprecations wove themselves into an odd refrain of point and counterpoint," he said. "They were praying and we were cursing, but we were all addressing the same listener."

Interestingly, Weinstein's "cursing" was somewhat responsible for comforting another patient. It happened that night as he and Al Liebert, who was assisting him, were working to remove a piece of shrapnel from the back of a wounded man's head.

"Liebert had been unusually slow and I was irritable, having worked

## 12. The Deliberate Bombing of Bataan Hospital No. 1

continuously for over ten hours," said Weinstein. "For God's sake, Liebert," he growled, "what the hell's the matter? You been hitting the hospital alcohol again?"

"I don't know. I've had a pounding headache ever since I got hit on the helmet with some shrapnel this morning," said Liebert, apologetically.

Seeing a ragged hole in the crown of his helmet, Weinstein slipped it off his head, discovering a deep wound two inches above his right ear.

"Al [and I] shaved his head, anesthetized the scalp … and removed an ugly chunk of shrapnel buried deep in [his] brain. While we were bandaging his head, I noticed he was grinning through the pain. I asked him, what the hell's so funny?

"He said, 'As long as I could hear you cussing, I knew everything was all right.'"[20]

Throughout the day and into the night, the gruesome task of uncovering bodies continued. Nineteen Filipinos were found entombed in a makeshift 15-foot section of metal drainage pipe they were using as a shelter. Concussion from one of the bombs that exploded near the entrance killed all nineteen.

The official count of those killed directly in the bombing was seventy-three. "Several of those who were dead died of shock," said Juanita Redmond. "They hadn't been hit, they were just too weak to live through the explosions."

One hundred and seventeen were wounded or re-wounded in the raid, of which 16 more would die of wounds sustained in the attack.

The physical damage to the hospital itself by the estimated ten bombs dropped on the compound was nearly fatal to its ability to function for any length of time. Destroyed were one ward and most of another, the Pharmacy and most of the drugs, the Receiving Ward, the doctors' and nurses' quarters, and the mess hall. Missed were half a dozen other wards, including the one housing forty-two Japanese wounded, and the vital operating pavilion.

Probably the most telling sign of the indirect effects of the bombing was in the number of beds left standing after the raid. "There had been about 1,600 beds, or makeshift beds, in our hospital," said Lt. Redmond. "Only 55 were left standing."

# The Fall of the Philippines

For the hospital staff, the rest of the day and night was mixed with fear, anger, and fatigue. Juanita Redmond summarized it best. "That night we stayed in our foxholes. I didn't sleep. We hadn't eaten since breakfast, but I wasn't hungry. We [felt] like hunted animals, waiting for the kill. But stronger than that was anger; anger and hate and a hot desire to fight back, to avenge our dead.

"What kind of human beings would deliberately bomb a hospital— defenseless, openly marked for what it was, filled with wounded and the sick?" she asked herself. There was no answer.[21]

For Al Weinstein, there had been no time for questioning or anger. "I operated all day and all night until after sunrise the next morning, for 24 hours straight, with only brief respites for coffee and sandwiches. I was so tired that I have no recollection of whom I operated on or what I did. Did these patients live? Did they die? To this day, I have no idea."[22]

As an exhausted Juanita Redmond crawled out of her foxhole the next morning, "head aching, a crick in [her] back, [and] legs cramped," little did she know that for her and all the Bataan nurses, it would be their last day on the peninsula. It was April 8, 1942. The white flag of surrender would be presented to the Japanese later that day. That night a boat would take them and three doctors lo Corregidor. Juanita Redmond, along with 21 other nurses, was flown to Australia by PBY before Corregidor fell.

Dr. Weinstein remained at Hospital No. 1 for several weeks after Corregidor surrendered before being transferred to the infamous POW Camp O'Donnell.

Al Poweliet was captured and survived the Death March.


(The "unofficial" count of the casualties sustained in the two deliberate bombings of Bataan Hospital Number 1 was 307, of which 112 were killed and 195 wounded.)

# 13

# The Fighting General of Bataan

Because of lost records and two and a half years as prisoners of war, many of those who fought and ultimately surrendered on Bataan never did receive recognition for their warranted contributions to the four-month campaign. One man, whose actions at the command level is well documented as one whose story should be told is Brigadier General Clifford Bluemel—a man who truly was "the fighting general of Bataan." Most of the direct quotes from General Bluemel in this story actually come from his private papers that are on file at the West Point library.

Fifty-six-year-old Brigadier General Clifford Bluemel, a 1909 graduate of West Point, was serving his second tour in the Philippines when the war broke out on December 8, 1941. Ten days before the Japanese attack, he had been given command of the Philippine Army's 31st Division. Considered a perfectionist by those who served under him, he did not hesitate to openly criticize or berate any of those he considered incompetent, including the young American officers within the division. One, who changed his mind once the battle started, actually claimed him to be the meanest man in the U.S. Army. Once the fighting began, however, it wasn't long before they all came to believe that his hard-driving, no-nonsense approach had molded the 31st into the best of the nine Philippine Army divisions on Bataan.

Through no fault of their own, the 31st was not critically involved in the events that would lead their commander to be recognized as Bataan's fighting general until the mid–January withdrawal from the first U.S. line at Abucay. The circumstances involving the difficult pullback to their new positions across central Bataan actually provided the stage, despite mass confusion, that would lead to him become known as the toughest and most resourceful general on Bataan.

What led to what would become one of the strangest and most confusing day Bataan would ever see occurred when the Philippine command reversed its initial decision to place the Philippine Division's 31st, 45th, and 57th Infantries on the newly established front line. Actually made while the withdrawal was under way, it involved placing what was considered the three most reliable U.S. regiments in reserve to be used, as needed, to plug any enemy breakthrough of the new line.

Relative to General Bluemel, he was told on January 25 that his entire 31st Division, along with the 51st Division that had been reorganized as a combat team, would occupy the 4,500-hundred-yard-wide Sector C on the new line. The position encompassed defending the important north-south Trail 2, through which a breakthrough by the Japanese would not only jeopardize the entire II Corps front, but perhaps all of Bataan as well.

The confusion began on the afternoon of the January 25th, as troops of the 32nd and 33rd moved into their assigned positions on the Sector C front. The 31st Infantry, less its 1st Battalion, unknown to its commander, had been reassigned to the beaches along Manila Bay. He found out early the next morning on Trail 2. On his way to inspect the positions the 51st had moved into during the night, he ran into a line of men stretched out along the trial behind an officer he recognized from the 1st Battalion. "Where in the hell are you going?" he shouted.

"Where's Colonel Irwin [31st Infantry's commanding officer]? He sent a message to join him."

"Hell, he's on Manila Bay."

"We've been ordered to join him."

"I'm the commanding officer of this division," he roared, "and no one else can give you an order! You put that battalion back in the line where I told you and keep it there 'til I tell you you can move."

As the line of men turned back up the trail, he yelled, "I don't care if Jesus Christ tells you to move it! You keep it there until I tell you to move it!"

As mentioned, the day that would be marked throughout by mass

## 13. The Fighting General of Bataan

confusion was just beginning. Continuing his inspection, when he reached the positions assigned to the 33rd Infantry, he was jolted again, this time by abandoned foxholes. The entire 33rd Infantry was gone, its absence leaving a 1,500-yard gap in not only his sector, but also the entire II Corps line.

Searching for answers, he said,

> Finally a Filipino told me, "I saw the assistant regimental supply officer, and he says the 33rd won't be with us." It was taken away from me and I wasn't told about it. Who took those regiments away from me, I don't know.
>
> I had a very bright young Filipino G-2 named Villa. The 32nd had two battalions on the line and one in reserve. I learned you never send oral messages in combat, so I wrote one and gave it to Villa to take to the colonel of the 32nd. It said, "You will have your reserve battalion occupy sector assigned to 33rd Infantry. That regiment has been taken away. You will move immediately."
>
> I told Villa, "You see all these foxholes? I want you to see a soldier in each foxhole before you get back to my headquarters, even if you're there until the day after tomorrow." When I got back about 7:00 that night, he said, "The battalion is in."

Meanwhile, the quest for the missing 33rd continued. Having to vent his anger on someone, he turned to his all–Filipino staff. "Listen, the general has a staff to help him and take care of him. You people are no goddamned good. I have to take care of you. What the hell good are you? Show me you're some good, any of you. Where's the 33rd Infantry?"

Then it was II Corps commander George Parker's turn. "I hollered murder to Parker. We had quite an argument. I never liked Parker, and he didn't like me. He said, 'We're sending you up another regiment from the 41st Division.' Of all the conglomerations, taking a regiment out of my division and sending it towards the Manila Bay side, then taking a regiment from another division and sending it over to me!" He was furious.

As the 41st arrived, yet another jolt. An American captain serving as an advisor to the regiment told Bluemel that General Vicente Lim, 41st Division commander, made them leave all of their machine guns behind. Obviously in no mood to be diplomatic, he got Lim on the telephone. "I gave him hell. 'What do you mean by taking away the machine guns?' He answered, 'They said the regiment was going to be in reserve and wouldn't need them.'"

With nothing that could be done about it, and still in search for troops to plug up the abandoned left side of Trail 2, he found 65 men from his division's headquarters battery who, equipped with 1917 Enfield rifles, he personally led to the abandoned 33rd positions. "Here you stay and here you die," he told their young Filipino commander. "I'm going to put in a battalion of the 32nd Infantry on your right with machine guns. Stop the Japs. If you don't, Bataan is finished."[1]

It was late in the afternoon when their feisty commander finally found out what happened to his 33rd. One of his staff officers told him the regiment's supply officer said that it had been pulled out to join the Philippine Division reserve in Sector A. With that news, Bluemel again called Parker to complain about yet another uninformed transfer of one of his regiments. Instead of talking to Parker, who doubtlessly didn't want to face more of the fiery general's ire, he had his operations officer Colonel Howard Johnson take the call. After listening to his complaint and still not providing an answer, Johnson jolted him again: the same 1st Battalion of 33rd Infantry that he had sent back into the line earlier that morning was soon to be on its way to join up with the rest of the regiment in Sector A.

As the Japanese prepared to open their attack against the Trail 2 corridor, Bluemel, stripped of two of his three regiments in one of the strangest, unexplained maneuvers of the entire campaign, prepared for the worst. Although reinforced at the last minute by the automatic weaponless 41st Infantry and remnants of the 51 Division, it would take a miracle and a forceful commander to stop the Japanese.

With Bluemel supplying the needed leadership, the miracle was actually perpetuated by a captured U.S. map that purportedly showed the final line of defense, called the Limay Line, had been established on an east-west line across the peninsula from the barrio of Limay, 3 miles south of the actual American positions. Fortunately, Japanese reaction to the map actually led them to believe that their attack at Trail 2 would only be against a thinly defended outpost line. This misconception, which led them to initially launch their assault with perhaps less preparation and less enthusiasm, would contribute greatly to the outcome.

## 13. The Fighting General of Bataan

The battle for Trail, which began with the Japanese attack on the afternoon of the 27th, followed by a second that lasted through the 29th, failed to break Bluemel's patchwork defense. On the evening of the 31st, reinforced by fresh troops and an intense air and artillery bombardment, they came on again.

Bluemel was waiting. Using the heavy enemy air and bombardment as a sign that a major ground attack would follow, he ordered his division artillery to lay heavy fire on the main trail route. Although slowed, the enemy came on, only to be met by a crescendo of fire from Bluemel's now-confident Filipinos. It wasn't long before the Japanese, staggered by the effects of artillery and now-accurate small arms fire, were forced to fall back for the last time. For all practical purposes, the battle for Trail 2 was over, as was their attempt to crack the U.S. line for another month.

Leap forward to April 3, the day the Japanese launched their opening attack against the final U.S. line. General Bluemel, between the Trail 2 battle and the 3rd, had remained in command of Sector C on the important eastern side of what would be the focal point of the attack against Mt. Samat. The only other general involved in his sector was Max Lough, commanding officer of the Philippine Division.

What brought Bluemel into the picture actually came on April 6, following the enemy's threat against the series of vital trails behind and east of the mountain. On April 5, in an effort to halt the overwhelming Japanese success against U.S. defenses on both flanks, General Wainwright ordered General Parker to counterattack the next morning.

With both Lough's 31st Infantry and Bluemel's 51st Combat Team scheduled to launch the attack at dawn, U.S. 31st commander Lt. Colonel Jasper Brady, prior to the attack, discovered that the Philippine Army's 21st Division, anchoring the important right flank of the scheduled assault, had been completely overrun during the night.

Realizing that the entire attack was now in jeopardy and unable to contact Lough, Brady got through to Bluemel. After explaining that because of the loss of 21st Division support and with just 800 men himself, would he confirm his decision to hold up the attack?

Bluemel wouldn't hear of it. "Why didn't you attack as ordered? The preparatory and supporting fire by my artillery is still coming as scheduled, and my 51st Combat Team is ready to accompany your advance."

Brady reiterated why he had held it up, saying again that it was impossible and asking for his support.

"Not by a damn sight!" he yelled. "Don't pass the buck to me. I advise you to launch your counterattack immediately. If you refuse ... I'm going to report your action to your sector commander."[2]

"Sir, I've tried but can't raise General Lough's headquarters."

"Then I advise you to report your failure to attack to General Parker," and then hung up.

It wasn't Brady, interestingly enough, who contacted Parker. It was Bluemel later that morning who, upon the failure of the planned counterattack, for the second time requested permission to pull back to the south bank of the San Vicente River.

The II Corps commander, reluctant to give up the vital Trail 2 without a fight, for the third time in two days refused Bluemel's request, ordering him instead to dig in on the original 31st jumping-off point.

However, Parker's hope was short lived, as by 1:00 that afternoon, before Bluemel could move up, the Japanese had successfully flanked the Americans and the 51st Combat Team at Trail 2. In fact, when men of the 31st began to withdraw, according to Major Eugene Conrad, they found "all trails ... denied," forcing them, "after successive delaying actions," to get to the San Vicente "across country," where they arrived around 3:00.

About that same time, as Bluemel was still in the process of moving into position, the order finally came to pull back and form a new line on the south bank of the San Vicente. From that afternoon until late that night, an all-out effort was made by the American command, or more specifically, General Bluemel, to organize the shattered Fil-American army on the south bank of the river.

If there was any doubt that describing General Clifford Bluemel as "Bataan's fighting general," it was answered on this and the subsequent three days. Few unit histories, including those of the 26th Cavalry, 57th Infantry, and Provisional Air Corps Regiment from adjacent Sector B,

## 13. The Fighting General of Bataan

who joined those already on the line, failed to mention the personal efforts of Bluemel during this time.

As men straggled across the river throughout the afternoon, many were met by Bluemel, who personally attempted to organize the resistance. With rifle in hand, he and several other officers by late that night had prodded, talked, threatened, but in most cases, physically forced the semblance of a line along the south bank. Interestingly, what he had been working so hard on had been his responsibility anyway, as by late that afternoon, General Parker had turned command of the entire II Corps east of Mt. Samat over to him.

It was early on the morning of the 7th when a worried Bluemel, after only an hour's sleep, with his two trusty Filipino staff officers, headed back to the front for a pre-dawn inspection of his positions. A few yards up the trail, they were met by a large group of men from his own division moving to the rear. After somehow herding them back to the front and finding all quiet along the river, they walked back to the command post. After snatching another hour's sleep—the last he would get in the next four days—he was awakened near dawn by the sound of men again shuffling away from the front.

This time it was remnants of the 51st Division, whom he again physically stopped and turned around. An American officer with the group told him that the Japanese had routed the entire northernmost sector of the line, including the Provisional Air Corps Regiment, his own 32nd Infantry, and the 51st Combat Team.

Not long afterwards, a truck heading away from the front at high speed ignored Bluemel, who had un-slung his trusty Garand rifle and waved for it to stop. Not far behind, the first of another column of trucks bore down on the rifle-waving general. As it, too, roared past, an American of the U.S. 31st Infantry leaned out and shouted, "The San Vicente Line has broken!"

This was followed by a ragged column of Filipino's, whom Bluemel, again threatening with his rifle, yelled to stop and "form a line on both sides of the road!" At that moment, several artillery shells exploded on the road behind them, stampeding the now-unstoppable, terrified men past him.

Major Clarence Bess of the U.S. 31st Infantry who witnessed

Bluemel's unsuccessful efforts wrote: "Rifle in hand and still trying to collect units streaming to the rear and form them along a delaying position, this he was unable to do."³

Although still not giving up, he walked back to his command post, picked up a jeep, and, after sending a runner back to Parker with the bad news, drove north toward the disintegrating line in hopes of stopping what may already have become the domino-effect abandonment of the San Vicente. Abandoning his jeep, he soon found a still-intact battalion from his own 31st Division, and he told its commander to follow him to a ridge overlooking the river and dig in. No sooner had he started than the area was rocked by a 10-minute artillery barrage which, by the time it ended, for all practical purposes the battalion had vanished. After helping the wounded and physically exhausted men stagger down the trail, he found that his jeep and driver had also disappeared.

Around 1:00 p.m., the exhausted, disheartened general got an unexpected lift. Moving slowly and reluctantly southward along Trail 2, he saw a scout car approaching from the south. As it pulled up, an officer leaned out and said, "Do you know where I can find General Bluemel?"

"Right here," he said. Surprised and even "cheered up a bit" to find that the officer, Major William Chandler of the 26th Cavalry, had been sent north to find him.

Bluemel was unaware that the 26th had been assigned to him until their meeting. By that time, General Parker, conceding all chances of holding the San Vicente, ordered him to try again on the south bank of the Mamala River, which was considered the next most defensible position.

To gain time to reestablish on the Mamala, Bluemel dispersed the relatively fresh 26th across vital Trail 2 and told Chandler to "execute a delaying action, with which," he wrote later, "they had become so familiar."⁴

However, Bluemel hadn't liked the chances the south bank of the Mamala presented him the moment he saw it. The higher, much steeper north bank would give the Japanese complete command of the line, making it virtually untenable even before the fight began. Additionally, the resulting breakup of those units on the San Vicente had, for

## 13. The Fighting General of Bataan

all practical purposes, rendered them impotent as organized fighting units.

Around nine that night, "Bluemel," wrote 26th Cavalry commander Colonel Lee Vance in his diary later, "assembled commanders of the 26th, 57th, and 31st Infantries, 14th Engineers, and miscellaneous army units, and ordered the establishment of a new line on the south bank of the Alangan River, to be in position by daylight of the 8th. There was great confusion during the movement; abandoned guns and broken-down trucks on the trail."[5]

And so, slowly, painfully, men, who had seemingly expended the last bit of energy preparing to dig in on the Mamala, arose to move south once more. "Move slowly," said Bluemel. "Fifty yards at a time, then stop."

As they arrived, Bluemel assigned the exhausted remnants of his army to their positions on the new line. For the third time within the past 48 hours, the battered remains of the II Corps found themselves hurried into a strange, unprepared, and un-reconnoitered position. Although on paper its strength was shown at eleven battalions, in reality, it was closer to just two—1,360 men.

"Rear guard reached Alangan River position about 7:45 a.m. Entire command exhausted but went into position immediately," read the first entry into Colonel Vance's diary for April 8. "Position occupied as follows from left to right: 14th Engineers—26th Cavalry—31st Inf. (US)—57th Inf. (PS)—803rd Aviat. Engineers."[6]

Col. Vance, however, was unaware of the crucial mix-up that had occurred between the 31st and 57th and the absence of the 803rd. In fact, the confusion by those ordered into the mile-and-a-half-wide center of the line precluded all hope of making a successful stand.

It came when the 57th, initially assigned to the left of the 31st, somehow ended up on its right, leaving a 600-yard gap between the Americans and the 26th Cavalry. The 803rd, meanwhile, apparently not informed of their assignment, had kept going south, leaving a second huge gap between it and Trail 20, two miles west of the East Road.

General Bluemel, with information about the fatal gaps, got word that General Parker wanted to talk to him. Those hearing only the response to his questions had no doubt about what was said on the other line. After asking to whom he was talking, he explained that there was a gaping hole in his line, that he had no troops to fill it with, and would they pull troops off beach defense to fill it?

Responding to the answer, he yelled, "That'll be too late! You can be damned sure the enemy will find that big gap before dark and rush through."

Questioned on what he needed, he said, "I need four staff officers, communication personnel, and equipment.... I have only two Filipino staff officers. Like me, they've been without food since breakfast on April 6 and have about one-and-a-half hours sleep a night. I have no communication personnel or equipment. The 31st Signal Company has disappeared."

After a long pause where he apparently learned that help wasn't on the way, he yelled, "Since you're not sending me any troops until dark to fill the gap, I can't possibly hold the line! What line do you want me to hold next?"

"Hold that line," was apparently the response, "and take staff officers from your own troops, and to use their communications and personnel."

"Damn it, I told you it's impossible unless the gap is filled immediately!" he said, slamming the phone down in response to the last answer.

It wasn't until two in the afternoon that the Japanese reached the Alangan opposite what was left of the 31st and 57th. Discovery of the enemy on its left flank was all the 200 or so totally spent Americans could take. Writing out a message for the commander of the 57th, Colonel Jasper Brady wrote, "Am being hit by strong enemy column. Am withdrawing." Commander Edmund Lilly, of the 57th, not surprised by Brady's message, also decided to withdraw his Scouts.

And so, by late afternoon of April 8, 1942, with little more than a single firefight to show for its efforts, the 57th pulled back from the center of what was to be the last U.S. line ever to be established in the defense of Bataan.

Meanwhile, Bluemel, by then, according to Major Chandler of the 26th Cavalry, "nearing a complete state of physical exhaustion, but still

## 13. The Fighting General of Bataan

refusing to spare himself," at 7:00 p.m. had ordered the 14th Engineers and 26th Cavalry to disengage and head south down Trail 20.[7]

By 11:00 o'clock., most of what was left of the Alangan River force that had literally stumbled their way down Trail 20 reached their destination on the Lamao. Bluemel, sitting on a rock soaking his feet in the middle of a river he didn't even know was the Lamao, was told that Parker wanted to talk to him.

Knowing that the II Corps command post was less than a mile down the river, Bluemel said if Parker wanted to talk to him, "tell him to get the phone to me."

Captain Franklin Anders, 57th intelligence officer, who helped run the wire from Parker's C.P. and who overheard the conversation that followed, remembered that Lt. Colonel Johnson, talking for Parker, who was down with malaria, told him to "form a line on the Lamao River."

"Where the hell is the Lamao River?"

"It's the stream near your phone."

"Why in the devil didn't you designate this position this morning as I asked? I could have had a daylight reconnaissance. Now it's too damned dark. None of my people knows a thing about this terrain. Why in hell didn't your staff of thirty make a reconnaissance for us? Why aren't they here to guide my troops into position or at least give us some advice?"

"It was not known how you desired to put the troops in," he weakly responded.

"I'm willing to put them any damn way as long as they get in. The least you can do is send me four of your staff officers and help me get my people into position."

To Johnson's response, "I'm sorry, we can't spare anyone!" Bluemel blew up. "You can't send me any one of your fat, underworked staff officers to show me where to deploy the handful of men I have? Where is the food we need to revive our starving bodies? I've told you, we haven't eaten for almost three days. Where is the ammunition we need to fire at the enemy? Where are the vehicles and medicines to treat and evacuate our wounded? I'll form a line, but don't expect it to hold much past daylight. Out!"[8]

(Referring specifically to his treatment by General Parker and his staff during that time, Bluemel, in his private papers written after the war, wrote the following: "Those God-damned bastards back there had been sitting on their damned asses for months, eating three squares a day before retiring to their comfy beds for a good night's sleep. They had their heads in the sand like a covey of ostriches. They didn't know what was going on, what had happened, and hadn't listened. And when it was all down the drain, I couldn't pull their dead asses out of the fire and don't know of anyone else who could except the Good Lord.")

After his tirade with Johnson, Bluemel made an effort to determine how many men he could put together to defend the line and if the terrain along the river was suitable for defense. For troops, he said they were the same men "who [had] fought the enemy and not run from them—Philippine Scouts from the 57th Infantry, 26th Cavalry, and 14th Engineers, plus some 300 Americans from the 31st Infantry."

With word that a quick reconnaissance of the south bank of the river in the dark had found it unsuitable for defense, even if given time to adequately prepare, Bluemel called Parker.

"General Parker," he said, "I cannot comply with such an order. I have no machine guns, no mortars, no AT guns, nothing to stop or even slow down a tank. I have no ammunition, no grenades, no dynamite. In the dark, no effective reconnaissance of the terrain can be made. Do you expect me to occupy and defend a position under these conditions?"

After the II Corps commander told him that he would send him what he could, Bluemel acquiesced. "All right, I'll form your line, but it won't hold."⁹

As he prepared to carry out what he knew was an impossible task, a weapons carrier arrived with several boxes of .30 caliber ammunition, but nothing else—no food, no water, and no hand grenades. When he discovered that the ammunition was in '03 Springfield 5-round clips and not usable in the M-1's most of his troops used, Bluemel again contacted Parker. It was 2:30 a.m. Before he could say anything, Parker told him that all he had to do was hold out until dawn.

"What's going to happen then?" he asked.

"A car caring a white flag will go through the lines on the East Road at daylight."

"Do you mean we're surrendering?"

## 13. The Fighting General of Bataan

"Yes. There must be no firing after the car passes through the lines. Did you get the ammunition and rations?"

"I got the ammo. No rations."

"I'll check personally."[10]

At that point, it was decided to pull back down Trail 20 to delay the chance of contact with the Japanese for as long as possible. And so, the 600 or so ragged, exhausted, half-starved men, all that was left of the entire II Corps that only 7 days earlier amounted to 28,000 in number, hit the trail one last time.

At 10 a.m., as Bluemel led what generously could be called the Lamao River force south, they were joined by Captain Mark Wohlfield and the only remnant from the Provisional Air Corps, whose regiment of Americans had been routed from Sector B three days earlier.

Ordered to make contact with the unit on his left flank, Wohlfield said, "We came upon some troops from the 31st Infantry. An officer asked who was in command. I told him I was. The officer was General Bluemel. 'How many men have you?' I asked. He said he had about 600. Now he had 675."[11]

An hour or so later as the staggering, ghost-like figures of Bluemel's army continued to move south, they unexpectedly stumbled into a regiment-size enemy force that had worked its way behind it and was blocking the trail. A firefight had erupted between the Japanese and the 26th Cavalry's 1st Squadron when the general arrived. Ordering his men to prepare to tangle with the Japanese, he was quickly approached by two American officers, including 26th's commander William Chandler.

"General," said one, "we were told to surrender this morning, and here it's near noon and you're starting a fight. Everyone has surrendered but you."

Bluemel told them to do what they wished, that he was going to keep fighting. Before it went much further, a runner approached with word that white flags had already been uncased across the U.S. front. The fiery general, according to Chandler, "reluctantly decided to send forward a white flag in hopes that the hostile unit had heard of the surrender. Whether or not they had was never determined, but they did accept it."[12]

And so, the war for Clifford Bluemel was at last over. At that moment, to look at a man holding the rank of brigadier general in the United States Army, and a man who, in the history of World War II to come, should have been acknowledged as one of America's true fighting generals, would not be believed. Identified as a general by the single star left hanging on the collar of his torn, tattered uniform; his once-shiny boots held on his feet by what was left of broken pieces of leather shoelaces; unshaved, one lens of his glasses missing, and cussing at the fact that it was over.

Perhaps the most tragic ending to Bluemel's career was that as a prisoner of war, he was denied the chance to put his ability to motivate and lead men of the young American army in the war to come. Judging by the results of early U.S. campaigns in both the Pacific and African theaters, there was a desperate need for leaders like him.

# 14

# Honorable But Not Easy

## *The Surrender of Bataan*

By late in the afternoon of April 8, 1941—just five days since the opening Japanese offensive against what would be the final U.S. line on Bataan—the battle for the beleaguered peninsula was over. The only thing left was how to bring it to a peaceful, honorable, and bloodless end. Anticipation on how it could be accomplished against an enemy known for its disdain for Americans in particular was one of apprehension.

Interestingly, the words "Not Easy" in the title of this chapter not only applied to the actual surrender, but to an order "not to surrender" on the U.S. side.

On April 5, the third day of what would be the final Japanese offensive on Bataan, a strange radio message was sent to General MacArthur in Australia from Philippine commander General Jonathan Wainwright. It said in part: "The operation suggested in your [radiogram of April 4] has been under consideration by me for some time, and I had about decided to adopt it if and when supplies became exhausted. The troops have been on half rations for three months and are now on less than that amount, which results in much loss of physical vigor and sickness. Nevertheless, before allowing a capitulation, the operation you suggested will be adopted.... I counterattack tomorrow."

What initiated it actually goes back to a March 28 message from Wainwright to General George Marshall in Washington, where, in closing wrote, "To be utterly frank, if additional supplies are not received for Bataan by April 15, the troops ... will be starved into submission."[1]

133

Four days later on April 1, in response to a message from Marshall to MacArthur where he quoted Wainwright's April 15 "starved into submission" statement, MacArthur responded with: "I believe ... that the supplies on Bataan will last beyond the date of April 15.... When I left on March 11th, it was my estimate that serious shortage would not develop at the earliest before May 1st....

"I am utterly opposed under any circumstances or conditions to the ultimate capitulation of this command as visualized in Wainwright's radio [of March 28]. If it was to be destroyed, it should be upon the actual field of battle.... To this end, I had long ago prepared a comprehensive plan to ... cut a way out if food or ammunition failed." After describing his plan, he added that he had not yet informed General Wainwright as "I feared it might tend to shake his morale and determination. I shall however, in view of his radio to you, inform him thereof in the near future."

What brought Wainwright's "I counterattack tomorrow" signal to MacArthur on the fifth was the radiogram to him explaining in detail the operational plan he had submitted to Marshall on April 1. After explaining that it was only to be implemented when the food supplies were completely exhausted, he closed by saying, "under no conditions should this command be surrendered."[2]

By the evening of April 8, the timing of the counterattack plan was at hand. Bataan's food supply, with the issuance of the last 45,000 C-rations two days earlier, was now exhausted.

At 11:30 p.m., Wainwright had the Corregidor switchboard connect him with Bataan commander Major General Edward King at his headquarters on the peninsula. Despite knowing that his exercise in futility could not be carried out, he told King that the pressure had to be taken off the II Corps before it was too late.

King told him that it was already too late.

Nevertheless, Wainwright ordered him to reinforce the beleaguered II Corps with units of General Albert Jones' I Corps and then attack "northward toward Olongapo" with the rest.

Stunned yet still answerable should he fail to notify I Corps of the plan, King called General Jones.

As anticipated, the outspoken Jones told King that MacArthur's

## 14. Honorable But Not Easy

plan was "ridiculous." His men had just completed a tortuous four-mile withdrawal to the banks of the Binuangan River in compliance with his order of the night before. They had nothing left.

King did not press it. He would not order an attack that was doomed to failure even before it started. There would be no counterattack by the I Corps. He looked at his watch. Both hands were at 12. It was Thursday, April 9, 1942—the beginning of what would be recorded as Bataan's last day.

The weary Bataan commander then called Brigadier General Arnold Funk and his operations officer, Col. James Collier, in for a conference. Together they reflected on the meeting they had had two days before with frontline commanders. When questioned about what percent of their units were still considered "effectives" (defined by King as a soldier who could walk 100 yards without staggering and still have the strength to shoot), all unanimously agreed it was no more than 15 percent. Together they retraced the four, hurriedly established lines on a map of Bataan, none of which had lasted a full day. The Japanese, they agreed, would be in Mariveles by tomorrow night, no matter what happened.

"II Corps as a tactical unit no longer existed," reflected Collier. Just behind the barrio of Cabcaben were the refugee camps and hospitals with over 13,000 defenseless patients already "within range of enemy light artillery"—no place to fight a battle.

"I've decided to surrender," said King. But knowing the position Wainwright was in with MacArthur's "no surrender" orders, he decided to put his own two stars on the line and not notify the commanding general until he had already contacted the Japanese. "I don't want [Wainwright] to be compelled to assume any part of the responsibility," he said.

Like the notification of the death of someone who had been terminally ill for some time, to everyone in the room, it was no surprise. Yet, remembered Col. Collier, it hit us "with an awful bang and terrible wallop." By the time Gen. King left to begin to outlining his surrender terms for the Japanese, "there wasn't a dry eye present."[3]

Slowly the agonizing wheels of capitulation began to turn. Word went out at 2:00 a.m. to the ordnance depots to destroy everything.

Motor pools were told to destroy all vehicles. Artillery and antiaircraft guns were ordered spiked. Of the remaining 50,000 gallons of precious gasoline, 40,000 were ordered dumped. The quartermaster was told to hold back 10,000 gallons to be used, hopefully, to transport the defeated garrison to POW camps. Unit commanders were told to bury their records and have their troops report to Mariveles at the southern tip of the peninsula at dawn.

Following his decision to surrender, Gen. King's primary task was to somehow communicate with the Japanese beforehand as to those desires. Colonel Everett Williams and Major Marshall Hurt, two bachelors on the general's staff, were selected to make the initial contact at dawn.

King handed Williams an official two-page "memo of instructions" to be used as a guideline in arranging a formal surrender meeting with Japanese commander, General Masaharu Homma, later that morning.

To cover the possibility that the Japanese should decline his offer, the memo instructed Williams to "ask him terms under which he [would] accept the surrender of Bataan."

Listed also were several points of "consideration" toward which he wanted Japanese attention drawn, points such as the dangerous proximity of the two hospitals to the current battle zone; to the fact that, because of the unusually poor physical condition of his command, it would take quite some time to organize and deliver them as prisoners of war; and that he had already "issued orders" to have them delivered "by motor transportation ... to places as might be directed." Lastly, hoping for their immediate release, he directed attention to "the vast number of civilians present in Bataan," who had remained "in no way connected with the American or Philippine forces."

It was decided that in order for Hurt and Williams to reach the Japanese lines by dawn, they should leave his headquarters around 3:30 a.m. At 2:00 a.m., the two men were sitting in one of the headquarters shacks when the II Corps ammunition and dynamite stores went up less than 800 yards away.

Hurt was talking on the telephone when "a terrific explosion occurred ... followed by a second." He started for the door when another blast rocked the "whole earth," and the shack began to break up. This

## 14. Honorable But Not Easy

was followed by a fourth explosion. "The window [fell] on my head," he dimly remembered, "and lumber [fell] all around," as did rocks, tree stumps, and chunks of concrete.[4]

Major Achille Tisdelle, General King's aide, who lived through the experience with Hurt and Williams, recorded the explosions in his diary as the most terrific he "had ever heard.... In the morning, our overhead cover (tops of the trees) was gone, and there were empty shell cases all over the camp. It is miraculous we came through this."[5]

A few minutes after the explosions, the light from General Wainwright's extension began flashing on the Corregidor switchboard. It was Brig. General Lewis Beebe, his chief of staff, asking to be patched through to Gen. King's headquarters. Wainwright, who had not heard from King since ordering him to counterattack at 11:30, was wondering how it was progressing.

The explosions, however, had momentarily disarranged the telephone communication system on the peninsula, and instead of getting King, Brig. General Clifford Bluemel answered. He was still up on what was the last line of defense, trying to organize the pitiful handful of men from his disintegrated II Corps into some kind of a fighting force. It was impossible.

Bluemel told Beebe that very thing. Beebe, relaying instructions from Wainwright, told him that he was on his own, that the commanding general would approve "whatever action he deemed best."

Meanwhile, Wainwright, anxious as ever about news of the counterattack, had Beebe call General Jones at I Corps. Beebe asked how his plans for the attack were progressing. Orders for the attack had not yet been given, Jones answered. Beebe told him to "stand by," that he would probably be receiving them at any minute from Gen. King, and then hung up.

The fact that Jones still had received no orders at that late hour drew no reaction from Wainwright, strongly indicating that the Philippine commander hadn't expected it anyway.

Further evidence along those lines surfaced a few minutes later at 3:00 a.m., when King, after hearing Beebe's conversation with Jones, phoned across to Wainwright.

Beebe picked up the receiver.

137

"I want a definite answer as to whether or not General Jones will be left in my command, regardless of what action I may take," said King.[6]

Beebe relayed the question to Wainwright, who nodded yes. "General Wainwright says you're still in command of all forces on Bataan," Beebe answered.

The subject of why King, after three-and-a-half hours, still hadn't informed his commanders of the counterattack, wasn't even broached by Wainwright. Nor did King mention that in less than 30 minutes he would be sending two men forward with white flags to implement the surrender he had order three hours earlier.

In a blacked-out dugout at Bataan headquarters, a man looked at the green, luminous dial of his watch. It was 3:15, time to get started for the front.

Colonel Williams and Maj. Hurt, the officers selected to carry word to the Japanese of Gen. King's desire to surrender, left the dugout and headed for the road.

After a quick stop at Hurt's tent for a piece of bed sheet that could be used as a white flag, they, as Hurt wrote later in his diary, "commandeered a reconnaissance car and motorcycle escort and [were] off." Latest word put the front somewhere around Kilometer Post 152, a little more than 8 miles away.

The two men started out but, finding the traffic impossible, decided to abandon the car. Hurt remembered that Williams looked at his watch, grabbed the white flag, "[climbed] on the rear of the motorcycle, and abruptly took off."

Left to follow the best he could, Hurt began working his way through the "maze of traffic, worming through crouching, demoralized, beaten foot soldiers." It was 4:00 a.m. He remembered what was written on the copy of instructions in his pocket: "You will proceed ... in time to arrive at our front lines by daylight." Bataan was down to its last two hours.

By 5:00 a.m., Hurt, after "saying a few prayers ... bumming a few rides, and [doing] a lot of walking," was within about three quarters of a mile from the barrio of Lamao. He had been virtually all alone on the road for the last half hour. There, in the faint, early morning light, sitting in a jeep parked next to Kilometer Post 155, he recognized Col. Williams and his driver.

## 14. Honorable But Not Easy

"Williams has learned that the front is at Km 151.8," wrote Hurt. "Everything is quiet now except for far-away explosions and the chattering teeth of our driver named Weaver. He is so scared he can't talk as we make our way forward."

After crossing the bridge over the Lamao River, there were still no Japanese, and it was now broad daylight. Interestingly, Bataan had folded up so fast within the last six hours that the Japanese army had found it tough to keep up.

Since "nothing has happened, we start slowly forward to make contact," said Hurt. "After a mile, everything is [still] deserted and quiet. We see and hear nothing."

After crossing a bridge over the Alangan River and starting up the hill on the other side, a large group of Japanese soldiers came onto the road. "We stop the jeep, raise our hands, and wave the white flag. Yelling, they rush us with their bayonets flashing. Is the end here?"[7]

Ironically, less than an hour earlier, a "yell" of a different kind was heard over the same question.

At 6:00 a.m., when General King was confident Hurt and Williams either had or would soon make contact with the Japanese, he phoned General Wainwright to tell him what he had done.

Lt. Col. Jesse Traywick, Wainwright's aide who took the call, rushed to the commanding general with the news.

Wainwright was shocked. "Go back and tell him not to do it!" he yelled.

The night-duty officer hurried back to the phone. It was too late, he was told. Contact with the Japanese had already been made.

"I had my orders from MacArthur not to surrender," wrote Wainwright later, "and therefore ... could not authorize King to do it." But he was quick to show that he had "no criticism" of the Bataan commander for doing what he had done. "It was a decision which required great courage and mental fortitude."[8]

Over on Bataan, meanwhile, the men who were on their way to deliver Gen. King's surrender terms were not at all sure they would live to do it.

Col. Williams and Maj. Hurt were being rushed by a platoon of bayonet-wielding Japanese soldiers. A minute or so later, a noncommissioned officer appeared and ordered the soldiers, who had already begun ransacking the jeep, to put everything back. "We heave a sigh of relief," wrote Hurt.

Williams pulled out Gen. King's surrender instructions and showed them to the sergeant. Seeming to understand, he climbed into the jeep and motioned them to drive on. They soon passed more enemy soldiers who "stare at us and do a lot of talking." Before long, they were turned over to an officer who, in turn, "relayed us further to the rear."[9]

"We pass several [exhausted] U.S. 31st Infantry soldiers being herded along by the Japs," wrote Hurt. "A rope is tied around the wrists of each, but they … tell us they are not being treated badly."

At Kilometer Post 146, they stopped and got out of the jeep. Seated at a small rickety table nearby were Maj. Kameichiro Nagano and an interpreter. The two Americans, carrying their white flag, entered the clearing and were introduced to Nagano. No one saluted. Nagano did not stand up.

The interpreter read Williams' surrender instructions. The two Americans answered several questions which, among other things, included challenges to their authority to surrender Corregidor. Nagano, at Williams' suggestion, agreed to set up a meeting with Gen. King at the Bataan Agricultural Experimental Farm Station back near the Lamao River Bridge.

Colonel Williams is left behind while Hurt, in the jeep, is escorted as far as the Lamao River by no less than four tanks. "We stop at the bridge, and my Jap escort asks me when I will return with Gen. King.

"'Two to four hours, depending on the traffic,'" I tell him. "Speedo," he says.

"After as very wild, rough, and fast ride past blown up tanks, burning trucks, broken guns, and unending strafing and dive bombing, we reach the command post," wrote Hurt. "I report to Gen. King. He is ready to leave at once.

"The General, his two aides, Maj. Wade Cothran and Capt. Achille Tisdelle, board a jeep and start out."[10]

Over on Corregidor, as soon as it became light enough, binoculars were broken out for a look-see at what was happening. Although it wasn't much, they could tell one thing for sure: "If King did surrender, some

## 14. Honorable But Not Easy

[of the] Japs don't know about it," said one man, alluding to the enemy planes seen still bombing and strafing.

He was right. Until Gen. King could make his surrender official, the Japanese air force had been instructed to continue their attacks on Bataan.

Major Tisdelle, carrying a white flag in Gen. King's jeep, wrote in his diary that they were bombed and strafed by "three fleets of dive bombers ... all the way, repeatedly." Colonel Collier, carrying a white flag in the lead jeep with Hurt, was a little more specific, stating that they were attacked no less than once every 200 yards, forcing everyone to dive into ditches or behind trees each time.

"Colonel Collier ... and I ... ran out of the ditch and waved the white flags hoping the Japs would see them," continued Tisdelle. "If they did," he said, "they paid no attention."[11]

It was now ten o'clock. The surrender party had been on the road for an hour and had only progressed a mile and a half. If the next couple of miles was to be as tough, chances were they wouldn't make the Japanese lines alive, and there would be no formal surrender of Bataan.

About that same time in the Press Relations Office back on Corregidor, Philippine army Major Salvador Lopez wasn't sure he could do what he had to, either. Word had come from Gen. Beebe, Wainwright's chief of staff, that although nothing official had been heard from Gen. King's headquarters, they should begin preparing the announcement of the fall of Bataan.

Lopez, one of the principal scriptwriters for the daily Voice of Freedom radio broadcasts from Corregidor, was given the job. He looked up at his companions, Lt. Francisco Isidoro, who would translate what he wrote into Taglog, the native language, and Lt. Norman Reyes, who would read it in both languages over the Voice of Freedom. "I don't think I can do it," he said.

"Mechanically," he remembered, "I placed a sheet of paper on the typewriter and began writing."

> Bataan has fallen. The Philippine-American troops on this war-ravaged and bloodstained peninsula have laid down their arms. With heads bloody but unbowed, they have yielded to the superior force and numbers of the enemy.

## The Fall of the Philippines

In all, Lopez would write 282 words of "the epic struggle that the Filipino and American soldier put up" on Bataan—a 282-word epitaph filled with praise befitting the "intrepid fighters [who had] done all that human endurance could bear."[12]

"The flesh must yield at last," he wrote in moving conclusion, "endurance melts away, and the end of the battle must come. Bataan has fallen, but the spirit that made it stand—a beacon to all liberty-loving peoples of the world—cannot fail!"

Yes, Bataan had fallen, but still not officially. The American half of the surrender party, about the time Lopez had finished writing his announcement, had been received by Maj. Nagano at the Agricultural Experimental Farm Station near Lamao. They had been two hours traveling the four miles from headquarters. They had been harassed and strafed continuously by the Japanese air force for the first half of their journey, until a reconnaissance plane acknowledged their white flags just outside the barrio of Cabcaben.

Through an interpreter, Nagano told the frazzled Americans that he was not authorized to make the arrangements himself, but that a member of Gen. Homma's 14th Army staff was on his way.

A few minutes later, a 1940 Cadillac, still shining through its coat of red Bataan dust, arrived and out stepped Col. Motoo Nakayama, Homma's senior operations officer. As Maj. Tisdelle remembered, "General King and all the rest of us stand up when he strides in. No one salutes on either side and no one [shook] hands."

"We arrange ourselves around the table. I cross my legs but a Jap officer knocks my feet down. I light a cigarette, but he knocks it down, too."[13]

Tisdelle glanced over at King, braced stiffly in his chair in front of Nakayama. "I never saw him look more a soldier than in this hour of defeat," he remembered.

General King, reflecting back on his history at that moment, remembered that almost to the minute, 77 years before, April 9, 1865, General Robert E. Lee was meeting with Gen. U.S. Grant at Appomattox. Like Lee, King lamented that he, too, "would rather die a thousand deaths" than do what he was about to do.

Nakayama's interpreter opened the conversation. "You are General Wainwright?" he asked.

## 14. Honorable But Not Easy

King identified himself as the commander of the army on Bataan. "Where is General Wainwright? We want to see General Wainwright." King told them that he had "no means of getting in touch with Wainwright" and that he was only representing his command in the negotiations.

"Japanese cannot accept surrender without [Wainwright]," emphasized the interpreter. Again, King patiently explained that he had no authority to speak for Wainwright or to surrender Corregidor either, as he had also been asked.

"Finally the Japs appear to be convinced," Tisdelle observed, "so the aide blurts: 'You will surrender unconditionally?'"

King explained that his forces "were no longer fighting units" and that he wished an armistice period so he could prepare his "army for deliverance as prisoners of war." He also requested that the air bombardment be lifted.

The Japanese air force was ordered to bomb until noon, he was told. "You will surrender unconditionally?"

"I desire to surrender with these four conditions," King went on, listing the points he wished the Japanese to honor. Would his men be treated as prisoners of war under the provisions of the Geneva Convention?

For the third time, "You will surrender unconditionally?" It was absolutely impossible, continued the interpreter, for Col. Nakayama to negotiate for the surrender of Bataan only. If the forces on the peninsula wished to give up, it would have to be done "voluntarily and unconditionally ... [by] each individual or each unit."

"How will the prisoners by treated?" Tisdelle remembers King asking. He receives no answer, only a cold stare. He repeats the question twice more. Then the interpreter jabbers with Nakayama, and finally says with a dry smile, "Of course, we are not barbarians. Then you will surrender?"

At that moment, a flight of Japanese planes roared over the trees heading south. Realizing that each minute of debate meant death to more and more of his shattered command, the Bataan commander nodded in agreement.

"Then King places his pistol on the table, and we do the same," continued Tisdelle.

Nakayama then asked him for his sword.

"I have none," replied King.

"They jabber some more, but finally decide that the crazy Americans can surrender without sabres. Then the Japs stomp out of the room."

With terms apparently agreed to, Gen. King called Col. Collier and Hurt over and instructed them to take a jeep south. "Move all American and Filipino troops south to Mariveles. They are to be assembled by unit for surrender."[14]

Although sounding routine, King's order to "assemble by unit for surrender," because of the rapid collapse of the Bataan forces, was nearly impossible to achieve.

The biggest culprit was the lack of communications. Aside from a few units in the virtually unchallenged I Corps area, for most in the II Corps after seven days of relentless, sustained Japanese attacks, it had become "every man for himself."

A frightening incident occurred in the I Corps' 11th Division sector, however, that was related to the lack of communication on the Japanese side. Major General William Brougher, 11th Division commander, on the evening of the ninth, after ordering his Filipino troops to stack arms in wait of the Japanese, had large bonfires built and white flags displayed across the division front.

"Instead of coming in to accept our surrender," he wrote later,

> the Japanese came in with machine guns blazing and shot into our soldiers disarmed and huddled in their bivouacs. The men were terrified and took off down Trail 7 toward Mariveles. They left their arms, equipment and even their food behind. In my CP, we debated the merits of sticking it out or following the men to the rear. I knew nothing of the terms of surrender, and with machine gun bullets whistling around, we all got the impression the Japanese were giving no quarter and that we would all be slaughtered if we remained where we were. Finally, we decided to follow our men to the rear and took off."

The next day, after succeeding in rounding up most of the division on the banks of the Sayasain River, the Japanese—this time peacefully—accepted their surrender.

By mid-day on April 9, at an abandoned U.S. fighter strip on the very southern tip of the peninsula, several thousand Americans had been rounded up or voluntarily gathered to officially surrender to the

## 14. Honorable But Not Easy

Japanese. Many had originally headed to the little port-of-entry town of Mariveles, hoping for a Dunkirk-like escape across the 2-mile North Channel to Corregidor. Fewer than 1,200 made it.

For those who were left, along with the hundreds of Filipino troops who had been captured or who had surrendered throughout the peninsula, little did they imagine as they lined up to begin their march to prison camp what was in store for them. History would record it as the Bataan Death March.

# 15

## "P-40 Something"

### *The Last of the Tomahawks*

Both before and during World War II, the Curtiss-Wright Airplane Company manufactured three versions of its P-40. The first, B model, called the Tomahawk, was used until April 1942 by the Flying Tigers in China and was responsible for most of the 286 "confirmed" kills made by the Tigers. Additionally, along with the nine squadrons in Hawaii that were partially outfitted with Tomahawks, thirty-one were shipped to the Philippines in May 1941.

This is the story of, by all accounts, the last P-40B Tomahawk fighter to see action in the Pacific in World War II.

In Hawaii, when the Japanese struck on December 7, of the 18 sorties flown by American fighters that day, nine were made in P-40Bs, which accounted for seven enemy fighters.

In the Philippines, of the four 24th Pursuit Group squadrons in the islands, three were later-version P-40E Kittyhawks. The fourth and only squadron equipped with P-40Bs was the 20th Pursuit Squadron at Clark Field. Sadly, of the 23 Tomahawks warming up on the ground when the Japanese struck at noon on December 8, only three got into the air. The rest, along with five that were unmanned, were all destroyed on the ground.

By the end of the day, only three P-40Bs were left on the Islands; and when what was left of the entire 24th Pursuit Group was ordered to Bataan in late December, they were down to two.

## 15. "P-40 Something"

Between then and February 12, the two fighters, along with no more than seven P-40Es, were involved in all the reconnaissance and combat missions flown.

On one of the more memorable missions, one of the Tomahawks, flown by Lt. Lloyd Stinson, was part of a surprise night raid on Nichols and Nielson Fields outside of Manila.

On February 24, two days before the attack, intelligence reports gathered from agents near the city indicated that the Japanese had concentrated a large number of fighters at the two fields. Assuming this meant that they had moved there to take advantage of the 10-minute, 30-mile, short-hop flight across Manila Bay to Bataan instead of the 120-mile-round-trip from Clark Field, it was decided that something had to be done.

Lieutenant Stimson, along with two other pilots, was assigned to attack Nielson. Although specific results of their attack was not known, intelligence reports claimed that between 14 and 17 Japanese planes were destroyed in the raids on the two fields, with over 30 more damaged by bombs and machine-gun fire. More importantly, it was reported that the enemy had ordered a general dispersal of all planes in the Manila area.

Not bad to claim that a single P-40B was one of the planes involved in momentarily chasing the entire Japanese fighter force in the Philippines out of town.

On the night of January 22, the Japanese successfully invaded the west coast of Bataan, some 900 men coming ashore on a beach below a headland identified as Quinauan Point.

Eleven days later in the early morning of February 2, a 13-barge Japanese force was spotted attempting to reinforce their positions on Quinauan. In response, two four-plane attacks involving both Tomahawks and two P-40Es strafed and bombed the enemy force, leading the pilots to believe their efforts had led to the repulse of the entire invasion. They were only half-right. Of the 700 enemy troops involved, the Japanese claimed some 350 never reached the shore.

On February 12, Brigadier General Harold George, commander of what was called the Bataan Flying Field Detachment, turned over operational control of the field to Captain Ed Dyess. It wasn't much of a promotion, as his entire operational force consisted of four P-40Es and just one flyable Tomahawk.

For the next 20 days, no combat activities for the tiny Bataan air force took place. On March 3, however, it all changed.

It began when an exceptionally large number of Japanese ships were spotted in Subic Bay, 20 miles north of the southern tip of the peninsula. At that time, the five-plane air force had been spread out amongst three fields—two at Bataan, one, the lone remaining Tomahawk, at Cabcaben, two miles north of Bataan Field, and two at Mariveles, southernmost of the three airfields.

With information on the heavy activity at Subic, George decided to "shoot the works," ordering four of the planes loaded with 30-pound fragmentaries. The fifth, Dyess' Kittyhawk, was rigged with a single 500-pound bomb on a homemade bomb rack.

Flying wingman for Dyess was Lt. Donald "Shorty" Crosland in the Tomahawk. Together they bombed and strafed enemy ships and shore installations before returning to Bataan. The two successfully repeated their efforts a second time, returning around 5:30 p.m.

Although shadows were covering both Bataan and Cabcaben runways by then, Dyess, with Crosland's replacement, Lt. John Burns getting his turn in the Tomahawk, took off at 6:00 p.m. for what would be Dyess' third sortie. At the same time, the two Mariveles fighters took off for their second crack at the big bay.

After the last and again successful attack, the four remaining Bataan air force fighters headed for home (the fifth fighter, a P-40E piloted by Lt. Erwin Crellin, was shot down in the first attack). Unbeknownst to the four pilots as they lined up for the approach to their respective fields, a strong tailwind had picked up off the bay that would affect the landings on all three airstrips. Of the four, only one pilot, Ed Dyess, was able to land without incident. It was not so for the two Mariveles pilots and John Burns at Cabcaben. Although none was hurt, unable to control their speed, all three overshot their respective fields, crashing at the end of the runways.

As for Burns in the Tomahawk, Dyess later wrote, "At George's headquarters I got the bad news. To avoid overshooting the field, he ground looped the plane, damaging it severely."[1]

## 15. "P-40 Something"

Despite sinking an estimating 26,000 tons of enemy shipping and killing several hundred Japanese in the process, by the end of the day, the Bataan Flying Field Detachment was down to only one plane—Dyess' P-40E, appropriately nicknamed "Kibosh."

Over at Cabcaben, meanwhile, ground crewmen surveyed the damage to the ground looped P-40B. The main damage, outside of one wing, was a bent propeller and a torn-out landing gear—all repairable. Under the supervision of capable engineer officer Lt. Leo Boelens, mechanics of the 21st Pursuit Squadron assigned to Cabcaben went to work on salvaging the last of the Tomahawks. Remarkably, two days later, with parts from three wrecked P-40Es and a rebuilt engine, the plane was ready to rejoin the Bataan air force.

Only one thing was missing. Without parts from the Kittyhawks, it would never fly again. And yet its main frame was still a P-40B. After discussing what to call it, someone said, "We have to call it something." That was it. All agreed to call it just that—"P-40 Something."

First to test "Something" was Lt. Bill Rowe. On March 14, headquarters on Corregidor ordered a reconnaissance of four Japanese airfields on Luzon to determine if a rumored buildup of planes was taking place. Although never having flown a P-40B, let alone the hybrid "Something," the veteran pilot had no trouble with the plane. His presence over all four fields being totally ignored, he returned safely to Cabcaben to report no unusual buildup on any of the airfields.

For the remainder of the month, there was no reconnaissance or combat activity for the two-plane air force. Because of this, on April 2, Ed Dyess sent Lt. Jack Donaldson to Cebu in "Something" to bring back some special items to help boost the sagging morale of his pilots, who had not seen the air for close to 30 days.

During the campaign, the island of Cebu had become the main quartermaster supply depot for Bataan and Corregidor. Although its warehouses were loaded with supplies of all kinds, because of the tight enemy blockade of Manila Bay, few ships had gotten through. Ironically, some of the supplies that did were flown in by military and civilian planes from Bataan. With Dyess' order, P-40 Something became a participant in the supply operation that had actually been going on for two months.

When the withdrawal to Bataan was ordered in late December, among others, three civilian planes were flown into Bataan Field—an 8-year-old Bellanca, a 1934 four-place Waco, and a Beechcraft Staggerwing—where, throughout the battle, they had somehow survived.

On February 3, Lt. David Obert was ordered to fly to Mindanao to deliver a secret codebook to Brigadier General William F. Sharp, Southern Islands' commander. On his return the next day, he stopped at Cebu where Col. John Cook, commander of the Army's quartermaster depot at Cebu City, loaded the cockpit of his Kittyhawk with "goodies" to take back to Bataan. Stuffed into his plane when he took off were, along with several miscellaneous items, candy, several bottles of cognac, and tobacco.

Wrote Obert of what followed: "Upon arrival at Bataan, the liquor, tobacco, and candy were turned over to General George who, in following days, passed it out to the pilots as sort of a reward for successfully completed missions. Probably could be classed as the maiden voyage of much-famed 'Bamboo Fleet.'"[2]

He was right. Because of it, the idea was born to use the three civilian planes and an occasional P-40 to fly not only candy and tobacco in for the pilots, but food and much-needed medical supplies for the Army as well.

What was called the "Bamboo Fleet" operated from that day on until the fall of Bataan, often ferrying VIP personnel south then returning with as much food, quinine, and other medical supplies as could be stuffed into the cabin and cockpits. Captain Roland Barnick, one of the pilots, said that they "… made about 35 round trips in all, evacuating 100 to 120 personnel and bringing in tons of supplies."

Meanwhile, the situation with the war on Bataan had reached its critical stage. On April 3, the Japanese launched what would be the final offensive against the starved and beleaguered American and Filipino garrison. Far beyond even the enemy's own expectations, the fall of Bataan was only five days away.

After an ordered reconnaissance flight on April 6, which pilot John McCown had to abort because of mechanical difficulties, the next time P-40 Something would leave dusty Cabcaben Field would be its last from Bataan.

## 15. "P-40 Something"

On the afternoon of April 8, former 20th Pursuit Squadron commander Captain Joe Moore was ordered to fly a P-40 to Cebu. His assignment, once there, along with two or three other P-40s, was to fly cover over a small convoy of supply ships through the Japanese blockade to Bataan and Corregidor.

When Moore arrived at Cabcaben that night, outside of identifying the plane he was to fly as number 41, he barely recognized the ship he had picked up brand new back in May, 1941. Interestingly, between the time he last flew it back in December, eight other pilots had flown it. Fittingly, he thought, that he would be the one to fly it out of harm's way.

Unknown to the 20th's old C.O., as he lifted "Something" off Cabcaben at 8:30 that night, Bataan was less than four hours away from surrendering.

Although the mechanical problems that had plagued his old fighter may have been evident, in Moore's familiar hands old number 41 gave him no problems. That was not to say that the flight was uneventful, though. To magnify the difficulty in flying at night, Moore ran into a large thunderstorm that forced him to divert west over the South China Sea to avoid it. When he finally touched down at Cebu with his fuel tank indicator leaning on the empty peg, the usual hour and a half flight had taken him an exhausting four hours.

The next day, April 9, when Moore, who had slept late, walked into the headquarters building, he was surprised to see the familiar faces of nine of his fellow 24th Pursuit Group pilots. Through various means, they had all escaped from Bataan that night, but at that moment appeared depressed and saddened about something. When Moore asked what was wrong, he was told they'd just heard over the radio that Bataan had fallen. It had, and with it, of course, was the mission to escort the supply ships through the enemy blockade.

That afternoon Moore was ordered to report to 24th Pursuit Group commander, Major Orrin Grover at Mindanao, and to use the new P-40E that had been flown in earlier by Lt. Dave Obert. Rightly irked by Grover's order to have Moore fly his Kittyhawk, Obert was told to follow in the P-40B—a model he, like several before him, had never flown.

Late that afternoon, a reconnaissance flight over the southeastern coast of Cebu located a convoy of Japanese ships heading toward Cebu

City. With the airfield just a mile outside the city, the handful of Bataan pilots who were still there were told to sleep near their planes in case the Japanese landed that night

"A report was received shortly after dark saying that the Japanese transports were moving toward the city," wrote Dave Obert in his diary later. "At about 4 o'clock, a report came that the landings were being made, and shortly thereafter demolition of stores and army supplies in Cebu started. The pilots of the planes at the airfield took off for Del Monte shortly before dawn just as the Japanese were reported entering the city."[3]

Last off was Obert in "Something"—the fifth different pilot to fly it. As he settled into the cockpit, the apprehensive feeling he had about flying a P-40B for the first time was suddenly forgotten, when demolition crews set off the huge gasoline storage tank near the edge of the airfield.

The magnitude of the explosion so unsettled Obert that, as he started down the runway, the trepidation he had felt before the takeoff was gone. As he felt the plane clear the runway, however, he suddenly realized that he'd forgotten about the hanger on the far end of the field. Saved by the surprisingly quick response of "Something," which barely cleared the building, Obert reflected that the heavier P-40E that he was used to flying would not have made it.

After his safe arrival at Del Monte on the morning of April 10, outside of transferring it to a nearby fighter strip known as Dalirig, the old fighter was not flown again until the thirteenth.

That morning, Lieutenants John Brownewell and Gus Williams were ordered to attack the Japanese airfield at Davao, 100 miles southeast of Del Monte. Just as Williams in "Something" and Brownewell in a Kittyhawk cleared the field, however, they spotted two Japanese floatplanes that had apparently come from working over the main field at Del Monte.

As the two planes started a steep climb toward the Japanese, Williams found old "Something" couldn't keep up with the faster P-40E. While still climbing to get himself into position, Brownewell shot down one of the enemy planes.

A thousand or so feet below the action, Williams, seeing the Japanese plane start to fall, banked "Something" in a relatively tight turn to visibly follow it to the ground. Without warning, the Tomahawk snapped

## 15. "P-40 Something"

violently to the outside, the force ripping off the slid-back canopy and the pilot's helmet and goggles as well (ironically, the P-40B Flight Manual actually warned of this happening if attempted with the canopy open).

Fortunately, with the engine still running wide open and Williams fighting the centrifugal pull from the spin, the motor suddenly quit, allowing the terrified pilot to slip back into his seat and pull the old fighter out of its uncontrollable 2,000-foot fall.

Williams, who guessed his altitude to be barely over 1,000 feet when he recovered, decided to try for a dead-stick, wheels-down landing on Dalirig. Concentrating on the problem at hand, he had forgotten to pull the throttle back from its wide-open position. Suddenly, as he approached the field, the engine kicked over again at full speed. Easing back on the throttle and making a wide, gentle circle over the field to avoid the possibility of another snap roll, Williams was able to bring "Something" down safely. Unknown to him and those who witnessed it, the incident was the death knell for the old P-40B.

It happened the next day, April 14. It was raining. Headquarters, with no possibility of enemy interference, decided to transfer all the fighters from Dalirig and the main field at Del Monte to the nearby strip at Maramag. Although not confirmed, the story was circulated that the veteran pilot assigned to make the short flight in "Something" didn't want to fly in the heavy rain.

Lieutenant Larry McDaniel, a P-35 pilot with virtually no time in a P-40 and who had not flown anything in weeks, volunteered. The plane that, according to an angry Gus Williams, should never have been allowed off the ground because of the incident the day before stalled on the approach to Maramag, the crash killing McDaniel and sadly closing the book on the history of the P-40B and its offspring "Something" in World War II in the Pacific.

# 16

# Corregidor Fights Back

## *May 6, 1942*

It was 21 days following the Japanese attack of the Philippines on December 8, 1941, before the first bombing of Corregidor. Between that December 29th day and its surrender on May 6, nary a day passed when Japanese bombers were not overhead. In fact, within that 128-day period, the island's air raid alarm would sound 300 times before it was over, often, as the end neared, four or more times a day. Despite the near 6 months of merciless bombings, all knew the end would not come from the air. There would be no surrender without an invasion and, for the dogged, gaunt men waiting for it, the long-awaited chance to fight back.

The job of defending Corregidor against the anticipated Japanese amphibious landing went to Marine Colonel Samuel Howard, commander of the Fourth Marine Regiment. Before Bataan fell, Howard laid out his defenses in anticipation of a seaward invasion of the three-mile-long island, with special emphasis on defending the western or Topside end. Of the 3,900 officers and men under his command, of which only 1,500 were Marines, he had assigned the bulk, some 2,000 men, to defend James, Cheney, and Ramsey Ravines on the western end of the tadpole-shaped island. Outside of the 580-man reserve located west of Malita Tunnel in Government Ravine, there were just 1,075 men left to defend over 5,000 yards of Bataan-facing beaches on the eastern tail of the island.

Of the men under his command, Howard supplemented his numbers by 1,245 escapees from Bataan, many of whom, when they arrived, were in such poor physical condition that, according to Philippine com-

## 16. Corregidor Fights Back

mander General Jonathan Wainwright, "they were incapable of even light work." Marine Lieutenant Robert Jenkins, upon seeing the contingent assigned to his 1st Battalion, said that he had never seen men in such poor physical condition. "Their clothing was ragged and stained from perspiration and dirt. Their gaunt, unshaven faces were strained and emaciated. Some were suffering from beri-beri as a result of weeks of a starvation diet of rice. We did what we could for them, and then put them to work on the beach defenses."[1]

Although the troops involved in the island's final battle fought under the colors of the 4th Marine Regiment, it could not exclusively be considered a Marine Corps battle. In round figures, of the 1,600 men who would be involved in the battle for the east end of the island on May 5–6, only 440 were Marines—less than one third. Of the 114 American officers involved, only 24 were Marines, and most of these at the command level. Outside of command, credit to those involved in the final battle must therefore be equally divided between men of the U.S. Marines, U.S. Army, U.S. Navy, Philippine Army, and Philippine Scouts.

Despite the signs after the fall of Bataan that the invasion would come from the peninsula and would be aimed at James Ravine and the eastern tip of the island, Howard made the fatal error of refusing to modify the strength and disposition of his troops until it was too late.

Although the Japanese invasion was still 24 hours away, on May 4, everyone on the island sensed it was near. On that day at 7:30 a.m., the Japanese opened up with air raid number 288 and concluded with number 294 at 6:08. In between, the island was shelled incessantly until dark. Wrote Harbor Defense commander, General George F. Moore, "Heaviest general bombardment yet falling on Corregidor; all calibers including 240 mm. Continuous drum-fire of bursting shells."

"Delving further into the matter of the fury," wrote Wainwright in his diary that night, "Moore and I estimated that at the end of the five incredible hours of bombardment, the Japs had hit the Rock with 1,800,000 pounds of shells."

The most ominous sign that the invasion was near was noted in Moore's 1:30 p.m. entry: "Observers report string of 15 invasion barges being towed north to south out of range beyond Hornos Point, Bataan." And later, "Bulk of enemy fire was switched today to beach defenses, especially James Ravine and the beach between North and Cavalry Points on the eastern end of the island."[2]

Of the results of the bombardment to the important North Shore beach defenses, Lieutenant Jenkins wrote that it was "practically impossible to get any rest or repair damage to our positions and barbed wire. Our field telephone system was knocked out; our water supply was ruined, requiring water to be hauled from the other end of the island in large powder cans. The island was enveloped in a cloud of smoke, dust, and the continuous roar of bursting shells and bombs. There were many more casualties than we had suffered in the previous five months."

Due to the intense shelling of the island, it didn't take much to guess exactly where the Japanese intended to invade. Initial enemy plans were to land on two successive nights. The first, to come just before midnight on May 5, was scheduled to land at two locations on the eastern end of the island. One was to come ashore near Cavalry Point. The second was to land at the narrow neck between Cavalry and Infantry Points. The landing scheduled for the night of the sixth was aimed at the beach below James Ravine, which provided the most immediate access to Topside and Malinta Tunnel.

One only has to read General Moore's diary for May 5 to know that it was D-day for the Japanese. It started at 8:35 a.m.: Air Raid Alarm No. 295. Corregidor under heavy fire from Bataan.

    0923—Corregidor being bombed, hit Bottomside.
    0955—All clear
    1055—Air Raid Alarm No. 296.
    1100—All clear
    1106—Air Raid Alarm No. 297. Five dive-bombers attack Corregidor.
    1130—All clear
    1203—Air Raid Alarm No. 298. Corregidor bombed.
    1327—Air Raid Alarm No. 299
    1400—All clear
    1447—Air Raid Alarm No. 300
    1515—Fort Hughes hit by bombs. Corregidor under intermittent artillery fire during afternoon.
    1837—All fortified islands under heavy fire. James Ravine, the North shore, and the tail of the island pounded terribly. Communications lines cut in many places; numerous beach defense guns and search-

## 16. Corregidor Fights Back

lights put out of action; many beach defense land mines blown up by artillery fire.

2100—Beach Defense reported manned.

2230—Message from "H" Station (General Moore's Harbor Defense command Post) to Beach Defense Commander: "Prepare for probable landing attack." Japs cannonading of tail of island very heavy; telephone communications out in many areas. Beach defense installations practically non-existent. Barbed wire entanglements, land mines, machine-gun emplacements, personnel shelters, and most of 75mm beach defense guns have been destroyed. North side of island bare of trees and vegetation, everything ground powdered dust. Intelligence obtained only by use of messengers. Estimate Japanese have 350 to 400 guns varying in caliber from 75mm to 240mm in Bataan.

2350—Runner arrived at "H" Station from North Point. Reported enemy landing.[3]

And so, it would be a mixed bag of 7,000 U.S. Army, Marine, and naval personnel and 2,700 Philippine Scout and army troops against a force of 5,000 men of the Japanese 4th Division and 7th Tank Regiment. More specifically, it came down to 2,000 Japanese of the 61st Infantry against little more than 1,000 troops of various units in defense of the east end of the island.

For the 2,000 61st Infantry troops crossing the North Channel,

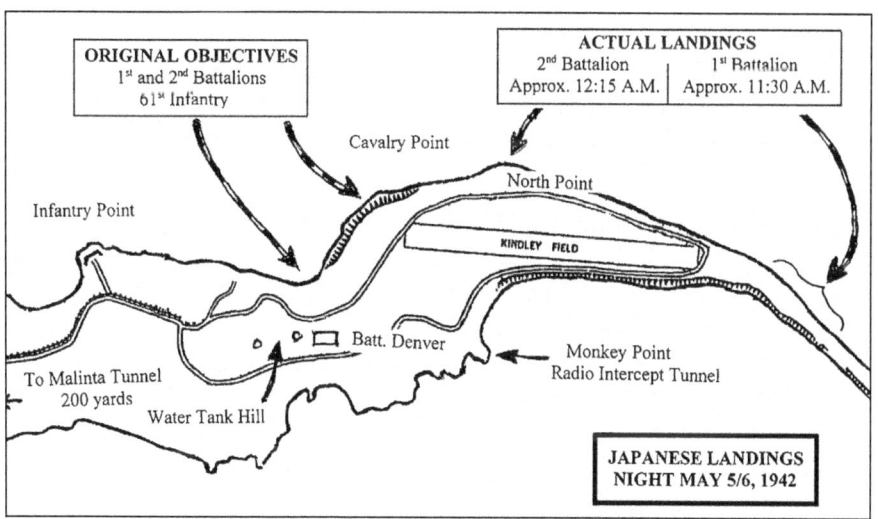

things up to then had not been easy. Malaria, which had ravaged the Filipinos and Americans on Bataan, had sent 28,000 Japanese troops into the hospital in the 21-day period between April 9 and May 1. Facing the postponement of the scheduled assault, only after the emergency delivery of 300,000 quinine tablets by air was the epidemic quelled in time to meet the scheduled date for the invasion.

To meet the Japanese invasion were members of a makeshift battalion of 367 Marines, American and Filipino army troops, a company of 803rd Engineers, 240 Philippine Scouts of the 91st and 92nd Coast Artillery, and a handful of Philippine army air corps and U.S. Navy Filipino mess boys—a total force of 1,024. Overall command of what was designated as the 1st Battalion went to Marine Lieutenant Colonel Curtis Beecher.

To cover the eastern end of the island, this diverse group was divided into three companies: Company A, under Marine Captain Lewis Pickup, was given the assignment of defending over two-and-a-half miles of North Shore beaches. Company B, under Lieutenant Alan Manning, was assigned defense of the South Shore. Weapons Company D, under Captain Noel Castle, was given the job of covering either side with his heavy machine guns and wooden-wheeled 37mm's. Also available were eight fixed .50-caliber antiaircraft machine guns from two platoons of what was called Mobile Battery, which were in position above Kindley Field.

Despite the fact that all his north-facing defenses had been pulverized into "powdered dust," Beecher's warning to Colonel Howard on May 3—that the defensive installations in his sector were practically destroyed and that he was "very dubious as to [his] ability to withstand a landing attack in force"—still drew no reaction from the Marine commander.

Although enemy bombardment of the island since April 29 often lasted well into the night, it was sporadic. Not on the night of May 5, however. It was 11:00 p.m., the exact moment the Japanese invasion force was shoving off from Lamao on Bataan for Corregidor. At that moment, instead of diminishing, there was a sudden increase in the shelling, as enemy gunners, firing white phosphorus shells from what General Moore guessed must have been 300 guns, blasted the anticipated landing

## 16. Corregidor Fights Back

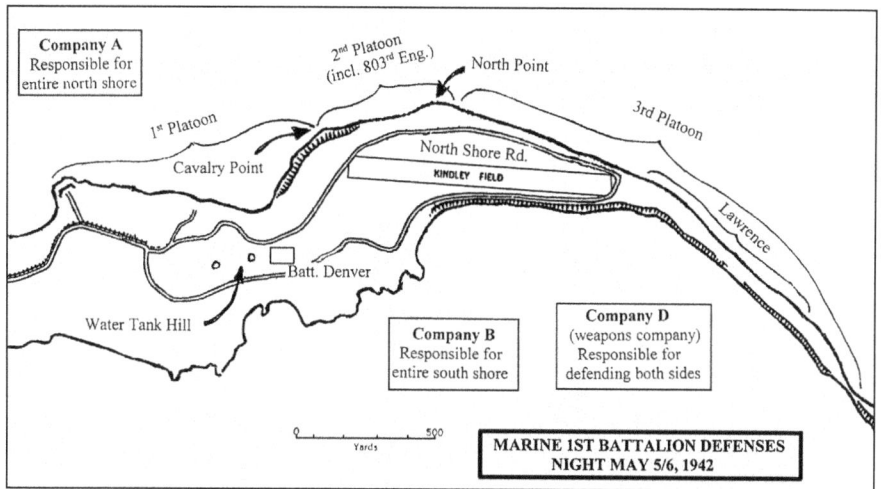

beaches. Although it was over in a few minutes, it was enough to alert General Wainwright in his living quarters in Malinta Tunnel that something was up.

"This sounds to me just like artillery preparation before an attack," he said to Lewis Beebe. "Let's go up and see what Moore thinks of it."

After discussing the situation with the two men and concluding, as Wainwright said, that they could "do nothing but wait for developments," an out-of-breath officer entered the lateral with the news that all anticipated. Diaries for that fateful moment read, "Runner arrived at 2350 at 'H' Station and reported enemy landing at North Point. As nearly as can be determined, the first wave hit the beach at 2330, 5 May 1942."[4]

As noted earlier, the objective of the first wave of Japanese invasion boats was Cavalry Point. Was the information Moore and Wainwright received that they had come ashore at North Point correct? It was.

As the fleet of landing craft rounded the southern tip of Bataan and entered the North Channel, much to their surprise they found the anticipated east-to-west-moving current running in the opposite direction.

In the confusion, the 1st Battalion boats, with regimental commander Colonel Gempachi Sato in the lead craft, soon were fighting a losing battle with the tide, which, by the time they were able to turn for shore, were over three quarters of a mile east of their objective.

Earlier, General Wainwright, writing about the effect of Japanese artillery on the island's 75mm guns, wrote that of the 48 available at the beginning of the siege, "forty-six were knocked out by the time the Japs landed." The two that had survived had done so only because General Moore had ordered their commander, army Lieutenant Ray Lawrence, not to reveal his position during the pre-invasion bombardment. It paid off.

Lawrence, who, for all practical purposes, was in command of the island from the eastern end of Kindley Field to Hooker Point, had a mixed complement of 82 men, including Marines, Philippine Scouts, and U.S. Army Bataan survivors.

Along with the two 75's, they were as well armed as any comparable unit on the island. This included two 37mm's, two heavy-machine guns, and eight Browning automatic rifles. To take advantage of the 50-foot bluffs that would face the enemy once they landed, each position was liberally stocked with grenades and surplus air corps 30-pound fragmentation bombs with improvised wooden chutes from which to drop them.

With H-hour originally scheduled for 11:30 p.m., Japanese shelling of the eastern end of the island had all but ceased several minutes before. Evidence that the enemy was approaching was therefore detected by motor sounds from their landing craft. At that, Lt. Lawrence ordered his beach defense searchlights turned on. Although quickly shot out by fire from the boats, unknown to the Japanese, their discovery had decided their fate.

First to open up on the Japanese was Marine Private Roy Hayes. Ordered to hold his fire until the barges got closer, he decided that they couldn't wait any longer and cut loose at the Japanese who, at that moment, were at near point-blank range. The initial burst from his .30-caliber machine gun was soon accompanied by small arms fire from all along the bluffs.

Illuminated by tracer fire, Lawrence's 75's then went to work on the enemy barges. His comment to the commander of one of the 75's who said he couldn't see the target through the sight was, "then use it like a shotgun, [like] you're shooting ducks on the pond." Supported by accurate .37mm fire from Scouts of the 91st Coast and .50-caliber fire from

## 16. Corregidor Fights Back

a Mobile Battery platoon on Kindley Field, few of the enemy barges ever reached shore.

For the handful of Japanese soldiers that were able to make it to the small, 30-foot-wide rocky beach, they were greeted by a fusillade of hand grenades, fragmentation bombs, and an unscalable 50-foot-high cliff. One observer said that the slaughter of the Japanese in their barges "was sickening." Lawrence said that they actually heard the enemy soldiers "crying for mercy, telling us to cease fire, that they were Filipinos."[5]

So complete was the repulse of the easternmost cluster of 1st Battalion boats that for all practical purposes, it ceased to exist.

With the enemy troops who had come ashore opposite Lt. Lawrence's positions reduced to a mere handful, the remaining 1st Battalion boats who hit the rocky shoreline further east near North Point found the going a little easier but not much.

Defending the bluffs above North Point was the 2nd Platoon of A Company on the left and Company A of the army's 803rd Engineers on the right.

Unlike the defensive positions occupied by Lt. Lawrence's men, those occupied by the two companies above North Point had taken a terrific pounding during the pre-invasion bombardment. Before they could recover, led by Colonel Sato himself, what was left of the 1st Battalion boats slipped ashore.

One of the first to discover the Japanese was Company D army Sergeant William Dudley, who quickly propped the trails of his 37mm gun so he could depress enough to fire on the beach. Enfilade fire from Marine Private Silas Barnes, operating a .30-caliber machine gun from Infantry Point, took a deadly toll on Japanese as they disembarked from their barges opposite Cavalry Point.

A few minutes after the Japanese disembarked, several were spotted coming up a ravine in front of A Company's positions. At that point, veteran Marine Gunnery Sergeant "Tex" Haynes went on a one-man crusade to stop them. After emptying two .45's and a rifle from a dead comrade, he yanked a .30-caliber machine gun off its damaged mount, slung an extra belt of ammunition over his shoulder, and started down the ravine, firing as he went. After expending both belts, a Japanese grenade felled the gallant marine—a man whose actions under different circumstances may have earned him the Medal of Honor.

Company A's 2nd Platoon, under the command of Gunnery Sergeant John Mercurio, along with the 803rd Engineers, soon had their hands full. Marine Corporal Edwin Franklin said that their positions were so close to the high-tide line that they could "reach out and touch the water," making it impossible to halt the enemy before they reached shore. Sgt. Mercurio killed a Japanese with his .45 the second he hit the beach: He was "so close [when I shot him], I could have touched him."[6]

Army Corporal Joseph Johnson, attached to the 2nd Platoon, said that moments after they landed, he could see enemy soldiers "... fleeting [and] darting in the shadows."

Along with the enemy suddenly being upon them, the effects of

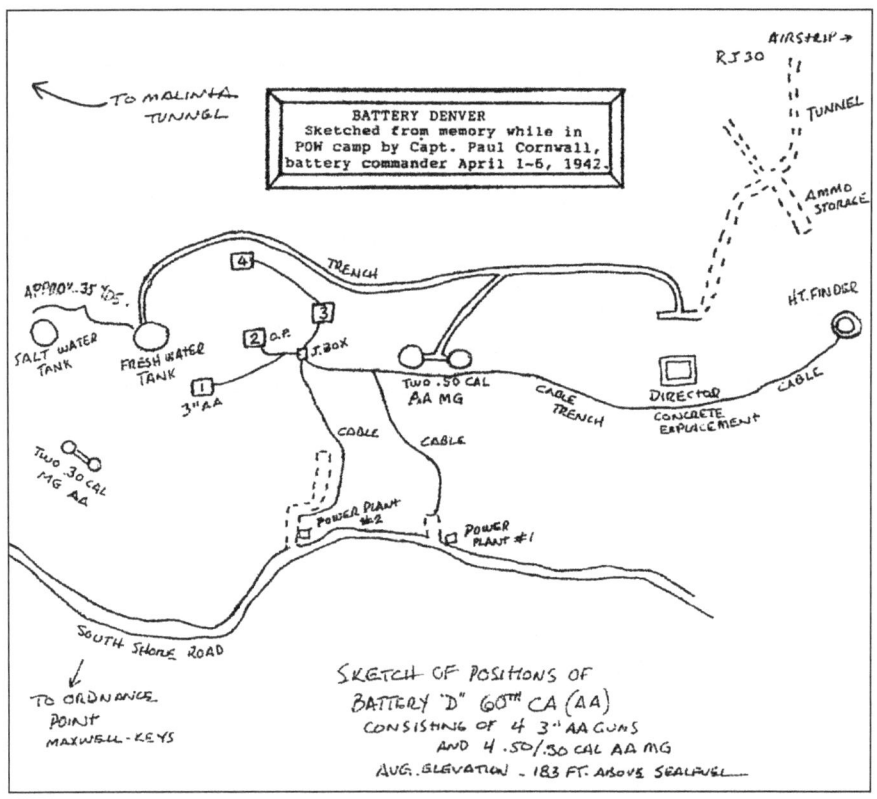

## 16. Corregidor Fights Back

what the Americans called Japanese "knee mortars" (actually grenade launchers) forced A Company to pull back some 200 yards across the entire North Point area to the western end of Kindley Field, leaving only the 803rd Aviation Engineers to cover the eastern end of the bluffs above North Point. With the Japanese having advanced to the edge of the airfield, the immediate fear was them crossing the field to the South Shore, thus cutting off the entire eastern end of the island.

Help came from the .50-caliber antiaircraft guns of Mobile Battery's 3rd Platoon, whose second section was in position on a little ridge on the south side of Kindley Field about halfway down the runway. Although forced to dig up the tripods of their guns to enable them to depress their barrels enough to fire on the Japanese, they were able to momentarily stop the infiltration across the little strip.

Before long, however, several enemy soldiers were spotted moving in on second section's position, forcing abandonment of their guns. Most of the men were able to work their way to either Battery Denver, a sandbagged, 4-gun antiaircraft battery near Water Tank Hill, or to the Radio Intercept Tunnel on Monkey Point. Those who escaped to Monkey Point were soon joined by a handful of men from Mobile's first section, whose guns had been destroyed by Japanese artillery.

Unfortunately, not only had the enemy shells knocked out their guns, but in wounding several of its crew in the process, it unknowingly set off a chain of events that helped assure the struggling Japanese of success on the island.

It occurred when a truck carrying first section's wounded back toward Malinta Tunnel was interpreted by a sergeant of Mobile's 2nd Platoon that the eastern end of the island was being evacuated. At that point, according to a prearranged plan, the commanding officer pulled his men back to an old World War I concrete infantry trench north of Malinta's East Portal near what was called RJ (Road Junction) 43, where it remained virtually out of the fight until the end. Had 2nd Platoon remained in its position on the ridge above the east end of Kindley Field, it very well could have blocked the Japanese from making the crucial move down the airfield toward Battery Denver and Water Tank Hill.

Although unaware that the Japanese were moving west across Kindley and along the North Shore Road behind them, A Company and the small band of 803rd Engineers, along with Lt. Lawrence, were still holding out.

Within an hour of Colonel Sato's 1st Battalion boats reaching shore, the 2nd Battalion barges, which were forced to reassemble because of confusion caused by the tides, were spotted a little over a quarter mile off North Point. Spotted much further out than the 1st Battalion and aided by the bright moon that had just come out, they would pay even a greater price for their attempted intrusion than their predecessors.

Along with those manning the North Shore guns, including Lt. Lawrence's two 75's, the most devastating results came from the mortars of Battery Way and Craighill on Fort Hughes, who were immediately ordered into action. They were soon joined by the 3-inch antiaircraft guns of Battery Idaho, whose direct fire on the Japanese from Fort Hughes added to the slaughter of the approaching Japanese.

"I doubt if any reached ... shore," remembered Lt. Lawrence. "I'm sure we sank at least a dozen...."[7]

A Japanese officer witnessing the event from three miles away at Cabcaben, Bataan described the scene as "a spectacle that confounded the imagination, surpassing in grim horror anything we had ever seen."

For those few who reached shore, one said, "Most of us just kept still ... lying against the slope—just waiting, hoping that reinforcements would arrive."

The price for helping create that "spectacle" was the enemy counterbattery fire that soon rained down on Battery Way.

Major Bill Massello and his made-over searchlight battery crew who had taken over Way had opened fire with the two remaining mortars, but a near-direct hit soon knocked one of them out. Before long, the last of the old 1890-model mortars, which were never built to sustain firing as many rounds as it was forced to, began to fall apart. First to go were the piston rods that cushioned the recoil. They froze up, bringing Massello to pour a can of lubricating oil on them. Amazingly, as the oil penetrated the cylinders, the barrel, stuck in the elevated position, slowly came back down.

As the chances of an accident increased with every shot, Massello, with firing-pin lanyard in hand, made his men clear the pit before firing

## 16. Corregidor Fights Back

the gun himself. Also, whenever it became impossible to traverse the gun because debris from enemy near misses had clogged the ring, he would clear and sweep the mechanism himself.

Fortunately, once the fire mission against the reeling 2nd Battalion boats ended, the intensity of Japanese counter-battery fire let up. This gave Massello and his crew time to recover and standby for the next mission, which would come at 3:00 a.m.

By 1:00 a.m. on the morning of the sixth, of the 2,000 men the Japanese anticipated they would have on shore, it is estimated that fewer than 800 had made it.

Until daylight, the battle for Corregidor would be recorded as one of the most confusing in the history of World War II. The biggest contributing factors on the U.S. side were the total lack of all communication between command and combat units and the continuous shelling and bombing of the 1,000 yards of open ground between Water Tank Hill and Malinta's East Portal.

In anticipation of a successful Japanese invasion of the eastern end of the island, it was planned to form a line of defense along what was called Wilson Park Ridge that ran northwest across the island 1,000 yards east of Malinta. The high point, known as Water Tank Hill, sat just a few yards west of what was considered the key link to the entire line—the four-gun antiaircraft battery called Battery Denver.

Anchoring both ends of the line were A Company on the north and B Company on the south, whose primary jobs still remained defending against a seaward invasion. If the Americans were unable to hold Battery Denver, both companies would be in jeopardy of being flanked. With no line to fall back on, success or failure to keep the Japanese out of Malinta depended on holding the center.

On April 24, 12 days prior to the Japanese invasion, Denver First Sergeant Dewey Brady and another man were killed while spotting enemy fire from on top of the fresh water tank next to the battery. Under most circumstances, the loss of one man wouldn't have the effect that the death of Brady had on the battery. The death of the "soldier's soldier," as one man who knew him said, devastated battery morale. Captain Paul Cornwall, who took over command of the battery from ill Captain Benson Guyton on May 1, said that after the loss of Brady, "the Battery was never the same; the spark had died." Ironically, he was killed on the very day the order awarding him a battlefield commission came down.

"On the night of May 5, a severe bombardment of the battery's position started about 7:00 p.m.," said Cornwall. "Members of the battery were ordered to take cover in the two power plant tunnels on the south side of the hill. After the shelling lifted around 10:30 p.m., a truck passed on its way to Malinta Tunnel. The occupants notified us that a landing had been made by the Japanese. Not long after that, Japanese machine gun fire alerted us from the vicinity of the water towers."[8]

Deciding that the defense of Denver itself, with its four sandbagged gun pits scattered in a half circle across the ridge, was all but impossible, Cornwall formed the hundred or so men from the battery along a line running "from Ordnance Point to the Marine positions on the Bataan side of Wilson Park Ridge." His earlier decision to bring one of the battery's two heavy .50-caliber antiaircraft guns with him would soon pay off.

About 20 yards off the North Coast Road was the entrance to a long access tunnel that led to the east end of Denver. Anticipating possible penetration by the Japanese through the tunnel, nine sharpshooting Marines had taken position behind a barricade of railroad ties in hopes of holding the tunnel. Although it worked, once it was discovered, the Japanese were able to slip past the entrance, moving west along the road a few yards before climbing to the top of the ridge.

When they reached the top and began to move toward the battery, they were spotted by the Denver Boys, who suddenly came to life. Particularly effective was one of the .50 calibers, but not for long, as sustained fire soon forced the gun to freeze up.

At that point, both sides went at each other with small arms and grenades. "I decided that an effort be made to clear the first water tower of a Japanese machine gun," said Cornwall. "Two men, Lieutenant Perkins and PFC Cisneros, carried hand grenades forward and succeeded in clearing the ridge and silencing the enemy machine gun nest." However, the Japanese, led by Colonel Sato himself, soon forced the Americans back off the hill some 150 yards to RJ (road junction) 21.[9]

Despite gaining the advantage, with only a piecemeal force himself, Sato was unwilling to attempt to capitalize further on his quick success.

## 16. Corregidor Fights Back

Thus, as the Japanese commander ordered his men back to dig in across the forward slope of Denver in wait of reinforcements, the second battle for Water Tank Hill would soon be joined.

Before the Japanese could get organized in their newly won positions, a hastily formed, five-man raiding party, led by army Lieutenant Robert Perkins, worked their way up to a spot behind Denver. From there they lobbed hand grenades into two of the gun pits, then dashed southward across the ridge and safely into Battery Maxwell-Keys on the south side. Unfortunately, their courageous efforts did nothing to weaken the enemy's hold on the position.

Marine Captain Lewis Pickup, commanding officer of A Company, whose job it was to defend the entire North Shore, because of the total absence of communications, was initially unaware of the Japanese landing until told that enemy troops had been spotted moving along the North Shore Road. Aware that the defense plan called for establishing a line across the island anchored by Battery Denver in the center, Pickup ordered a squad, led by Gunnery Sergeant Harold Ferrell, to reconnoiter the battery to make sure it was still in U.S. hands. Of course, it wasn't.

When Ferrell got close to the battery area he said, "I heard voices, and not American. Corporal Morris crept close enough to observe that the place seemed to have Japs all over it, digging in."[10]

With news of the enemy's capture of Denver, Pickup, upon his return, was perplexed as to what to do. On the one hand, he couldn't afford not to go after them, nor could he could not pull troops off beach defense to do it.

The answer came when Captain Noel Castle, commanding officer of the Company D weapons company, volunteered to attack the Japanese with a patrol of his own men and a few stragglers. Castle, a member of the Marine Corps rifle team and who famously carried two pearl-handled .45s, moved his men into position below the hill. "Let's go up there and run the bastards off," Sergeant Ferrell heard him tell his men.

At that point, Ferrell warned him of the enemy's control of the battery. Ignoring the warning, he told him that he was going to take his men up there and "shoot those people's eyes out."[11]

Marine Corporal Joseph Kopacz, who survived the attack, said that they ran head on into the Japanese near the first water tower. At that point, Castle picked up an abandoned .30-caliber machine gun and opened up on the advancing Japanese, almost single-handedly forcing them to fall back into one of the Denver pits. While leading his men forward, however, the young captain was killed by machine gun fire. At that point, the assault ground to a halt, the men falling back to the bottom of the hill.

With news of Castle's death and the failure to retake the hill, Captain Pickup sent a runner to 1st Battalion command post in Malinta Tunnel informing Colonel Beecher of the situation. At that moment, had the Japanese known, the U.S. line across Water Tank Hill was totally nonexistent. But help, as it was, was on the way.

First to react was Lieutenant Colonel Lloyd Biggs of the 92nd Coast Artillery, who had hastily put together a makeshift group of his Scouts, stragglers from Denver and a few Marines, placing them on a line from the South Shore Road to a position just west of Water Tank Hill. There they were joined by another hurriedly formed group who, when linked up, formed a continuous but dangerously thin line across the island.

As the night wore on, what was mentioned as the two major contributing factors to the outcome of the battle—lack of communication and relentless enemy artillery fire on U.S. positions—began to take its toll.

Relying on runners to keep Beecher and Colonel Howard informed of the progress of the battle was all but impossible. So devastating was the artillery fire on the open ground between Water Tank Hill and Malinta's east entrance that no one will ever know how many messengers were either killed, wounded, or failed to show up. Because of this, it wasn't until after 1:30 a.m. that word reached Colonel Beecher of the desperate situation and plea for reinforcements from Captain Pickup.

Despite the fact that the enemy was only 1,000 yards away from the east entrance, Beecher still had a difficult time convincing Colonel Howard that it was the main Japanese invasion effort. Still convinced that the main assault would come against the middle or western end of the island, the Marine commander was still reluctant to commit

## 16. Corregidor Fights Back

his reserve forces in Government Ravine in case they were needed there.

Finally, at about 2:00 a.m., Howard acceded, ordering only the 1st Battalion, made up of companies O and P, which had moved into Malinta just after midnight, to counterattack the Japanese positions on Water Tank. Had he chosen instead to commit his four 4th Battalion reserve companies at the same time, it is possible the Japanese could have been forced out of Denver and off the ridge.

First out into the now bright moonlit night was Marine Lieutenant William Hogaboom's Company P. Along with Captain Robert Chambers' O Company, this reserve force was made up of 215 Marine and Navy Headquarters and Service Company personnel and 90 men of the fledgling Philippine army air corps who had escaped from Bataan—hardly a force to be reckoned with.

Guided by Captain Golland Clark, 1st Battalion adjutant, as the men formed into a skirmish line a few yards outside the tunnel, someone spotted some "shadowy figures" moving along a ridge to the left, at which a couple of men fired at with their 1917 Enfields.

Marine Quartermaster Clerk Frank Ferguson of Company O, whose 1st Platoon had followed them out of the tunnel, witnessed what happened. "The men who shot at the forms quickly learned of their mistake when sulfurous [four-letter] oaths came back from men on the ridge," said Ferguson.

Recognizing the booming voice as that of army Lieutenant William King, who was nearly hit by the shots, he remarked that, "No Japs could cuss like that." He was right, as it seems the targets were men of Mobile Battery, who, it will be recalled, had prematurely withdrawn back to the old concrete infantry trench near Malinta earlier that morning. Fortunately, no one was hit in the "friendly-fire" episode.

Moments later, as Ferguson led his men forward, he spotted something that instinctively told him all hell was about to break loose.

"I saw a couple of white flares go up some distance ahead of us," he remembered. "Word was passed to the men [to seek] immediate shelter for I suspected that the flares were a Jap signal for artillery support. My estimate was not wrong.... This particular barrage was the most severe and concentrated I had ever come under."[12]

Unfortunately, the two O Company platoons that followed Ferguson out of Malinta were caught in the open when the barrage hit. Unaware of their fate and therefore still anticipating their participation, the Quartermaster Clerk turned company commander ordered his men to move out.

The original plan was for the Ferguson's 1st and Sergeant John Haskin's 3rd Platoon to form a line from the south shore across the ridge to a point above the North Shore Road, where it would link up with Lt. Hogaboom's P Company. Together they would attack the enemy positions on Water Tank and Denver.

"I deployed my platoon straight to the front with my right resting on the road," he said. "Sergeant Haskin's 3rd Platoon was expected to deploy to my right, and I presumed the 2nd Platoon was in my rear for support."[13]

Not waiting for Haskin to join him, Ferguson ordered his men forward. When they reached the top of the ridge behind the two water tanks, they were halted by heavy machine-gun and automatic weapon fire from Battery Denver. Although resigned to wait for reinforcements, the resourceful Japanese, using the sandbagged Denver gun pits, had done a masterful job of establishing a defense line across the ridge.

"The Japs seemed to have a machine gun or automatic weapons every few yards or so placed to offer [interlocking] support," said Ferguson. "Three times I sent men forward, and three times they were repulsed."[14]

Expecting 3rd Platoon support from his right during the attacks but not hearing any firing, he investigated only to find it wide open. Ordering two of his machine guns to cover the exposed area, he went to find out what happened. Unable to communicate with Ferguson as to his plight, Haskin, along with Quartermaster Clerk Herman Snellings' 2nd Platoon, had been caught out in the open in the devastating barrage that hit just as they came out of the tunnel.

"All but about five of Haskin's men had been killed or wounded when caught in the barrage," said Ferguson. "Snellings had [only] four left [out of the 50 men] in his platoon." Realizing that both his flanks were unprotected, Ferguson sent Snellings and a handful of men to make contact with P Company on his left. "Soon word came back that P Company had been joined. My relief was great," he said, "but not for long."

## 16. Corregidor Fights Back

Because of the effective defense the Japanese had put up, Ferguson found himself in a quandary as to what to do. With nothing heavier that a few BARs and ancient Lewis machine
guns, "frontal assaults had proven foolish," he said. "Since [our] line [was] no more than 30 yards from the enemy, we ... tried to rout them with grenades, but the trees that had been felled by shell fire interfered with their use."[15]

At that point, Sergeant Harold Ferrell was ordered to have a crack at them with his old Stokes mortars that had been converted to fire 81mm ammunition. However, after firing 20 World War I vintage rounds that, at best, were considered "so unreliable as to be practically worthless from mortars for which there were no sights," it, too, was called off.

Sometime during the attempt to rout the Japanese from Denver, two Marine veterans, Sergeant Major Thomas Sweeney and 3rd Platoon commander John Haskin, were able to climb to the top of one of the water tanks from where they successfully hurled grenades down on the enemy machine guns that had been holding up the advance. Haskins, however, was shot and killed while climbing up to the tower with a musette bag of full of grenades. How many times the courageous Marine made the trip is not known, nor is when a Japanese sniper finally killed his buddy, Tom Sweeney. When informed of their deaths, Frank Ferguson, knowing that the two were very close friends, said that it was "almost fitting that they should go out together."

When word of the successful Japanese landing on the island reached General Wainwright earlier that night, he sent a brief message to General Marshall in Washington, announcing that, "Landing attack on Corregidor in progress. Enemy landed North Point. Further details as the situation develops."

At 2:30 a.m., Lt. Colonel Johnny Pugh, Wainwright's senior aide, handed the General a handwritten message that had been scribbled on a piece of lined legal pad paper. Pugh apologized, adding that communications had run out of official message forms. It read:

> During recent weeks, we have been following with growing admiration the day-by-day accounts of your heroic stand against the mounting intensity of

bombardment by enemy planes and heavy siege guns. In spite of all the handicaps of complete isolation, lack of food, and ammunition, you have given the world a shining example of patriotic fortitude and self-sacrifice.

The American people ask no finer example of tenacity, resourcefulness, and steadfast courage. The calm determination of your personal leadership in a desperate situation sets a standard of duty for our soldiers throughout the world.

In every camp and on every naval vessel soldiers, sailors, and Marines are inspired by the gallant struggle of their comrades in the Philippines. The workmen in our shipyards and munitions plants redouble their efforts because of you.

You and your devoted followers have become the living symbols of our war aims and the guarantee of victory.

Franklin D. Roosevelt

Wainwright, so moved by the words, vowed to keep the message and hopefully someday pass it on to his son.

Ironically and possibly never known by the General, the President did not write the message. In fact, he may never have seen it. At General Marshall's request, Major General Dwight Eisenhower, at the time deputy director of Army War Plans in Washington, wrote it.

An hour later, Wainwright sent off a reply to the President. After expressing "gratitude and appreciation" for his "gracious and generous message" and describing the enemy landings and terrific bombardment during the past seven days, he concluded with, "As I write this at 3:30 a.m., our patrols are attempting to locate the enemy positions.... I will counterattack at dawn to drive him into the sea or destroy him...."[16]

If Wainwright's message sounds as if he was unaware of what was really happening in the battle, it is true. As mentioned, because of the lack of communications, everyone from the commanding general to General Moore and Colonel Howard were in the dark as to the tactical situation. However, both Wainwright and Moore, according to their diaries, did receive information about results of the enemy's third attempt to land. Wrote Wainwright: "A third assault wave of landing boats approaching Corregidor; broken up and practically annihilated by artillery fire from Fort Drum, Battery Way, and roving 155mm gun batteries Stockade, Wright, and Gulick."[17]

Their targets were, as Wainwright said, boats of the enemy's third

## 16. Corregidor Fights Back

wave that were not only carrying reinforcements, but ammunition which was expected to run out by mid-morning. Few Japanese barges would make it.

One battery that would reap success against the Japanese was Battery Gulick. In his diary, General Moore made reference to the effectiveness of the four "roving" 155mm gun batteries on the Rock that became its "main dependence for counter-battery fire against the Japanese."

On the night of the fifth, Captain Jack Gulick, commander of his own Battery Gulick, had moved his gun to a spot on Topside between two buildings from which the flash from his gun muzzle could not be detected. When the order came to open up on the enemy's third assault wave, Gulick was ready, firing on the helpless boats with deadly accuracy. Try as they might, however, the Japanese were unable to spot the muzzle flashes from Gulick's 155, believing that it was coming from somewhere near the golf course. Although innocent Battery Globe, located near the course, got pounded, the Japanese were never able to find or stop the resourceful captain until the end.

When the order to fire on the enemy boats in the North Channel was given to the commander on tiny Fort Drum, it wasn't that the battleship-shaped island's four 14-inch guns couldn't reach the target, it was, as he said, that they couldn't see it. "Just fire anywhere at that smoke between you and Cabcaben, and you can't miss them," was the reply.

Effects of U.S. fire, which included machine gun and small arms fire from shore, like on the two previous attempts that night, had a devastating effect on the enemy. For the boats carrying ammunition that were well behind those with reinforcements, results of the fire from the big guns actually forced them to turn back. Recalled one Japanese officer, "[We] threw the ammunition into the nearby waters and returned to Bataan."

For those carrying reinforcements, as they neared Corregidor, it was fire from machine guns and small arms more than artillery that apparently had the most effect. Wrote one boat commander who survived the attack, "American high-powered machine guns poured a stream of bullets on us from all directions. Rifle fire added to the hail of death. Men who huddled in the center of the boat were all either killed or wounded. Those who clung to the sides were hit by shells that penetrated the steel plating. The boat had sprung several leaks when we finally came within landing distance of Corregidor. Desperately, I gave the signal and led the charge against the shore defenses. I don't know how many men responded. In that mad dash for shore, many drowned as they dropped into the water mortally wounded. Many were killed outright.... If it had not been for the fact that it was the dark hour before dawn, I doubt if any of us would [have made it]."[18]

If the U.S. command was in the dark about what was happening, so was General Homma at his 14th Army headquarters on Bataan. Word of the progress of the invasion had been filtering piecemeal back to him throughout the night, and none of the news was encouraging. With no clear picture of the situation other than what could be seen from the southern tip of Bataan, "every time I was disappointed [at the news]," he said.

When information reached him on what happened in the pre-dawn attempt to reinforce Colonel Sato and that only 21 of the 52 landing craft that started out that night were left, he panicked. "My God," he thought to himself, "I have failed miserably on the assault. I had plenty of troops on this side of the sea [but] could not send reinforcements with the 21 boats that were left." Unknown to the Japanese commander, the answer to his dilemma was at that moment being loaded onto three of the remaining 21 landing craft—tanks.[19]

It was a little after 4:00 a.m. when Colonel Howard got word of the plight of O and P Companies in the battle to dislodge the Japanese from Battery Denver. At that point, he ordered the last of his reserves into the fight.

As men of what was designated as the 4th Battalion moved out of the confines of Malinta as dawn was breaking that morning, never was a U.S. Marine unit so under-represented by Marines and non-combatants than companies Q, R, S, and T of the battalion. Of the 303 men listed, only one officer, Major Francis Williams, and three NCO's were Marines. Of the remainder, 278 were naval personnel from the U.S. Navy section base on Bataan or off the scuttled sub-tender *USS Canopus*. Although equipped to match its men, with 1917 Enfields and a few Lewis

## 16. Corregidor Fights Back

machine guns, they had trained hard for the impossible task they faced as they solemnly made their way out into the open.

About 500 yards out, the brief lull in enemy artillery fire that had so devastated the area throughout the night ended. The results, along with causing many casualties, temporarily scattered and disorganized the planned attack. By 5:00 a.m., however, Major Williams had reassembled his troops, sending two companies, Q and R, to the left to help A and P Companies contain the Japanese north of Battery Denver.

It was daylight by the time the two got into position, at which the men of Company Q, on the extreme end of the line near the water, spotted two enemy barges loaded with Japanese troops that were hung up on some rocks about a hundred yards offshore. A small group of the best sharpshooting sailors in the company was sent to pick off the helpless enemy. Thirty minutes later and after several hundred rounds from their old World War I Enfield rifles, the job was done.

Meanwhile, Major Williams, who had also taken over command of the decimated 1st Battalion, assigned Company T, under navy Lieutenant Bethel Otter, to help contain the Japanese in Battery Denver and brought S Company to cover the extreme right or southern flank of the line. For the first time since the Japanese were discovered in Denver, the Americans were in a position, although tenuous at best, to make a coordinated attack against them.

Scheduled for 6:15, everything went well for Q and R Companies on the left, who easily pushed the enemy back some 200 to 300 yards.

In the assault, army Captain Harold Dahlness, commanding officer of Company R, and Lieutenant Otis Saalman led several men against a Japanese machine-gun position at the head of a draw. Under covering fire, one of the men crawled up close enough to throw a grenade. The toss looked perfect, but to everyone's aghast, a Japanese soldier with grenade in hand, rose up to throw it back. But it was too late—his frantic effort to save himself and his comrades gone when it blew up in his hand.

With news of Q and R Companies' success, Williams ordered them to pinch in toward Denver where it was hoped T Company would also have made some headway. But it hadn't happened.

## The Fall of the Philippines

It wasn't for the lack of trying, however. Six navy men, including Lieutenant Otter and Ensign James Lloyd, crawled close enough to attack one of the enemy machine gun nests—a gun that, as one man remembered, "had dealt so much misery to Company T and the rest of the battalion." Armed with grenades, when they got close enough, the six men made a suicidal charge at the enemy position. Although they knocked it out, five of the six were killed, including both officers.

At approximately the same time, a third T Company officer, army Captain Calvin Chunn, was wounded while leading a successful attack on the Japanese who were attempting to set up a 75mm mountain gun near the water towers. Chunn would survive.

On the right of the water towers, Quartermaster Clerk Frank Ferguson, commander of O Company's 3rd Platoon, and army corporal Alvin Stewart of the 803rd Engineers, had worked their way to a spot a few yards below what Ferguson recalled as a "beautiful and well-nigh impregnable position," at which they prepared to throw grenades. Apparently believing, after the first two grenades, that they'd been flanked, Japanese soldiers began to abandon the position. Silhouetted against the pre-dawn sky as they ran back, rifles were quickly substituted for grenades. "They were like ducks in a shooting gallery," said Ferguson, who, along with Stewart, estimated they shot down some twenty enemy soldiers before they were spotted.[20]

As he looked to congratulate Ferguson, Stewart saw that he had been shot in the face. Bandaging him the best he could, the two men crawled back to their own lines. With the wound, as Ferguson said, "looking like part of my face had been shot away," he worked his way back to Malinta, dodging not only enemy artillery fire on the way back, but bombs and machine-gun fire from planes of the Imperial Japanese Air Force, which had joined the attack at dawn.

As soon as it was light enough to see, the unmistakable sound of a .50-caliber machine gun was heard from the vicinity of Battery Maxwell-Keys on the U.S. right flank. It was from a machine-gun emplacement near the battery that had been manned by a makeshift crew of Bataan survivors. From their position, they were able to get an occasional glimpse of Japanese soldiers moving along the south side of the ridge below Denver, at which they cut loose with the big navy water-cooled

## 16. Corregidor Fights Back

.50. Until discovered and chased from their position by Japanese knee-mortar fire, they, along with the Scouts from Battery Keys who had joined in with rifles and machine guns, were, for the moment, able to discourage any idea Colonel Sato had of infiltrating the American right flank.

Upon learning of the enemy landing early that morning, General Moore had ordered the men of destroyed Batteries B, C, D, and H of the 59th Coast Artillery to form as infantry and standby for use when needed. As things began to develop on the East Sector during the night, Moore ordered Battery B, formerly assigned to Battery Crockett, to move into Malinta as a reserve force. With men of the other three 59th batteries still being held by Colonel Howard in anticipation of a possible landing on the west end of the island, the 60 American artillerymen of Captain Herman Hauck's battery, now ordered into the fight, were the last to be sent.

Reflecting the anxiousness and zeal of their commander, but unknown to the men of the battery, with daylight Japanese artillery observers from an observation balloon on Bataan had apparently spotted them as they moved out of Malinta, bringing a rain of 240mm shells down on the small column. Fortunately, Hauck's men were able to escape the heavy losses that had been inflicted on 1st Battalion companies earlier, reporting to Major Williams around 8:30.

With the American line opposite the entrenched enemy in Denver barely but still holding, Williams sent the 59th to the south shore against several Japanese who had been spotted trying to work their way behind U.S. lines.

As successful as Companies Q and R had been against Col. Sato's right flank, so was Hauck's effort against his left. The 59th, reinforced by a few Scouts and men from Mobile Battery's 3rd Platoon, after disposing of the few infiltrating Japanese, launched an attack out of the vicinity of Battery Maxwell-Keys against Sato's left flank. Although successful, it would be for naught.

A little before 10:00 a.m. from his R Company position overlooking Kindley Field, Lieutenant Otis Saalman spotted the weapons that meant doom to Corregidor once they reached the island—Japanese tanks. Three of them were already moving up the slope toward the airstrip when he saw them. They had come ashore around 8:30, but for an hour and a half had struggled unsuccessfully to negotiate the steep bluffs above the beach. Ironically, if it hadn't been for one of the tanks, a captured American Stuart M-3, towing the two Japanese Type 97's up from the beach, threat from the enemy armor may never have occurred.

At that point, apparently prearranged with the movement of the tanks, two white flares were fired from the Japanese position in Denver, which, moments later, brought another fusillade of artillery fire down on the area between Denver and Malinta.

Moments before, Lieutenant William Hogaboom, commanding officer of P Company, in position near the North Shore Road, noticed a handful of men on his right "beginning to fall back in disorder. I detected Major Williams attempting to stop the withdrawal," he said, "and ran over to find out from him the cause. He told me that tanks had been brought into action and that there were no antitank weapons available to stop them."

Realizing that even if it was possible to stop the retreat, it was too late to reestablish the line. Williams ordered Hogaboom to pull his men out and fall back to the old concrete trench near RJ 43, and there to prepare to make a final stand.

"I passed word down into the ravine," said Hogaboom. "Men came streaming out, and although dazed by the intense action they'd been through, indicated resentment of the unexplained order to fall back."[21]

Getting them back to the trench wasn't easy. "We had to pass through two 240mm barrages to reach the road cut near the trench. It was each man for himself. Casualties were heavy."

When Captain Harold Dahlness was ordered to pull R Company back from their position on the enemy's right flank, not only were his men "resentful" of the order, but, with further to go along the more exposed north side of the island, were chewed to pieces by Japanese artillery. "Dirt, rocks, trees, bodies, and debris literally filled the air all the way back," remembered Dahlness. Only a handful made it.

When Hogaboom and Williams took stock of the number and condition of the exhausted group of men who had made it safely into the trench, it was obvious that, tanks or no tanks, it was all but over.

"Those of us who reached what had been the concrete trench before

## 16. Corregidor Fights Back

the 240's worked it over prepared to set up a defense line," recalled Hogaboom. "Major Williams went to Malinta to report the situation and obtain reinforcements. Lieutenant Harris of A Company joined me in the trench I had occupied with little more than a couple dozen of my men."[22]

One battery that had tried unsuccessfully to hit one of the barges carrying the tanks across was Battery Way. For every shot fired by the old 12-incher, however, it was being hit by at least one in return.

The story of Major Bill Massello and his gun crews, who had somehow kept the gun in action steadily since 3:00 a.m., was one of both heroism and tenacity. With three of the four guns previously knocked out, there were plenty of gun crews standing by to take over if needed. Like substitutes on the sidelines of a football game, they couldn't wait to get in. However, despite wounds and the ultimate danger of being killed at any moment, each crew was reluctant to give up or concede what they considered an earned privilege of servicing the gun.

Sergeant Walter Kulinski, who witnessed one in action, said that he had never seen men like that crew. "They were wounded, but wanted to fire the gun." One man refused to be replaced despite a severe stomach wound. "You couldn't keep them down. That's the funny thing—I couldn't understand it. They were fighting fools."[23]

With enemy counter-battery fire salvos coming in every few minutes, at 5:00 a.m. when the last trained crew went down, it was clerks, cooks, radio operators, and motor pool personnel who, without hesitation, jumped in to keep the old mortar firing.

The man behind it all was Bill Massello—a man who motivated his men by example. Together for three months on Bataan and now on Corregidor, it was his undying spirit, leadership, and courage under fire that brought Kulinski to label him "a fighting man, a real Coast Artillery officer." There were even rumors that "Wild Bill," as some of his men called him, had the telephones ripped off the walls so he couldn't be ordered to surrender.

Around 10:30, Massello, with his luck far overextended, for the umpteenth time, had gone out to sweep the debris off the gun's traverse ring, when shrapnel from an enemy shell that hit on the far side of the pit felled the gallant soldier. Crewmen rushed out and carried him to shelter. The wounds to both legs and one arm, although not life threatening, forced him to turn over command of the battery to Captain Fred Miller. Not long after that, the old mortar, whose life, like Massello's, was also far overextended, gave out, its breechblock finally freezing up.

Overheard as he ran out to sweep off the traverse ring for what would be the last time, he said, "If they ever get me, what a way for a soldier to go with a goddamn broom in my hand."[24]

With a casualty rate of close to 75 percent, what was left of the game men of "the last big gun on Corregidor to fire on the enemy," as Massello said, sat down in wait of the Japanese.

It was after 11:00 a.m. when Major Williams reported to Colonel Howard in his Navy Tunnel headquarters, asking him for antitank guns and reinforcements. The Marine commander told him that there wasn't anything he could do, that General Wainwright had decided to surrender at noon. Ironically, it was Howard who, an hour earlier, had informed the Philippine commander that the enemy had landed tanks on the island.

When informed of the tanks, "I had to make up my mind," said Wainwright, about "the task of trying to find ways and means of averting the inevitable. I went over our position in my mind: shaken troops, beach defenses literally pulverized, concrete machine gun nests reduced to powder, the majority of seacoast guns destroyed, fifty-six beach-defense 75mm guns knocked out, communications gone, movement of troops all but impossible because of the continued shelling, new and uncontested landings....

"But it was the terror that is vested in the tank that was the deciding factor," he said. "I thought of the havoc that even one could wreak if it nosed into the tunnel where lay helpless wounded and their brave nurses."

Pacing up and down in one of the darkened laterals trying to decide what to do, "my head came up and I entered my own headquarters and called General Moore and Beebe. I had come to a decision which I never regretted. "[The two men] agreed that I had taken the only steps possible under the circumstances."[25]

Wainwright then told Beebe to get out the previously prepared sur-

## 16. Corregidor Fights Back

render message that had been readied in case of his death and to broadcast it to the Japanese over the "Voice of Freedom" transmitter at 10:30, adding that he would cease fire at noon. He then instructed Moore to have Colonel Howard initiate Plan Pontiac, the order to destroy all weapons greater than .45 caliber, by 12:00 noon.

At his regimental headquarters in the Navy Tunnel, Colonel Sam Howard, with head in hands, openly wept at what he had to do. "My God," he said to his executive officer, Donald Curtis, "I had to be the first Marine officer ever to surrender a regiment."

After issuing the order, Howard wrote out a critique of the situation. "All general reserves have been committed, the enemy was making additional landings; ammunition in the East Sector was practically exhausted and it was impossible to get any into the area. Practically all of our guns were destroyed, and it became only a question of hours before our lines would be overrun." He felt better.[26]

Beebe, meanwhile, hurried to the communications lateral and at 10:30 began reading the message. Since there was no way to directly communicate with General Homma, it was hoped the Japanese, who had monitored the "Voice of Freedom" broadcasts since their inception in early January, would hear the cease fire message to notify the 14th Army commander.

To stress the importance of the message, Beebe repeated "Message for General Homma or present commander-in-chief of the Imperial Japanese forces in Luzon," twice, followed by: "Anyone receiving this message, please transmit it to the commander-in-chief of the Imperial Japanese Forces in Luzon."

The text, emphasizing, among other things, that a white flag would be displayed in a prominent position on Corregidor and that all firing from harbor forts would cease at 12:00, was repeated in Japanese by Japanese-American Sergeant Richard Sakakida.

With no way of knowing if the message had successfully gotten through, other than to wait for Japanese reaction to the noon raising of the white flag, Beebe repeated it at 11:00 and again at 11:45.

Twelve noon came and went, and although the few U.S. troops who had been notified of the surrender ceased firing, there was no appreciable let up in the bombing and shelling of the island. At 12:30 the message was read for the fourth and last time, and still no response. In fact, there would never be one, as General Homma neither heard nor was told of it. Quite the opposite. Believing at last report that his entire operation was in jeopardy, he had diverted the troops originally scheduled to land at James Ravine that night to reinforce Colonel Sato on the eastern end of the island.

Although it is not known what brought the Japanese to let up their attack a half hour later at 1:00, it may have been that the white flag, which had gone up at noon on the old 100-foot ship's mast flagpole on the edge of the Parade Ground, had been spotted, possibly by aircraft.

The job of replacing the American flag with a white bed sheet was given to Colonel Paul Bunker, Seaward Defense Commander on Corregidor. Despite the continued enemy shelling, which at the time was still focused on the East Sector, the two-time All-American from West Point vowed the occasion would be ceremonial. Accompanied by his deputy, Lieutenant Colonel Dwight Edison, and a bugler, the three men walked out of the tunnel leading to Bunker's command post below Battery Wheeler, up the hill, and across the Parade Ground to the flagpole. There, with the two officers standing at attention, tears welling up in their eyes, the bugler played taps. Edison then lowered the flag, running up the white bed sheet in its place.

When Bunker got back to his headquarters, he cut off a small corner of the flag, which he later sewed under the shoulder patch of his uniform, then solemnly burned the flag. (Although Bunker died in prison camp, the tiny corner of the flag was recovered and is on display at the museum at West Point.)

Meanwhile, back in Malinta, a touching scene occurred after General Moore was informed that the white flag had been raised over the island. Several of his staff officers had gathered in "H" Station when the word came in. Despite knowing that the most difficult part of the surrender process lay ahead, one by one they all came forward, saluted and shook hands, each congratulating Moore on the good fight he had put up.

After the last man came forward, Moore said, "Thank you for your support. With your guidance, Corregidor did its job for almost 5 months. I don't know what history will say about the Rock and our part in the

## 16. Corregidor Fights Back

war, but from the bottom of my heart, I'm proud to have been your commander."

One of the officers there, Major Steve Mellnik, said that what followed was one of the most emotional experiences he had ever witnessed. "With tears streaming down [our] cheeks, officers and everyone in "H" Station cheered and applauded for five minutes."[27]

Assuming that the decided lull in the enemy bombardment meant that they had recognized the white flag, four men, Marine Captain Golland Clark, Lieutenant Alan Manning, a Marine musician, and a flag bearer carrying a torn strip of white bed sheet tied on to a broom handle, walked out of Malinta's East Portal, hoping to be recognized as an advanced surrender party.

When they passed the old concrete trench outside the tunnel entrance, realizing that the end was here, Major Williams ordered the handful of survivors to take shelter inside the tunnel. Of the many men deserving to be called "heroes" for their efforts that night, one was the commander of the makeshift 4th Battalion sailors, Major Francis Williams. Having taken over command of both battalions, of those survivors few hesitated to heap praise on him for his courage, leadership, and determination under the most harrowing of circumstances.

With the flag bearer holding the broom handle high over his head, the four men marched into the early afternoon sun looking for the first Japanese officer they could find.

A few anxious yards down what was left of the road, a Japanese officer, spotting the white flag, stepped out of the brush. At that point, with the bugler probably blowing "Carry On," someone in the party, most likely one of the two Chinese Marine officers, explained that they wanted to be taken to his commanding officer. They were led down the North Shore Road, across Kindley Field to Water Tank Hill, where they met with Colonel Motoo Nakayama, Homma's senior operations officer. It was the same Colonel Nakayama who had negotiated with the surrender party on Bataan nearly a month earlier.

Nakayama, through an English-speaking lieutenant, insisted that he would only talk to General Wainwright. At that point, the four men turned and started back for Malinta.

During the three hours between General Wainwright's 10:00 a.m.

decision to surrender and the initial meeting with the Japanese, a lot had been going on both inside and outside of the tunnel.

Ironically, the last to learn of the surrender that day were the Japanese. By the time they were notified of U.S. intentions to give up, the whole world knew it was over.

Once General Beebe began reading the surrender message over the "Voice of Freedom," word spread through the tunnel like wild fire.

Army radio operator Corporal Irving Strobing, in touch with station WTJ in Honolulu, sent what was supposed to be the last message. When he was handed it, he was told to send it in the clear, and that there would be no more official messages. Simple and undramatic but omitting the word "surrender," it said, "Notify any and all vessels headed toward this area to return to their home base."

Although it may have been the last official message from the Rock, Ensign Kenneth Hoeffel, over the navy's own transmitter, sent what was to be its "final message" to the Navy Department in Washington. Although also omitting the word "surrender," it left little doubt that it was over.

"Our few remaining ships being sunk," it read. "Now destroying all military equipment. 172 officers and 2,126 men of the navy send last expression of loyalty and devotion to country, to families, and to friends. Going off the air."

At 11:55, Commander Melvin McCoy, the navy's communications officer, handed what was its last message to the radioman. "Beam it for Radio Honolulu," he said, "and don't bother with code."

"Going off the air now. Goodbye, and good luck. Callahan and McCoy."[28]

Meanwhile, back in the army's communication lateral, Corporal Strobing, who later said that he was "afraid to let his contact [with Honolulu] go even for a second," was giving the world his own unofficial, dramatic, and sometimes rambling account of Corregidor's last hours. His words, which were also picked up by a few ham radio operators along the U.S. West Coast who happened to be listening at 3:40 a.m., would appear in newspapers and magazines all over America. Without them, no one would have any idea what the last hours on Corregidor were like until after the war.

## 16. Corregidor Fights Back

"They are not here yet," he began. "We are waiting for God-only-knows what.... Lots of heavy fighting going on. We've only got about an hour and twenty minutes before we may have to give up.... We don't know yet. They are throwing men and shell at us and we may not be able to stand it. They have been shelling faster than you can count...."

At 11:05, after pausing for a few minutes, he came back on the air. "We've got about 55 minutes, and I feel sick at my stomach.... They are around smashing rifles. They bring in the wounded every minute.... General Wainwright is a right guy, and we are willing to go on for him, but shells were dropping all night, faster than hell. Damage terrific. Too much for guys to take.... Corregidor used to be a nice place, but it's haunted now.... The jig is up. Everyone is bawling like a baby. I know how a mouse feels, caught in a trap waiting for guys to come along and finish up. My name is Irving Strobing. Get this to my mother, Mrs. Minnie Strobing, 605 Barbey Street, Brooklyn, New York. My love to Pa, Joe, Sue, Mac, Joy, and Paul. Tell Joe wherever he is to give 'em hell for us. My love to you all. Sign my name and tell my mother you heard from me." Strobing added, "ZZA, Standby..." but it was the last word from Corregidor.[29]

Although the world had heard the last from the Rock, there were two more messages out of Corregidor of official nature, sent by General Wainwright to President Roosevelt and General Douglas MacArthur. Written in pencil on a yellow legal pad, to Roosevelt via the Chief of Staff General Marshall, he wrote,

> For the President of the United States. With broken heart and head bowed in sadness but not in shame, I report to your Excellency that today I must arrange terms for the surrender of the fortified islands of Manila Bay....
> There is a limit of human endurance, and that limit had long since been past. Without prospect of relief, I feel it is my duty to my country and to my gallant troops to end this useless effusion of blood and human sacrifice. Please say to the nation that my troops and I have accomplished all that is humanly possible and that we have upheld the best traditions of the United States and its army.... With profound regret and with continued pride in my gallant troops, I go to meet the Japanese commander. Goodbye, Mr. President.[30]

The message to MacArthur was similar in content, with these exceptions: "I feel it is my duty to the nation and my troops to end this useless slaughter.... American and Filipino troops have engaged and held the enemy for nearly five months. We have done our full duty for you and for our country. We are sad but unashamed. I have fought to the best of my ability from Linguyen Gulf to Bataan to Corregidor, always hoping relief was on the way.... Goodbye, General. My regards to you and our comrades in Australia..."

Although the world knew that Corregidor had surrendered, they had no idea of the difficulty that lay ahead in carrying it out.

When the "Execute Pontiac" order was received by the 2nd and 3rd Battalion Marines defending the unchallenged Middleside and Topside beaches, it was devastating psychologically as if they'd been winning and told to surrender. Outside of the approximate 200 who had seen combat against the Japanese on Bataan in the battle for Longoskawayan Point in January, it was particularly difficult. After weeks of preparations in anticipation of finally getting their licks in against the Japanese, the order to lay down their arms without firing a shot was too much to take for all of the old Shanghai Marines. One Marine had to be corralled when he threatened to kill the messenger who had told them to surrender.

A 2nd Battalion Marine, Private William Coghlan, expressing the feelings and reactions of most at "Pontiac," said, "We tore [our weapons] apart, stomped on them, cracked them across the wall, threw rifle bolts into the bay, [while] all the time giving vent to our anger with lusty curses at the Japs." With Japanese artillery still continuing to pound the Rock, after destroying his weapon, Private 1st Class Ben Lohman said, "We didn't know what to do. The word was finally passed to go into Malinta Tunnel."[31]

Battery commanders in those still-functioning coast artillery and antiaircraft batteries ordered their guns spiked and their breaches thrown deep into the jungle or tossed into the sea. Recoil cylinders were smashed or made useless, antiaircraft height finders were wrecked, and all records and operating manuals burned—all of this punctuated no doubt with plenty of "lusty curses" at the Japanese.

The real difficulty with the order to surrender happened in the East Sector, where because of the lack of communications, many never heard it. The continued bombing and shelling of the area by the Japanese also

## 16. Corregidor Fights Back

made it impossible to believe, even when word somehow got through that it was over.

Although it is not known how or to whom Captain Herman Hauck's makeshift 59th Regiment reserve force surrendered, they, it will be recalled, had been successful in forcing Colonel Sato's left flank defenders back off the ridge.

Unaware of the order to surrender, led by the aggressive Hauck, they had actually driven the Japanese north over the ridge and down onto the airfield and were advancing on the lead Japanese tank when word came to give up. Hauck's men, disbelieving at first, disgustedly threw down their weapons and raised their hands in surrender.

Further south at the Radio Intercept Tunnel on Monkey Point, a makeshift group of defenders, composed of marines, sailors, Philippine Scouts, and army Bataan survivors, had withdrawn to the area earlier that morning when the Japanese gained control of the north side of Kindley Field.

One of the Bataan veterans, air corps Lieutenant Edgar Whitcomb, was initially assigned to B Company when he arrived and put in charge of the 37mm gun and a ten-man crew of Philippine Scouts. Unchallenged during the night, at dawn he had thrown the breach block of the old "wooden-wheeled antique," as he called it, "into the sea" and proceeded with his Scouts to Monkey Point.

When they arrived, Whitcomb reported to marine Captain James Bromeyer and Lieutenant Mason Chronister, who were attempting to establish a line of defense above the entrance to the tunnel on the edge of the South Shore Road.

Whitcomb was quickly enlisted to help. Finding the men "gathered in small groups," he said, "I spent most of my time running up and down the line ordering them to scatter and take a protected position."

From their position overlooking Kindley Field, the "mixed conglomeration of fighting talent," as he called them, was initially able to keep the Japanese at bay. "We had no idea of the progress of the battle," recalled the young air force officer. "All we knew was that over the hill, the Japs were firing at us and that we were firing back."

As the morning wore on, Japanese accuracy improved. Along with their machine guns, particularly effective were the enemy "knee" mortars. Although casualties began to mount up, it was not enough to force the Americans off the ridge.

From his position on the ridge, Whitcomb, for the first time, got a look at the precision of the Japanese artillery fire on U.S. positions between Water Tank Hill and Malinta Tunnel, leaving him with little doubt that the end was near." The coordination between the artillery on Bataan and the forces that had landed on the island [was surprising]," he said. "[Whenever] flares would go up, the artillery would shell a sector into which the Japs had not yet moved. While the shelling went on, dive bombers continued to fly in so low that we could actually see the faces of the pilots."

Around 11:00, a runner appeared with information that General Wainwright would surrender the island at noon. "With that information," said Whitcomb, "we withdrew down the South Shore road to the navy tunnel, where we could stand off any attack until that time."[32]

For Wainwright, the wait for the return of the advance surrender party was, as he said, "a torturous hour." Finally, at close to 2:00, Captain Clark entered the Headquarters lateral with news of the meeting with the Japanese.

"He won't come to see you, sir," said Clark. "He insists that you go and meet him."

Wainwright stood up, removed his pistol belt and .45, then he and his aides, Johnny Pugh and Tom Dooley, General Moore and his aide, Major Bob Brown, and Clark all climbed into Moore's battered Chevrolet and headed out of the tunnel. It was a rough ride over the cratered, torn-up road, but something that Tom Dooley, Wainwright's driver on Bataan, handled without difficulty.

Despite the white flag, which had been tied onto the front of the car, "enemy machine gunners from Denver Hill sprayed shots at us as we approached," said Wainwright. "We got out of the car at the foot of Denver Hill and, following Clark, began its ascent. As we did, Jap bombers opened up with heavy attacks on nearby Fort Hughes, more than two hours after I put up the white flag."

Near the top of the hill, the six men were met by an English-speaking Japanese lieutenant, whom Wainwright sized up as being "wiry and fit and reeking with arrogance." Identifying himself as Lieutenant

## 16. Corregidor Fights Back

Uramura, "he shouted at Wainwright, who, cupping his good ear with his hand to hear over the noise, was told that they would not accept the surrender unless it included 'all American and Filipino troops in the whole archipelago.'"

Not about to discuss the surrender with a Japanese lieutenant, Wainwright fired back, "I do not choose to discuss surrender terms with you. Take me to the senior officer present on Corregidor!"

At that moment, Colonel Motoo Nakayama, whom Homma had sent over to bring Wainwright back if he was ready to surrender all the islands, walked up. Through Uramura, Wainwright told him that he was there to "tender the surrender of the four fortified islands at the mouth of Manila Bay."

Uramura translated it to Nakayama, who "in an angry torrent of Japanese," as Wainwright remembered it, "told me without translation what I already knew—that my surrender must include all forces in the entire Philippines."

"In that case, I will deal only with General Homma and with no one of less rank," replied Wainwright sternly. "I want an appointment with him."

Nakayama agreed to take him to Cabcaben to meet with the Japanese commander, at which Wainwright invited the two men to go with him to the North Dock and take his personal boat across. They agreed.

Johnny Pugh, in the meantime, had started for the tunnel and the South Dock where Wainwright's boat was tied, to bring it around to the North Dock. He almost didn't make it.

"Pugh's path back to the east entrance ... became beset with a sudden and tremendous barrage," said Wainwright. "But by crawling, crouching, and edging along, using whatever cover he could find, he made it—an act of striking heroism. But the shelling which Pugh had survived caused the Jap colonel to stop in his tracks, for the road [around Malinta Hill] to the North Dock lay through the same bombardment."

The two Japanese, fearing being killed by their own shells, insisted that they turn back.

It was the chance Wainwright had been waiting for. "Why the hell

189

don't you people stop shelling?" he shouted angrily. "I put up my white flag an hour ago."

Colonel Nakayama murmured something to Uramura, who remarked, "We have not accepted any surrender from you as yet," at which the Japanese invited Wainwright and Dooley to cross in one of their barges from the safer eastern end of the island.

"He took us to Corregidor's tiny airfield in the vicinity of Cavalry Point," remembered Wainwright, "[where he] contacted Bataan by radio and ordered a boat to come over and fetch us. It was nearly four o'clock by the time it arrived. We shoved off for Bataan ... and Homma."[33]

# 17

# "You will, repeat, *will* surrender"

It has been well documented that the honorable surrenders of the British at Hong Kong and Singapore, and the Americans at Bataan and Corregidor, were filled with trepidation and fear. If Japanese demands were not immediately met, the slaughter of hundreds of helpless prisoners would occur. When General Jonathan Wainwright met with the Japanese to negotiate the surrender of Corregidor on May 7, 1942, he found himself faced with having to surrender every island in the Philippines on which American and Filipino forces still occupied, including Mindanao, Cebu, Panay, Negros, Leyte, and Samar—or face the consequences.

The sequence of events that led to a near collapse of negotiations, and the possibility of having to face those consequences, began on the veranda of a house at Cabcaben, Bataan where the Americans met to negotiate for what they hoped would be a smooth transition.

Before leaving Corregidor to meet with Japanese Army commander General Masaharu Homma, Wainwright had acknowledged to himself that the Japanese might demand he surrender all of the Philippines rather than just Corregidor. His initial reluctance to do so, however, almost blew up in his face.

With both surrender parties sitting facing each other at a long table, Wainwright handed his "formally signed surrender document" to Homma. Although the Japanese commander could read and speak English, he passed it on to his interpreter, Lieutenant Nakamura, who read it aloud in Japanese. The document stated that he only had the authority to surrender the four island forts in Manila Bay, and nothing else.

"With a look or two at me," said Wainwright, "[Homma] spoke sharply to Nakamura." In a stern voice, Nakamura said that no surrender would be considered unless it included all American and Filipino troops in the archipelago.

"I can only surrender my men on Corregidor and the three other fortified islands," replied Wainwright. "The troops in the Visayan Islands and Mindanao are no longer under my command. They are commanded by General Sharp, who in turn is under General MacArthur's command."

Nakamura said that Homma didn't believe him. "It has been reported many times by the United States radio that you command all troops in the Philippines. He will not accept any surrender unless it includes all forces." He was asked when General Sharp was released from his command.

Although he had done it earlier that day, playing his trump card, Wainwright replied, "Several days ago. Besides, even if I did command General Sharp's troops, I have no means left for communicating with them. I have destroyed my radio equipment."

"Send a staff officer to Sharp," Homma replied through Nakamura. "I will furnish the plane."

Wainwright refused, still insisting he no longer had authority over Sharp. After bantering back and forth for a few minutes, Homma, after conferring with the other officers at the table, turned, banged on the table with his fist and said without an interpreter, "At the time of General King's surrender in Bataan, I did not see you! Neither have I any reason to see you if you are only the commander of a unit of the American forces. I wish only to negotiate with my equal. Since you are not in supreme command, I see no further necessity for my presence here." At that point, all the Japanese stood up.[1]

All the while, the four Americans seated alongside Wainwright—Brig. General Lewis Beebe, his chief of staff; his two aides, Major John Pugh and Captain Tom Dooley; and Major William Lawrence, his administrative assistant—had been nervously listening to his puzzling

## 17. "You will, repeat, will *surrender*"

attempt to bluff his way out of the inevitable. Realizing that the entire surrender process was in jeopardy, Pugh, who was sitting next to him said, "Wait!"

After a quick conference between the five men, Wainwright, nodding his head in compliance, turned and said, "In the face of the fact that further bloodshed … is unnecessary and futile, I will assume command of the entire American forces in the Philippines at the risk of serious reprimand by my government following the war."

Homma wasn't convinced. Through Nakamura, he responded that Wainwright had denied his authority. "Your momentary decision may be regretted by your men. He advises you to return to Corregidor and think the matter over. If you see fit to surrender, then surrender to the commander of the regiment on Corregidor. He in turn will bring you to General Homma in Manila. This meeting is over. Good day." At that point, Homma and another officer walked down the veranda steps, got into the Cadillac they had arrived in, and drove away.

The Americans were dumbfounded. With the words, "…your decision may be regretted by your men" foremost in their minds, Dooley turned to Wainwright and, in a panicked voice said, "General, you'll have to arrange something. Corregidor and the other harbor islands disarmed this afternoon. The Japs will slaughter our unarmed people."

As the five Americans walked off the porch, Wainwright spotted Colonel Motoo Nakayama, who, along with English-speaking Lieutenant Uramura, had come across with them from Corregidor. "What do you want us to do now?" he asked.

Through Uramura, Nakayama tersely replied, "We will take you and your party back to Corregidor, and you can do what you damn please!"

Fortunately, Beebe and Johnny Pugh had cornered a sharp-looking young Japanese lieutenant who said he spoke English. They told him it wasn't exactly clear what Homma wanted them to do.

"Wainwright should return to Corregidor," he said, "and either resume fighting or surrender to the Japanese commander there."

The two men hurried over to Wainwright. After telling him what the lieutenant had said, the three men then walked over to Nakayama.

"General Wainwright will surrender all American forces to General

## The Fall of the Philippines

Homma unconditionally," said Pugh. "Take us to General Homma, and General Wainwright will dispatch me to Mindanao to instruct General Sharp to comply with his demands."

Although it was out of his hands now, Wainwright, as he said later, continued to "strongly hope that some way would still be found to avert the surrender of all forces. But each time I thought of the continued organized resistance on Mindanao, I thought, too, of the perilous position of close to 11,000 men, nurses, and wounded on Corregidor." He also remembered that earlier he had released all of the Philippines except Corregidor to General Sharp.[2]

Early the next morning on Corregidor, Wainwright, realizing the urgency of notifying General Sharp that he was reassuming command and to prepare to surrender, he sent for his assistant chief of staff, Colonel Jesse Traywick. Telling him that to avoid any misunderstanding, he was going to send him to Mindanao to hand deliver a written copy of the surrender.

After dictating it and Traywick writing it down, Wainwright was then told that he was being taken to Manila to broadcast the instructions to Sharp over the radio, to which he agreed would give the southern islands commander time to "inform General MacArthur of the situation and obtain his approval of the proposed surrender."

At 11:43 that night, sitting at a small bamboo table at Manila radio station KZRH, he began reading virtually the same message Colonel Traywick would be delivering to General Sharp the next day. In part it read:

> This is Lieutenant General J. M. Wainwright. Message for General William F. Sharp, commanding the Mindanao and Visayan Forces. Anyone receiving this message, please notify General Sharp at once. I, as Commanding General of the United States Forces in the Philippine Islands, hereby resume direct command of Major General Sharp ... and of all troops under his command.
>
> I now give a direct order to William Sharp. Subject: Surrender! ... General Homma declined to accept my surrender unless it included the forces under your command.... After leaving General Homma, with no agreement between us, I've decided to accept, in the name of humanity, his proposal and ... surrender all of American and Filipino Army troops in the Philippine Islands. You will, therefore, be guided accordingly and will, I repeat, *will*, surrender all troops under your command to the proper Japanese officers.

## 17. "You will, repeat, will *surrender*"

After mentioning that Colonel Traywick would deliver a copy of the message and was empowered to act for him, he concluded with: "The Japanese Army and Navy will not cease their operations until they recognize the faithfulness of execution of these orders. [They] must be carried out faithfully and accurately; otherwise, [they will] continue their operations. If and when such faithfulness is recognized, the commander ... of the Japanese forces ... will order that all firing be ceased."[3]

It was 12:30 a.m., May 8, 1942, and it was over—or was it?

Before meeting with Homma on Bataan, Wainwright had messaged MacArthur in Australia that he had decided to surrender. Unknown to him, what followed would set off a firestorm of messages and actions that would go on for another month. It started with a message from MacArthur to Sharp that said: "Wainwright has surrendered. From now on, communicate on all matters directly with me...."

In response, Sharp radioed back the gist of Wainwright's broadcast, asking for further instructions. Before answering, MacArthur fired off a terse message to Washington, saying that he placed no credence in the alleged broadcast by Wainwright.

His "further instructions" answer to Sharp was that orders emanating from General Wainwright had no validity. This was tempered, however, by giving him full authority to make any decision that an immediate emergency might demand.

Confused by the "do/don't" tenor of the message, and concerned that the Japanese would continue their operations against the helpless men and nurses on Corregidor, he was perplexed as to whether he should accept "no validity," or surrender "in the name of humanity?"

To further cloud his decision, while waiting for Colonel Traywick, he had released the four island commanders from his command, telling them that although surrender was imminent, they could escape into the mountains and fight as guerrillas if they wished.

When Traywick arrived the next afternoon, the two men discussed the situation, prompting Sharp to unhesitatingly send the following radiogram to his island commanders:

As I have not yet surrendered, the instructions given you yesterday releasing you from my command are withdrawn. I resume command and direct you to cease all operations against the Japanese army at once.... This is imperative and must be carried out in order to save further bloodshed. Acknowledge.

MacArthur was next. Sent at 7:15 p.m., it read: "I have seen Wainwright's staff officer and have withdrawn my order releasing commanders on other islands and directed surrender. Dire necessity alone has prompted this action."

Realizing at that point that it was out of his hands, MacArthur did not reply to Sharp, contacting General Marshall in Washington instead. After indicating that he had received word that Wainwright had reassumed command of all the forces in the Philippines and directed their surrender, with more disdain than regret, he concluded with: "I believe Wainwright has temporarily become unbalanced and his condition renders him susceptible of enemy use."[4]

Although for Wainwright the immediate threat of massacre of the troops on Corregidor had now subsided, unknown to Sharp, he was still one arduous month away from concluding the surrender of the southern islands. Based on the number and quality of troops and lack of equipment and weapons he had to work with, however, it's difficult to believe that it would take another 30 days to bring a formal end to the battle for the Philippine Islands.

Unlike the seven Philippine Army divisions located on Luzon before the war started, only three, the 61st, 81st, and 101st were in the south. Along with one regiment each from the 71st and 91st Divisions, a few Constabulary and provisional units, that was all that were available to cover the islands of Mindanao, Cebu, Panay, Negros, Leyte, and Samar.

As far as weapons and equipment, it was much the same. Individual weapons were 1917 Enfields, many of which were defective and quickly broke down. It was the same for the .30- and .50-caliber machine guns that were issued. There were no antitank guns, grenades, or steel helmets. A shortage of ammunition had even limited the number of target rounds fired. According to one American officer, most of the men who fought on Mindanao had never fired a live round before they went into battle. For artillery weapons, until December 12 there was not one field artillery piece in all of the southern islands. On that date, Sharp received eight World War I-vintage 2.95-inch mountain guns, of which two were knocked out of action ten days later.

## 17. "You will, repeat, will *surrender*"

Of the battles for the six islands, Mindanao was over the quickest. On May 10, just four days after the initial invasion and on the same day he negotiated Wainwright's surrender order, Sharp surrendered the largest island in the Philippines. If that was any indication of what to expect with the remaining five, on paper it looked to be all over in a matter of days, if not hours.

One week before he left the Philippines, General MacArthur, in anticipation of using Mindanao as the first step in fulfilling his "I shall return" promise, divided his southern islands command. For this, General Sharp was given Mindanao, and Brig. Gen. Bradford Chynoweth, then on Cebu, given what was designated as the Visayan Force. Despite this, when it came time to surrender, it would be Sharp alone who had to carry it out, placing him in relatively the same position Wainwright had found himself in.

What could loosely be called the "army" that was spread out amongst the five islands amounted to some 20,000 in number. Although designated as being under the command of General Chynoweth, it amounted to four small, independent commands, of which each acted independently as it related to the surrender.

On Cebu, despite the efforts of the 6,500-man garrison, which included two Philippine Army regiments, the organized fight for the island lasted only two days, ending on April 12. But control of the island was another matter, for although there was little or no organized resistance past that date, there was no formal surrender, either.

As far as Chynoweth was concerned, the efforts he made immediately after the war started were now going to pay off—the stockpile of food and ammunition, the setup of communications, and the establishment of remote, inaccessible mountain hideouts from which to launch guerrilla operations.

However, on May 8, nearly a month of hearing nothing, he heard General Wainwright's surrender broadcast. This was soon followed by the two messages from Sharp, where, as aforementioned, after releasing his Visayan commanders and encouraging them to escape and fight as guerrillas, he signaled that he had taken the command back, with orders to immediately cease all operations against the Japanese.

To say that this was confusing to Chynoweth and the rest of his

## The Fall of the Philippines

island commanders is an understatement. Because of the don't/do orders that had practically come in back to back, Chynoweth, believing the sudden change had come at the point of a Japanese bayonet, ordered his communications officer to both ignore and not acknowledge any further messages from Sharp. In deciding to do this, however, he not only relinquished his command of the entire Visayan Force, but also placed the decision and execution of any orders emanating from Sharp in the hands of individual island commanders.

He next received a hand-carried note from the commander of Japanese forces on the island urging him to surrender "to avoid further bloodshed." His written response was that the request to surrender was not "legally binding" since it was obviously made under duress and that "We do not believe that we can honorably surrender."[5]

At that point, while contemplating taking his staff across to Panay to link up with Colonel Albert Christie's force, his communications officer told him they had just heard a faint radio message from that island that said: "Where is General Chynoweth? Tell him to come back over here and command us."

Cheered after hearing the message and while preparing to leave, a courier arrived with a message from Colonel Roger Hilsman, commander on nearby Negros. It stated that Sharp's previous order to surrender was authentic and that a staff officer would be arriving to negotiate the surrender of his entire Visayan command.

Although hearing that, as he said, "knocked us into a tailspin," he still decided not to go forward with the surrender until hearing directly from General MacArthur, whom he hoped would "tell us … to hang on."

Ironically, what he was waiting for but hoped would not come came that same night when listening to a shortwave radio broadcast from station KGEI in San Francisco. General MacArthur, it said, was no longer in contact with the Philippines.

The next day, May 15, exactly seven days since Wainwright's meeting with General Homma, Sharp's emissary, Captain Gray, arrived with the order directing his surrender and another one from Wainwright that said, "On no account were any commanders to make any attacks to evade the terms of surrender." To emphasize the consequences of not following

## 17. "You will, repeat, will *surrender*"

orders, Gray told Chynoweth that the Japanese were set to kill the Americans on Corregidor "if the surrender was not faithfully executed."

The next morning Chynoweth told his men about the surrender but that they were free to hide out in the hills and continue guerrilla operations. Later that afternoon, the man who, as far as Sharp knew, was going forward to negotiate the surrender of his entire Visayan command, instead met the Japanese with his staff, a few naval officers, and 50 Filipino soldiers, surrendering only the island of Cebu.

Although General Sharp probably held out hope that Chynoweth would include the entire Visayan command in his surrender negotiations, realistically he had his doubts that Colonel Albert Christie on Panay would be included.

Christie, whose garrison included close to 7,000 men, from the very beginning had prepared his troops to wage guerrilla warfare until reinforcements arrived. Planning not to oppose the Japanese landings, which occurred on April 16, Christie, from his well-fortified and supplied mountain retreat, immediately began hit-and-run raids against the Japanese.

When he received Sharp's surrender order on May 10, like Chynoweth's, his initial reaction was much the same. Questioning his authority to order it, he replied that there "wasn't even one small reason" to give up because "some other unit has gone to hell or some Corregidor shell-shocked (influenced-surrender) terms (had been made)." He also said, "I must have MacArthur's okay; otherwise, it may be treason."

Obviously exasperated for having to convince Christie of the dangers of failing to obey his orders as he had done with Chynoweth, Sharp responded that the Japanese would not accept Wainwright's surrender until all the Visayan islands commanders had capitulated. Failure to do so, he stressed, meant they would resume offensive operations. He then told him that MacArthur had been informed of the situation and that Lt. Col. Allen Thayer had been dispatched by plane with further written instructions. He concluded with a stern warning that his "failure to comply [would] produce disastrous results" and to immediately reply of his "actions and compliance."

As requested, Christie did reply immediately, but not in the affirmative. "Your radio surrender of my forces," he said, "[is] totally unnecessary. I strongly urge you to have the approval of the War Department through MacArthur.... In this delicate situation, please do not issue me any peremptory orders that will embarrass or get us into mutual conflict.... No army surrenders portions still free, intact, and having a good chance of helping the general mission. Make me independent. Do not put me on the sacrifice block."

While awaiting Thayer's arrival, he sent a follow-up message to see if MacArthur had responded to his request. As there had been no reply, Sharp ignored it, saying that "No further comments from [him were] desired" and to "acknowledge this message and state actions taken at once."[6]

Ironically, Colonel Thayer arrived just minutes after Christie had received the above message. Along with presenting the Panay commander a copy of Wainwright's letter, he was handed one written by Sharp.

Acknowledging the predicament Christie was in, Sharp wrote, "Be it understood that I have the highest regard for your courageous and resolute stand.... However, developments of the war make such action utterly impractical, regardless of the capabilities of your forces. If any other course were open to me, I would most assuredly have taken it."

After again mentioning the possible fate of the Corregidor prisoners for his failure to cooperate, he concluded with Wainwright's words—that the only course of action was to surrender "in the name of humanity."

The next day, May 19, Christie informed Sharp of his talk with Colonel Thayer, and decided "to comply faithfully with your orders for the surrender of my division." Two days later, the man who had originally commanded a garrison of some 7,000 men led his army, 90 percent of which had vanished into the hills or gone home, forward to meet with the Japanese.[7]

In command of the islands of Leyte and Samar, separated by a narrow strait of less than three miles, was Colonel Theodore Cornell. Like everyone, he had received General Sharp's surrender message on May 10. However, believing that since it had been sent in the clear or in "plain text" that it was not authentic, he refused to acknowledge it.

Although the Japanese had not yet landed on either island, he made

## 17. "You will, repeat, will *surrender*"

plans to separate his 2,500-man force, preparing them to carry on guerrilla operations. Meanwhile, Sharp, who had heard nothing from him for 10 days, as he had done with Cebu and Panay, dispatched a courier with a written order to surrender.

On May 26, two days after the Japanese landed unopposed on Leyte and with Sharp's order in hand, Cornell surrendered. Of his original contingent of 2,500, however, only 62 men—40 Philippine Army and 11 American officers and eleven enlisted men—surrendered, the rest having disappeared into the hills.

General Jonathan Wainwright, following his "You … will surrender…" radio broadcast to General Sharp on the night of May 7, was taken with his staff and General Beebe to the University Club in Manila, where he remained until June 9.

Although his month-long stay at the club, by later POW camp standards, was reasonably accommodating, the situation remained tenuous until the surrender of one troublesome island in particular was settled and the threat "that Jap guns would be turned on the unarmed thousands on Corregidor."

The island in question was Negros. Geographically sandwiched between Panay and Cebu, it was not occupied by the Japanese until May 21, eleven days after its commander, Colonel Roger Hilsman, received General Sharp's surrender message.

Despite the threat of invasion, and like the decisions initially made by the other three island commanders, efforts were directed more on successfully establishing guerrilla operations than on defending the narrow, 125-mile-long island. After dividing his 2,000-man force into five separate battalions and assigning each to a specific sector, Hilsman mistakenly released each commander from his direct control to allow them to operate independently as guerrillas.

After receiving Sharp's order on May 10, like all the Visayan commanders had done, he decided to wait until he received written instructions. Arriving on May 18, a meeting with his sector commanders was immediately called. After telling them of the Japanese threat to kill a certain number of American captives on Corregidor each day until the surrender was accepted, he said that he had decided to give up the island.

Since Negros had not yet been invaded, Sharp instructed Hilsman

## The Fall of the Philippines

to go to Iloilo on Panay to make arrangements with the Japanese to surrender. Realizing it would take both time and persuasion to get all five of his sector commanders together and convince them to surrender, he decided to send Colonel Carter McLennon to Iloilo as his representative.

In the meantime, as anticipated, not only was there trouble with his sector commanders, but his personal attempt to compel them to give up actually led to a threat to kill any American or Filipino officer who attempted to enforce it. Perhaps even more serious was a promise by one mutinous section leader to kill all 196 Japanese civilians who had been interned when the war broke out if any effort was made to force him to surrender.

In fact, so serious had the situation become that twice after the Japanese occupied the island on May 21, Hilsman had to appeal to the enemy commander to extend once more the deadline to settle the situation. He was given until June 3.

When the date came and went without any change, the Japanese agreed to accept the surrender of the troops he had by then persuaded to come down out of the hills. Of his original complement of 2,000, fewer than 700 Americans and Filipinos came forward.

General Wainwright, who had been kept abreast of the Negros situation, when told of the surrender, wrote: "I did not know [until later] how close I was to being required to witness the murder of ten of my officers each day the mutineers held out."

Finally, on June 9, 1942, three days short of a month since he had given his "You will surrender" broadcast, he was told by the Japanese that all organized resistance in the Philippines had ended and that "Your high command ceases immediately. You are now a prisoner of war...."[8]

Outside of guerrilla activities on Mindanao, of which much has been written, nothing of what occurred on the Visayas has been documented. Judging by the difficulties described in this story, however, chances were that if the Japanese chose to occupy the island, there was guerrilla activity.

# Chapter Notes

## Chapter 1
1. Army Air Action in Philippines and Netherlands East Indies—1941-2 (hereafter USAF Studies)
2. Ind, Allison. *Bataan the Judgment Seat*. New York: Macmillan, 1944 (hereafter Ind).
3. Sakai, Saburo. *Samurai*. New York: Doubleday, 1957 (hereafter Sakai).

## Chapter 2
1. White, W. L. *They Were Expendable*. New York: Harcourt & Brace, 1942 (hereafter White).
2. White, W. L. *Queens Die Proudly*. New York: Harcourt & Brace, 1943.
3. Dyess, William E. *The Dyess Story*. New York: Putnam, 1944 (hereafter Dyess).
4. 24th Pursuit Diaries of Majors Ben Brown, David Obert, and Stewart Robb, "Army Air Action in Philippines and Netherlands East Indies, 1941–1942, U.S. Air Force Studies (hereafter 24th Pursuit Diaries).
5. Bartsch, William H. *Doomed at the Start*. College Station: Texas A&M Press, 1992 (hereafter Bartsch).
6. Bartsch.
7. White.

## Chapter 3
1. Chapple, Wreford G. "War Patrol Report for Period 8 December 1941 to 27 December 1941."
2. Blair, Clay Jr. *Silent Victory: The U.S. Submarine War Against Japan*. New York: J.B. Lippincott Co., 1975.
3. Winslow, W. G. *The Fleet the Gods Forgot*. Annapolis, MD: Naval Institute Press, 1982.

## Chapter 4
1. Brown, Cecil. *Suez to Singapore*. New York: Random House, 1942.
2. Sakai.
3. Edmonds, Walter D. *They Fought with What They Had*. Boston: Little, Brown, 1959.
4. "Boyd Wagner's Story," *LIFE*; December 29, 1941.

## Chapter 5
1. Sackett, Commander E. L. "History of the USS *Canopus*," Ship's History Section, Office of Naval Records and History, Navy Department, Washington, D.C. (hereafter Sackett).
2. Sackett.
3. Harrington, Joseph. *Yankee Samurai*. Detroit: Pettigrew Enterprises, 1979.
4. Sackett.
5. *Ibid*.
6. Redmond, Juanita. *I Served on Bataan*. Philadelphia: Lippincott, 1943 (hereafter Redmond).
7. Sackett.
8. *Ibid*.

## Chapter 6
1. Miller, Ernest. *Bataan Uncensored*. Long Prairie, MN: Hart Publications, 1949.
2. White.

## Chapter 7

1. Ramsey. Edwin. *Lieutenant Ramsey's War.* New York: Knightsbridge, 1990 (hereafter Ramsey).
2. *Ibid.*
3. Capt. John Wheeler, "January 18, 1942 Action Report, 26th Cavalry," *LIFE*, March 23, 1942 (hereafter Wheeler).
4. Wheeler.
5. DeLong, Lt. Edward. Combat Report, January 18, 1942, Microfilm Section, Navy Publications Office, Washington, D.C. (hereafter DeLong).
6. *Ibid.*
7. Bulkeley, Lt. John. Combat Report January 18, 1942, Microfilm Section, Navy Publications Office, Washington, D.C. (hereafter Bulkeley).
8. DeLong.
9. *Ibid.*

## Chapter 8

1. Brown, Ernest L. "Operations of 57th Infantry at Abucay, January 1942." Prepared for U.S. Army Infantry School, 1947, Annex V, Office of Chief of Military History, Washington, D.C. (hereafter Brown).
2. Olson, Major John E. Monograph: "Operations of 57th Infantry at Abucay. Jan. 1942." Prepared for U.S. Army Infantry School, 1948, Annex V, Office of Chief of Military History, Washington, D.C. (hereafter Olson).
3. Brown.
4. *Ibid.*
5. Olson.
6. Webb, William E. "Operations of 41st Infantry in Defense of Abucay Line." Prepared for U.S. Army Infantry School, 1950, Annex V, Office of Chief of Military History, Washington, D.C.
7. Brown.
8. Olson.
9. *Ibid.*
10. Brown.
11. Olson.
12. Brown.
13. Olson.
14. *Ibid.*
15. Brown.

## Chapter 9

1. 24th Pursuit Diaries.
2. Ind.
3. *Ibid.*
4. *Ibid.*
5. Grashio, Samuel C. *Return to Freedom.* Tulsa, OK: MCN Press, 1982 (hereafter Grashio).
6. 24th Pursuit Diaries.
7. Ind.
8. Grashio.

## Chapter 10

1. Ind.
2. Dyess.
3. *Ibid.*
4. Grashio.
5. Dyess.
6. *Ibid.*

## Chapter 11

1. Morton, Lewis. *The Fall of the Philippines.* Washington, D.C.: U.S. Army, 1953 (hereafter Morton).
2. Poweleit, Alvin C. *USAFFE.* Privately printed, 1975 (hereafter Poweleit).
3. Tisdelle, Achille, Maj. *Diary of Major A.L. Tisdelle. Military Affairs,* Summer 1947 (hereafter Tisdelle).
4. Ashton, Paul. *Bataan Diary.* Privately printed, 1964.
5. Morton.
6. Tagarao, Silvestre. *All This Was Bataan.* Quezon City, Philippines: New Day Publishers, 1991.

## Chapter 12

1. Weinstein, Alfred A. *Barbed-Wire Surgeon.* New York: Macmillan, 1948 (hereafter Weinstein).
2. *Ibid.*
3. Poweleit.
4. Blasingame, Wyatt. *Combat Nurses of World War II.* New York: Random House, 1967.
5. Redmond.
6. Weinstein.
7. Redmond.
8. Weinstein.

## Chapter Notes

9. Redmond.
10. Weinstein.
11. Redmond.
12. Weinstein.
13. Norman, Elizabeth. *We Band of Angels*. New York: Random House, 1999.
14. Redmond.
15. *Ibid.*
16. Poweleit.
17. Redmond.
18. Holdbrook, Stewart. *None More Courageous*. New York: Macmillan, 1942.
19. Weinstein.
20. *Ibid.*
21. Redmond.
22. Weinstein.

## Chapter 13

1. Whitman, John. *Bataan: Our List Ditch*. New York: Hippocrene, 1990 (hereafter Whitman); Bluemel, Clifford. Private Papers. West Point Library (hereafter Bluemel Papers).
2. Whitman.
3. Bess, Clarence, Maj. Operations of Service Company, 31st Infantry, 5 January–9 April,1942. U.S. Army Infantry School.
4. Chandler, William F. "26th Cavalry—Battles to Glory." *Armored Cavalry Journal*, March-August 1947 (hereafter Chandler).
5. Lee C. Vance. 26th Cavalry Diary of Col. Lee C. Vance, Commanding Officer, 26th Cavalry Regiment (hereafter Vance).
6. *Ibid.*
7. Chandler.
8. Astor, Gerald. *Crisis in the Pacific*. New York: Dell, 1996.
9. Bluemel Papers.
10. *Ibid.*
11. Knox, Donald. *Death March: The Survivors of Bataan*. New York: Harcourt, Brace Jovanovich, 1981.
12. Chandler.

## Chapter 14

1. Wainwright, Gen. Jonathan. *General Wainwright's Story*. Garden City, New York: Doubleday, 1946 (hereafter Wainwright).
2. Beck, John. *MacArthur and Wainwright*. Albuquerque: University of New Mexico Press, 1947 (hereafter Beck).

3. Morton.
4. Chunn, Calvin. *Of Rice and Men*. Los Angeles: Veterans Publishing, 1946 (hereafterChunn).
5. Tisdelle.
6. Wainwright.
7. Chunn.
8. Wainwright.
9. Chunn.
10. *Ibid.*
11. Tisdelle.
12. Lopez, Salvador P. "When Bataan Fell," *Voice of the Veteran*, Manuel Buenafe, ed. Manila: Philippines Educational Promotion, 1971.
13. Tisdelle.
14. *Ibid.*

## Chapter 15

1. Dyess.
2. Obert.
3. *Ibid.*

## Chapter 16

1. Wainwright, John M., and Celedonio Ancheta, *The Wainwright Papers*, Vol. 1 & 2. Quezon City, Philippines: New Day, 1980 (hereafter Wainwright Papers).
2. Moore, George F. *Diary of Gen. George F. Moore*. Quezon City, Philippines: New Day, 1980 (hereafter Moore)
3. *Ibid.*
4. Wainwright Papers.
5. Miller, Michael J. *From Shanghai to Corregidor: Marines to the Defense of the Philippines*. Washington, D.C.: History and Museums Division, Marine Corps Historical Center, 1997.
6. *Ibid.*
7. *Ibid.*
8. Capt. Paul Cornwall. "War History of Battery 'D' 60th CA (AA),written in POW camp from memory of May 5–6, 1942" (hereafter Cornwall). http://corregidor.org/ca/btty_denver/denver_2.htm.
9. *Ibid.*
10. Miller.
11. Miller; Belote, James, and William Belote. *Corregidor: The Saga of a Fortress*. New York: Harper & Row, 1967 (hereafter Belote).

205

12. Miller.
13. Hogaboom, William F., "Action Report: Bataan" *Marine Corps Gazette* (April 1946), 27–41 (hereafter Hogaboom).
14. Miller.
15. *Ibid.*
16. Morton.
17. Wainwright Papers.
18. Miller.
19. Morton.
20. Miller.
21. Hogaboom.
22. *Ibid.*
23. Morris.
24. *Ibid.*
25. Wainwright Papers.
26. Hough, Frank, Verle Ludwig, and Henry Shaw, *U.S. Marine Corps Operations in WorldWar II,* Vol. l. Washington, D.C.: U.S. Government Printing Office, 1959.
27. Mellnik, Stephen M. *Philippine Diary, 1939–1943.* New York: Van Nostrand Reinhold Co., 1969.
28. Mellnik, S. M., and Melvyn H. MacCoy, *Ten Escape from Tojo.* New York: Farrar and Rinehart, 1944.
29. Toland, John. *But Not in Shame.* New York: Random House, 1961.
30. Wainwright.
31. Hough; Miller.
32. Whitcomb, Edgar D. *Escape from Corregidor.* New York: Macmillan, 1958.
33. Wainwright Papers; Wainwright.

## Chapter 17

1. Wainwright.
2. *Ibid.*; Morton.
3. Wainwright.
4. Beck.
5. Morton.
6. *Ibid.*
7. *Ibid.*
8. Wainwright.

# Bibliography

Ashton, Paul. *Bataan Diary*. Privately printed, 1964.

Astor, Gerald. *Crisis in the Pacific*. New York: Dell, 1996.

Bartsch, William H. *Doomed at the Start*. College Station: Texas A&M University Press, 1992.

Beck, John Jacob. *Macarthur and Wainwright*. Albuquerque: University of New Mexico Press, 1974.

Belote, James H., and William M. Belote. *Corregidor: The Saga of a Fortress*. New York: Harper & Row, 1967.

Blair, Clay Jr. *Silent Victory: The U.S. Submarine War Against Japan*. New York: J.B. Lippincott, 1975.

Blasingame, Wyatt. *Combat Nurses of World War II*. New York: Random House, 1967.

Bluemel, Gen. Clifford. Private Papers. West Point Library.

Brougher, W.E. *South to Bataan, North to Mukden*. Athens: University of Georgia Press, 1971.

Brown, Ben S., David L. Obert and Stewart Robb. Diaries of 24th Pursuit Group Activities. "Army Air Action in Philippines and Netherlands East Indies, 1941–1942," part of U.S. Air Force Studies.

Brown, Maj. Ernest L.: *Operations of the 57th Infantry, Abucay, January 1942*. Prepared for U.S. Army Infantry School, 1950, Annex V, Office of Chief of Military History, Washington, D.C.

Bulkeley, John D. "Summary of Operations—Motor Torpedo Boat Squadron Three, December 7 1941-April 10, 1942." Microfilm Section, Navy Publications Office, Washington D.C.

Chandler, William F. "26th Cavalry—Battles to Glory." *Armored Cavalry Journal*, March-August 1947.

Chapple, Wreford G. "War Patrol Report for Period 8 December 1941 to 27 December 1941." Operational Archival Branch, U.S. Naval Historical Center, Washington, D.C.

Cornwall, Capt. Paul. "War History of Battery 'D' 60th CA (AA)," written in POW camp from memory of May 5–6, 1942. http://corregidor.org/ca/btty_denver/denver_2.htm.

Chunn, Calvin E. *Of Rice and Men*. Los Angeles: Veteran's Publishing, 1946.

DeLong, Edward. "Combat Report -January 18, 1942." Microfilm Section, Navy Publications Office, Washington, D.C.

Dyess, Lt. Colonel William E. *The Dyess Story*. New York: G. P. Putnam, 1944.

Edmonds, Walter D. *They Fought With What They Had*. Boston: Little-Brown, 1959.

Grashio, Samuel C. *Return to Freedom: The War Memoirs of Samuel C. Grashio, USAF.* Tulsa: MCN Press, 1982.

Harrington, Joseph D. *Yankee Samurai*. Detroit: Pettigrew Enterprises, 1979.

Hough, Frank, Verle Ludwig and Henry Shaw. *U.S. Marine Corps Operations in World War II, Vol. l.* Washington, D.C.: U.S. Government Printing Office, 1959.

Ind, Allison. *Bataan, the Judgment Seat*. New York: Macmillan, 1944.

# Bibliography

Jablonski, Edward. *Flying Fortress.* Garden City, New York: Doubleday, 1965.

Knox, Donald. *Death March: The Survivors of Bataan.* New York: Harcourt, Brace Jovanovich, 1981.

Lopez, Salvador P. "When Bataan Fell." *Voice of the Veteran.* Manuel Buenafe, ed. Manila: Philippines Educational Promotion, 1971.

MacArthur, Douglas. *Reminiscences.* New York: McGraw-Hill, 1964.

Mellnik, Stephen M. *Philippine Diary, 1939-1945.* New York: Van Nostrand Reinhold Co, 1969.

Mellnik, S. M., and Melvyn H. Mac Coy. *Ten Escape from Tojo.* New York: Farrar and Rinehart, 1944.

Miller, Ernest B. *Bataan Uncensored.* Long Prairie, Minnesota: Hart Publications, 1949.

Miller, J. Michael. *From Shanghai to Corregidor: Marines in the Defense of the Philippines.* Washington, D.C.: History and Museums Division, Marine Corps Historical Center, 1997.

Moore, George F. *Diary of Gen. George F. Moore.* Quezon City, Philippines: New Day, 1980.

Morris, Eric. *Corregidor-The End of the Line.* New York: Stein and Day, 1981.

Morton, Louis. *The Fall of the Philippines.* Washington, D.C.: Center for Military History, U.S. Army, 1953.

Norman, Elizabeth . *We Band of Angels.* New York: Random House, 1999.

Olson, Maj. John E.: *Operations of the 57th Infantry at Abucay, January 1942.* Prepared for U.S. Army Infantry School, 1950, Annex V, Office of Chief of Military History, Washington, D.C.

Poweleit, Alvin C. *USAFFE.* Privately printed, 1975.

Ramsey, Edwin P. *Lt. Ramsey's War.* New York: Knightsbridge, 1990.

Redmond, Juanita. *I Served on Bataan.* Philadelphia: J.B Lippincott, 1943.

Romulo, Carlos. *I Saw The Fall Of The Philippines.* Garden City, New York: Doubleday, Doran, 1942.

Sackett, Commander E.L.. "History of the USS *Canopus*." Ship's History Section, Office of Naval Records and History, Navy Department, Washington, D.C.

Schultz, Duane. *Hero of Bataan.* New York: St. Martin's Press, 1981.

Tagarao, Silvestre. *All This Was Bataan.* Quezon City, Philippines: New Day Publishers, 1991.

Toland, John. *But Not in Shame.* New York: Random House, 1961.

Wainwright, John M., and Celedonio Ancheta. *The Wainwright Papers, Vol. 1 & 2.* Quezon City, Philippines: New Day, 1980.

Wainwright, Jonathan M. *General Wainwright's Story.* Garden City, New York: Doubleday, 1946.

Weinstein, Alfred A. *Barbed-Wire Surgeon.* New York: Macmillan, 1948.

Wheeler, Captain John. "26th Cavalry January 16, 1942 Action Report." *LIFE*, March 23, 1942.

White, W.L. *They Were Expendable.* New York: Harcourt, Brace, 1942.

Whitman, John W. *Our Last Ditch.* New York: Hippocrene Books, 1990.

Winslow, W.G. *The Fleet the Gods Forgot.* Annapolis, MD: Naval Institute Press, 1982.

Young, Donald J. *The Battle of Bataan: A Complete History.* Jefferson, NC: McFarland, 2009.

# Index

Abucay 76
Abucay Line 75, 78, 83, 119
Adams, Lt. Jack 39, 41
Air Force 3
Alangan River 127–129, 139
Alder Lt. Glen 12, 19
Alexander, Col. George 5
Anders, Capt. Franklin 129
Aparri 15, 28, 44, 45
Armstrong, Lt. Fred 8, 9
Ashton, Capt. Paul 102
Associated Press (AP) 79
Australia 39, 133, 195

B-17D 15–17, 19, 28–29, 38–42
B-29 43
Baker, Lt. Bill 87–89
Ballanca 102
Bamboo Fleet 150
Barnes Pvt. Silas 161
Barnick, Capt. Roland 150
Bataan Death March 107, 145
Bataan Field 84, 87, 89, 92–94, 148, 150
Bataan Flying Field Detachment 84, 147, 149
Bataan Hospital No. 1 118
Batalan River 66, 72
Battery Craighill 164
Battery Crockett 177
Battery Denver 163, 165–170, 174, 178
Battery Gulick 172
Battery Hughes 164
Battery Idaho 164
Battery Stockade 172
Battery Way 164, 179
Battery Wright 172
Beebe, Maj. Gen. Lewis 141, 159, 180, 184, 192–193

Beechcraft Staggerwing 150
Beecher, Lt. Col. Curtis 158, 168
Bell, Don 4
Bell P-390 Airacobra 46
Bellanca 150
Benning, Fort 75, 58
Benson, Lt. Gordon 34
Biggs, Lt. Col. Lloyd 168
Blass, Dan 7, 8, 13
Bluemel, Brig. Gen Clifford 119–120, 122–127, 130–132, 137
Boelens, Lt. Leo 149
Brady, Sgt. Dewey 165
Brady, Col. Jasper 128
Bridget, Commander Frank 52–53
Brougher, Brig. Gen William 144
Brown, Lt. Ben 18, 20
Brown, Capt. Ernest 75–81, 83
Brownewell, Lt. John 16, 152
Bulkeley, Lt. John 14–15, 28, 56, 69, 71–72, 74
Bums, Lt. John 95, 96, 148
Bunker, Brig. Gen. Paul 182
Burks, PFC David 109–110, 113
Burma 98

Cabanatuan 58
Cabcaben 135, 141–142, 148–151, 164, 173, 189, 191
Cabcaben Field 92, 94–96
Cagayan 42–43
Callahan 184
Campbell, Col. Alexander 5–6
*Canopus*, USS 48–57, 174
Capinpin Gen. Mateo 103, 105
Cardona 62
Carey, Harry 3, 8
Castle, Capt. Noel 158, 167–168

# Index

Cavalry Point 156, 159, 161, 190
Cavite 20, 23, 26–27, 48
Cebu 150–152, 191, 196–197, 199–200
Cebu City 150–152
Chambers, Capt. Robt. 169, 183, 188
Chandler, Ensign Barron 70
Chandler, Maj. William 126, 128, 131
Chapple, Lt. W.G. "Moon" 30–37
Cheney Ravine 154
China 146
Christie, Col. Albert 198–200
Chronister, Lt. Mason 187
Chunn, Capt. Calvin 176
Chynoweth, Brig. Gen. Bradford 197–199
Cicneros, PFC. 166
Clark, Capt. Goland 169, 183, 188
Clark Field 3–6, 8, 12–14, 18–23, 27–29, 38, 46, 82, 85, 146–147
Coats, Lt. Lee 39
Coleman, Lt. John 24
Collier, Col. James 135, 141–142, 148–151, 164, 173, 189, 191
Connally, Lt. Jim 39
Conrad, Maj. Eugene 124
Cook, Col. John 150–152
Cornell, Col. Thoedore 200–201
Cornwall, Capt. Paul 165–166
Cothran, Maj. Wade 140
Crellen, Lt. Erwin 93
Crosland, Lt. Shorty 18, 93–95, 148
Curtiss-Wright Airplane Co. 146

Dahlness, Capt. Harold 175, 178
Dale, Lt. Jack 21
Dalirig Field 152–153
Davao 152
deBeneditti, Pvt. Edmond 60, 62–63
Del Carmen Field 11–12, 17–18, 20–22
Del Monte Field 15–16, 28–29, 39, 42, 84, 92–94, 152–153
DeLong, Lt. Edward 70–74
Denver Hill 188
Distinguished Service Cross (DSC) 43, 46, 68, 78
Donaldson, Lt. Jack 149
Dooley, Capt. Tom 188, 190, 192
Drake, Lt. Jim 10–11
Dudley, Sgt. William 161
Dutch East Indies 98
Dyess, Capt. Edwin 20, 22, 54–55, 95–97, 147–149

East Portal 163, 165
East Road 76, 83, 93, 127, 130
East Sector 186
Easter Sunday 105
Eckles, Sgt. Alfred 5
Edison, Lt. Col. Dwight 182
803rd Aviation Engineers 161–164
Erickson, Lt. Edward 24
Euperio, Pvt. Pedro 68

Far East Air Force 15–16, 85
Fealock, Lt. Willie 23, 25
Ferguson, Frank 169–171, 176
Ferrell, Sgt. Harold 171, 176
5th Interceptor Command 4, 5
51st Combat Team 123–125
51st Division 83, 120, 122
59th Coast Artillery Regiment 177, 187
57th Infantry Regiment 75, 77–78, 81, 120, 127–128, 130
1st Corps 66, 99, 101, 134, 137, 144
1st Infantry Regiment 58
1st Regular Division 66
Ford, Lt. Walter 54
Formosa 16, 28, 106
Fort Benning 75
Fort Drum 172
Fort Hughes 188
45th Infantry Regiment 120
41st Division 78, 102–103, 121
41st Field Artillery Regiment 106
41st Infantry Regiment 103
42nd Infantry Regiment 104
43rd Infantry Regiment 104–105
Fossey, Lt. Jim 9, 13, 96–97
14th Army (Jap.) 142
14th Engineer Regiment 127, 129–130
4th Division (Jap.) 105, 157
4th Marine Regiment 154–155
Franklin Cpl. Edwin 162
Fry, Col. Phillip 74
Funk, Brig. Gen. Arnold 135

Geis, Lt. Parker 8, 10, 21
General Hospital No. 1 107–109, 112, 118
Geneva Convention 143
George, Brig. Gen. Harold 5, 6, 85–88, 90–92, 97, 147–148, 150
Gonzales, Pvt. 68
Goodall, Lt. Commander Hap 52–53, 55

210

# Index

Gootee, Sgt. John 41
Government Ravine 154, 169
Gozar, Lt. Jose 26
Grace Line 48
Grande Island 92–93, 95–96
Grant, Gen. U.S. 142
Grashio, Lt. Sam 88–90, 94
Gray, Capt. 198–199
Grover, Maj. Orrin 5–7, 151
Guderian, Gen. Hans 98
Gulick, Capt. John 172
Guyton, Capt. Benson 165

H-Station 157, 182–183
Hall, Lt. Jack 18, 87–88
Halverson Lt. Max 9, 11
Hamilton Field 13
Harris, Lt. 179
Hart, Adm. Thomas 15
Haskins, Sgt. John 170–171
Hauck, Capt. Herman 177, 187
Hayes, Lt. Roy 160
Hayes, Sgt. Tex 161
Hede, Lt. Cmdr. Al 49
Hennon, Lt. Bill 17
Hilsman, Col. Roger 198, 201–202
Hobrecht, Lt. Forrest 24
Hoeffel, Ensign Ken 184
Hogaboom, Lt. William 169, 178
Hogan, Lt. Rosemary 115
Homma, Gen. Masaharu 98, 105–107, 142, 174, 181–182, 189 195, 198
Homos Point 155, 168
Hong Kong 98
Honolulu 184
Hook, Lt. Willa 116
Hooker Point 160
Hospital No. 2 108
Howard, Col. Samuel 154–155, 169, 172–174, 177, 180–181
Hughes, Lt. Harrison 7, 8
Hurt, Maj. Marshall 136–140, 144

Iba Field 5, 27, 93
Ibold, Lt. Robert 85, 87–88
II Corps 120–121, 127, 137, 144
Ilinin Point 71
Iloilo 202
Imperial High Command (Jap.) 106
Ind, Capt. Allison 87–88, 90–91, 96–97
Indo-China 99

Infantry Point 161
Interceptor Command 19, 23
Irwin, Col. John 120
Iverson, Lt. Guy 9, 11

James Ravine 154–156, 182
Johnson, Lt. Colonel 129–130
Johnson, Lt. Gus 50
Johnson, Maj. Harold K. 81–82
Johnson, Cpl. Joseph 162
Jones, Brig. Gen. Albert 134, 137–138

Keator, Lt. Randy 7–8, 11, 13
Kelly, Capt. Colin 29, 38, 47
Kelly, Cpl. Robert 15, 58
KGEI radio station 198
Kibosh 95–97
"Kickapoo" 6
Killin, Cpl. W.G. 41
Kindley Field 160–161, 163, 183, 187
King, Sgt. Bill 7
King, Maj. Gen. Edward P. 100, 133–137, 139–141, 192
King, Lt. William 169, 183, 188
Kopacz, Cpl. Joseph 167
Kramb, GM Charles 55
Krieger, Lt. Andy 26
Kulinski, Sgt. Walter 179
Kurtz, Capt. Frank 19

Lae 46
Lamao 158
Lamao River 129, 131, 140
Lamon Bay 58
Lang, Pfc. Fred 111
Lawrence, Lt. Ray 160–161, 164
Lawrence, Maj. William 192
Lee, Gen. Robert E. 142
Legaspi 41
Lemay, Gen. Curtis 43
Leyte 191, 200
Liebert, Cpl. Al 116–117
Lilimbon Cove 56

Mabatang 76
MacArthur, Gen. Douglas 36, 44, 62–63, 76, 84, 91, 133–135, 185, 194–200
*Mactan* 11
Mahar, Col. William 67–68
Mahoney, Lt. Grant 16, 23, 27
Malaria 158, 167, 168

# Index

Malaya 98–99
Malinta Tunnel 154, 159, 163, 165–167, 170, 177–179, 182–183, 188
Mamala River 126
Manila 5, 22–23, 30, 35, 44, 58, 62, 86, 107, 112, 147, 193–194
Manila Bay 65, 76, 89, 101, 120, 149, 189
Manning, Lt. Alan 158, 183
Mareti, Lt. Sam 18
Mariveles 48, 55–56, 63, 92–94, 96, 136, 144–145, 148
Marshall, Gen. George 133–134, 171–172, 185, 196
Martino, John 71
Massello, Maj. Bill 164, 179, 180
Mauban 66
Mayagao Point 70–72
Mays, Sgt. 114
McCowan, Lt. Morgan 12–13, 19
McCown, Lt. John 150
McCoy, Commander Melvin 184
McDaniel, Lt. Larry 153
McLennon, Col. Carter 202
McManus, Chaplin 49
Medal of Honor 45, 80, 162
Mellnick, Maj. Steve 183
Mercurio, Sgt. John 162
"Mickey Mouse Battleship" 53, 54
Midway 43
Miller, Lt. Col. Ernest 58
Miller, Capt. Fred 180
Mindanao 15, 28, 38, 42, 85, 151
Mindoro 31
Mitchell, Sgt. Robert 59–60, 63
Mitsubishi A6M2 "Zero" 21, 26–27, 39, 41
Mitsubishi G3M "Nell" 13
Mitsubishi G4M "Bettie" 13
Mobile Battery 158, 161, 163, 169, 177
Moore, Brig. Gen. George 155–160, 173, 177, 181–182, 188
Moore, Lt. Joe 3–8, 10, 92
Morong 66, 69, 72, 73–74
Morris 167
Motor Torpedo Boat Squadron 3 14, 56, 69
Mt. Samat 102–103, 105–106
Mulcahy, Lt. Lloyd 10–11

Nakamura, Lt. 191–192
Nakayama, Col. Motoo 143–144, 183, 189–190, 193

Napo Point 73
Nara, Akira 104
Naval Academy 36
Naval Battalion 52–53
Navy Tunnel 51, 181
Negano, Maj. Kameichiro 140
Negano Detachment 101
Negros Island 191, 196, 201
New Guinea 46
Nichols Field 14, 20, 23–24, 27–28, 85–89
Nielson Field 23, 85–86
19th Bombardment Group 4, 13, 38
91st Coast Artillery Regiment 160
92nd Infantry Regiment 74
Nininger, Arthur 82
North Channel 145, 173
North Point 156–157, 161, 163
North Shore Road 164, 166–167, 170, 183

Obert, Lt. David 85–86, 88–89, 150–152
Olongapo 66, 92–93
Olson, Lt. John 75–83
194th Tank Battalion 58, 100
122nd Infantry Regiment (Jap.) 67
Ordnance Point 166
Otter, Lt. Bethel 175–176

P-26 25, 26
P-35 Seversky 12, 14, 16, 18, 20
P-39 Airacobra 46
P-40 Something 149–153
P-40B Tomahawk 7–9, 12, 19, 96, 146
P-40E Kittyhawk 11–12, 16–17, 20–22, 24, 26–27, 44–45, 81, 93–94, 97, 146
Panay Island 191, 196, 198–202
Parker, Brig. Gen. George 121–127, 129–130
Patrol Wing 10 (Patwing 10) 52
PBY Catalina 24–25
Pearl Harbor 28, 43
Perkins, Lt. 166
Philippine Army 75, 196
Philippine Army Air Corps 25, 158
Philippine Constabulary 102
Philippine Division 75–76, 120, 122
Philippine Red Cross 63
Philippine Scouts 16, 65, 155
Phillips, Lt. Jim 24, 25
Photo Joe (Jap. reconnaissance plane) 52
Pickup, Capt. Lewis 158, 167–168
Pilar 102

# Index

Plan Pontiac 181, 186
Posten, Lt. John 22, 92, 94
Poweleit, Capt. Alvin 100, 109–111, 115–116
Power, Brig. Gen. Thomas 43
Press Relations Office 141
Provisional Air Corps Regiment 124–125, 131
PT-31 71
PT-34 71–72
Pugh, Lt. Col. John 171, 188, 191–194

Quinauan Point 54–55, 147
Quirino, Capt. Carlos 102

Radio Intercept Tunnel 136, 187
Ramsey, Lt. Edwin 66–68, 74
Rancke, Lt. Henry 21
Reagan, Ronald 40
Redmond, Lt. Juanita 56, 110–118
*Return to Freedom* (book) 90
Reyes, Lt. Norman 141
Roosevelt, Franklin D. 40, 42–33, 185
Rowe, Lt. Bill 149
Rumbold, Maj. Ralph 59

S-38 30
S-40 30
Saalman, Lt. Otis 175, 177
Sackett, Capt. Earl 48–51
Sakai, Saburo 10, 41
Sakakida, Sgt. Russell 52, 181
Sakdalistas 86–87
Salinas, California 61
Salinas National Guard 61
Samal 78
Samar 196, 200
Samat, Mt. 98–106, 123, 125
San Marcelino 28
San Vicente River 124–126
Sangley Pt. 25
Sato, Col. Gembachi 150, 160, 164, 166, 174, 177, 182, 187
Saysain River 144
Schlotte, Lt. 41
Schrieber, Lt. Harry 39
17th Pursuit Squadron 5, 6, 12–13, 16, 18, 20
7th Tank Regiment (Jap.) 104, 157
Shanghai Marines 186
Sharp, Brig. Gen. William 150, 192, 194–201

Sheppard, Lt. Bill 17
Signal Hill 96
Sisiman Bay 74
16th Division (Jap.) 101
61st Infantry Regiment (Jap.) 157
Smith, Maj. (Dr.) Charles 110
South China Sea 84, 91, 101
South Dock 189
South Luzon Force 58, 62
South Shore Road 76
Steel, Lt. Don 27
Sternburg Hospital 11
Stinson, Lt. Lloyd 88–89, 96, 147
Stockton Field 13
Stone, Lt. Earl 88–89
Strobing, Irving 184–185
Strobing Minnie 185
Stuart M3 Tank 59, 61, 63, 178
Subic Bay 70, 95–96, 148
Sutherland, Maj. Gen. Richard 91–92
Sweeney, Sgt. Thomas 171

Tagalog 53
Tagarao, Sgt. Silvestro 124
Thayer, Lt. Col. Allen 190, 200
3rd Pursuit Squadron 4, 5
31st Division (PA) 119–120
31st Infantry Regiment 127, 130
31st Signal Company 128
34th Pursuit Squadron 11, 18, 20
32nd Infantry Regiment (PA) 125
33rd Infantry Regiment (PA) 121
Tisdale, Maj. Achille 100, 130, 140–143
Tokyo 43
Tokyo Radio 97
Tolentino, Sgt. 68–69
Trail 4 105
Trail 429 104
Trail 7 144
Trail 6 104
Trail 20 129, 131, 140
Trail 29 104
Trail 2 122–124, 126
Traywick, Lt. Col. 139, 194–195
20th Infantry Regiment (Jap.) 52
20th Pursuit Squadron 3, 6, 20, 151
21st Division (Jap.) 101
21st Division 102–103
21st Pursuit Squadron 4, 20, 54, 92
24th Field Artillery Regiment 77–78
24th Pursuit Group 14, 84

# Index

24th Pursuit Squadron  14, 20, 54
26th Cavalry  65–66, 75–76, 127

University Club Manila  201

Vance, nCol. Lee  127
Vandevanter, Lt. Elliot  39, 40
Vickers 2.5 Packhowitzer  106
Vigan  15–19, 28, 45–46
Villamor, Capt. Jesus  25–26
Visayas  199, 201–202
Voice of Freedom Radio  141, 184

Waco  150
Wagner, Lt. "Buzz"  5, 22, 38, 43–47
Wainwright, Gen. Jonathan  54, 56, 66–67, 69, 123, 133–135, 137–140, 142–143, 159–160, 171–172, 183, 185, 189–197, 200–202

Wake Island  38
Water Tank Hill  168–170, 183
Weaver, Pvt.  139
Webb, Maj. William  77
Weinstein Dr. Alfred  109–118
Wermuth, Capt. Arthur  56, 78, 82–83, 89
Wheeler, Capt. John  66–68
Wheless, Capt. Hewitt  38–40, 42–43, 47
Whitcomb, Lt. Edgar  187–188
White, Lt. Kiefer  93
Wilkins, Capt. John  30
Williams, Col. Everett  136–138
Williams, Maj. Francis  175, 177–180, 183
Williams, Lt. Gus  152–153
Williams, Cpl. W.W.  41
Wilson Park Ridge  166
Wohlfield, Capt. Mark  131
Woolery, Lt. Edward  85, 88–89

Milton Keynes UK
Ingram Content Group UK Ltd.
UKHW042042271124
451814UK00014B/127